Contents

Acknowledgements   2

Preface to 2nd Edition   4

Foreword   5

Introduction   6

1. The Genus Hydrangea
The Name 'Hydrangea'   10
Hydrangea Fossils   10
Natural Distribution   10
Introduction into Cultivation   11
General Description   12
Flowers   12
Flower Colour   14
Leaves   14
Species in Cultivation   22
Some Problems and Peculiarities of
    Hydrangea macrophylla   35

2. Hydrangeas in Gardens   40

3. Cultivation
Site   45
Soil and Colour Change   51
Planting   55
Feeding and Mulching   55
Pruning   57
Pests and Diseases   60

4. Propagation
Softwood and Semi-ripe Cuttings   64
Hardwood Cuttings   69
Buds   71
Layering   72
Suckering   72
Seed   73
Division   74

5. Other Aspects of Hydrangeas
Pot Plants   75
Cut Fresh Flowers   75
Dried Flowers   75
Well Dressing   77
Paper-making   77
Adverse Effects of Hydrangeas   78
Hana Matsuri   79

**6. Descriptions of Cultivars and
Subspecies**   80
Flower Head Types of Subspecies   161
Flowering Times   163
Glossary of Terms   165
List of Gardens   168
Sources and Further Reading   170
Useful Addresses   172
Index   173

Preface to 2nd Edition

Nine years on from the publication of the first edition many changes have taken place in the hydrangea world, both at home and abroad. Brian Rothera, co-author, sadly died in 1997 but he lived long enough to know that hydrangeas were increasing in popularity. John Bond who wrote the Foreword has also died but his support of our efforts never failed. Two additional National Collections of Hydrangea have been established in Great Britain, in Ayrshire and North Wales. In France, Robert and Corinne Mallet's collection has been moved to a new site and greatly extended, supported by the flourishing Shamrock Society. The Aldridge Garden in Alabama, USA, has opened in a woodland setting with a heavy emphasis on hydrangeas. The American Hydrangea Society, based in Atlanta, encourages worldwide membership and is unflagging in its promotion of the genus (see details of all these in List of Gardens, page 168). More cultivars continue to come from Japan and numbers of hydrangeas in *The Plant Finder* increase every year.

This second edition is based mainly on knowledge and experience gained from working with the expanding National Collection maintained in the Lakeland Horticultural Society's garden at Holehird, Windermere. The Collection now numbers around 250 named species/cultivars of hydrangea. The splendid display which they make from July to September/October has attracted much media attention and continues to encourage large numbers of visitors to the garden. Nurserymen too are finding the Collection useful to check and extend their stock.

In 2000, five more plants in the Collection were given Awards of Garden Merit by the RHS and these have been noted. There are 20 new inclusions in the book and additionally, four of the Tellers have been given amplified entries. Careful observation over many years has shown that all new inclusions are 'Good Growers'. Not all are yet available in the trade but one purpose of a National Collection is to get correctly named good plants into commercial production. The Collection holders are keen to encourage this and therefore I justify the inclusion of some as yet unfamiliar plants. Others which I might have included have been omitted because evaluating them, over many years, is not yet complete. I trust that this volume helps to maintain the present surge of interest in hydrangeas.

I would like to express particular thanks to Geert Boering for his inspired help with the new cover design: Trevor Nicholson-Christie for his generosity with slides; Shelagh Newman (the present curator of the Collection in Cumbria) for the paragraphs on seed propagation; Sylvia Nichols for additions to the section on Well Dressing; Elizabeth Dean (American Hydrangea Society); Eddy Aldridge (Aldridge Garden, Alabama, USA); Allen Coomes (Hillier Garden and Arboretum); Michael Hickson (Knightshayes); Sally Gregson; Maurice Foster; all of whom have given freely of time and expertise. Lastly, my husband Griff, for help with the photography, proof-reading and for bearing patiently with a second run of hydrangea preoccupation.

Toni Lawson-Hall

Hydrangeas

A Gardener's Guide

Revised Edition

Toni Lawson-Hall and Brian Rothera

Timber Press
Portland, Oregon

Acknowledgements

The authors wish to thank a very large number of people, for help has been generally and generously given. It would be unwise to attempt a list of individuals, for it would never be complete, and unintentional omissions would surely occur. We should like, however, to mention particularly those who have corrected text: Elizabeth McClintock, who kindly checked the descriptions of species; Norman Yock, Martha Aldridge and Hélène Bertrand who checked descriptions of some cultivars, and gave patient help and advice; Takeomi Yamamoto, for slides and information from Japan, and Kazuko Wood for kindly translating text; many members of the Lakeland Horticultural Society, for their continuous help and tolerance; the National Council for Conservation of Plants and Gardens, whose central staff have given us constant support; those responsible for all the gardens we have visited, for the generous giving of their time and expertise, and for allowing us to take photographs; the library and herbarium staff at the Royal Botanic Gardens, Kew and Edinburgh; the staff at the RHS Library, Vincent Square, and the Plant Pathology Department, Wisley; Floral B committee of the RHS Awards Department; Ray Cooper for his untiring research into references; Timber Press Inc., Portland, Oregon, and B.T. Batsford Ltd, London, for permission to reproduce the Hardiness Zone maps from *A Manual of Broad-Leaved Trees and Shrubs* by Gerd Krussmann; the 'hydrangea contacts' we have made, in England, Scotland, Ireland, USA, France, Switzerland, Holland and Belgium, who have offered us such kindness and hospitality – many in these countries, and also in Japan, Australia, South Africa, New Zealand and Canada, who have been kind enough to answer our letters; our friends, families and especially our partners, who have borne patiently with us and the hydrangeas while this book was being prepared.

Our sincere thanks to them all.

Toni Lawson-Hall and Brian Rothera

First published 1995. Reprinted 1999

New edition 2004

Drawings/illustrations © Toni Lawson-Hall.

ISBN 0-88192-669-8

Printed in Singapore

Published in North America in 2005
by Timber Press, Inc.
The Haseltine Building
133 S.W. Second Avenue, Suite 450
Portland, Oregon 97204-3527, USA.
www.timberpress.com

A catalog record for this book is available from the Library of Congress

All photographs © the authors and photographed at the Lakeland Horticultural Gardens, Holehird, Windermere, Cumbria, UK unless stated otherwise (GL-H: Griff Lawson-Hall; TN-C: Trevor Nicholson Christie).

Foreword

I am writing this foreword as a gardener responsible for an extensive area of woodland garden which is situated some distance from the sea. It would have been equally appropriate to invite a person who is involved with a garden with maritime influence to write this foreword, such is the adaptability of this valuable summer-flowering genus.

There is no problem in planting a woodland garden for a long spring display, and autumn is also well catered for. It is the summer period that presents a problem and here the hydrangea provides the answer with a wealth of colour over many weeks. My great favourites are *Hydrangea aspera* 'Macrophylla', the perfect lacecap, *H. arborescens* 'Grandiflora', so very reliable, *H. macrophylla* 'Blue Wave', *H. macrophylla* 'Générale Vicomtesse de Vibraye', so very attractive and so hardy, and almost all of the *H. paniculata* cultivars.

We have for a very long time been in need of a really good work on the genus *Hydrangea*, and Toni Lawson-Hall and Brian Rothera have certainly not given me cause for disappointment. I am equally confident that all those interested in the genus will find this book the answer to all aspects of their needs. The book is clearly written for gardeners, beginning with an excellent introduction to the history and botany of the genus; a thorough glossary on page 165 will help the reader understand this section. The chapters on cultivation and propagation are particularly impressive and will be of great value to all levels of gardeners. The identification of the species is in most cases straightforward; this is not the case, however, with the numerous cultivars of *Hydrangea macrophylla*, and confusion reigns in many gardens and nurseries. The many excellent colour photographs (each cultivar described has its own photograph) will help tremendously to alleviate these problems.

I referred earlier to the great need for this book, the only relatively recent work of value being Michael Haworth-Booth's *The Hydrangeas*. I had the privilege of meeting him shortly before his death when I visited his nursery and garden, my purpose to collect some superb late-flowering evergreen azaleas. On this occasion he kindly gave me his three superb cultivars of *Hydrangea serrata* 'Diadem', 'Miranda' and 'Blue Deckle'. I propagated large numbers of these and I believe I was responsible for distributing them to many gardens and nurseries in Britain.

I am confident that this exceptionally well-written book on this most exciting and valuable genus will find its way on to a great many bookshelves, and will be the standard work on the genus for many years.

J.D. Bond M.V.O., V.M.H.
Keeper of the Gardens
The Great Park, Windsor

Introduction

What does the name 'Hydrangea' conjure up in the reader's mind? Is it a colourful pot plant, given as a present that will last well? Is it an array of many such plants on a concert platform or decorating a hotel foyer? Perhaps it is a shrub in his or her own garden, easy, undemanding, little noticed? Or maybe a massed planting giving a late summer display in a public park? Most readers will have some image for the shrub is widely grown. As a garden plant, however, it is not held in the same esteem as perhaps a rose or a rhododendron, and is undervalued in spite of the long-lasting colour which it gives. In Cornwall, in the west of England, where hydrangeas are prolific and spectacular, they are rated as common shrubs by those who live there. Nor is a great deal known about the plants, beyond the fact that the flowers tend to change colour. Nurseries frequently sell them simply labelled 'Red', 'White' or 'Blue' as that seems to be all that the customer wants, and names of hydrangea varieties are not a familiar part of gardening vocabulary. Yet there are hundreds of named varieties in cultivation, many of which are readily available and could add colour and interest to our gardens and parks.

One of the reasons why so little is known about the common shrub is that very little has been written about it in English. Earlier last century there were publications in France and Germany, and many articles in horticultural journals in these and other countries, dealing mostly with hydrangeas as popular pot plants. Specialist literature is still being produced, but there is little for the ordinary gardener to use except brief sentences in major reference works. The main reference book written in English is Michael Haworth-Booth's *The Hydrangeas*, first published in 1950 and now in its fifth edition. This excellent volume covers the species and the cultivars, listing and describing some 400 of the latter. However, the few colour photographs it contains are not sufficiently detailed to enable the reader to make a positive identification of a particular shrub. Without a reference to good colour photographs today's gardener is lost, as is the garden centre salesman if a customer questions a plant's name.

Two shorter books, published in 1958, are *The Hydrangeas* by A.G. Puttock and *Hydrangeas and Viburnums* by D. Bartrum. Both outline the species as understood by them, and D. Bartrum describes some hundred cultivars. Illustrations are all black-and-white and many of the plants are no longer obtainable. In 1992, Corinne Mallet produced a book, first in French and later the same year translated into English – *Hydrangeas: Species and Cultivars*. The beautiful colour photographs which accompany the plant descriptions make an artistic volume, most welcome after so many years without any updating of information on hydrangeas. Volume 2, also by Corinne Mallet, was added in 1994, and a delightful book by G. Church of New Zealand came out in 1999.

The major botanical reference is Dr Elizabeth McClintock's *A Monograph of the Genus Hydrangea*, published in California in 1957. This comprehensive work is devoted to the taxonomy of the species, and does not include cultivars. Dr McClintock, the botanist, and M. Haworth-Booth, the horticulturalist, do not always agree, especially on the subject of the classification of *Hydrangea macrophylla*. The authors of this book, being gardeners, accept Dr McClintock's findings with gratitude, but do admit to sympathy with some of Haworth-Booth's opinions.

The plant itself, of course, can provide us with all the information we could wish, but this knowledge is only valuable if the shrub is correctly labelled. Sadly this is often not the case. The botanical institutions grow mainly species and these are accurately named. Cultivars, however, are used by these gardens more as a decoration than a source of reference, and no claim is made as to the correctness of the names. Nurseries vary in the care which they devote to this aspect, and errors are common. These mistakes, however, are not necessarily due to careless practice, for hydrangeas present special problems. One is the very large number of cultivars which has been developed. Also, unlike most flowering shrubs, the flowers of some of the most commonly grown hydrangea cultivars can change colour when the plant is grown on soils of differing acidity and alkalinity. This, and other variations to which the genus is prone, increase the naming hazards.

It is only by checking the name and form of a plant carefully in several different locations that a degree of certainty can be established about its identity. In Britain, this is part of the work of National Collection holders. In 1986 Derby County Council started to make the first National Collection of Hydrangeas in their garden at Darley Abbey Park, Derby, and this collection is now established. In the Lakeland Horticultural Society's garden at Holehird, Windermere, Cumbria, a second National Hydrangea Collection is being developed, and its care was the responsibility of the authors of this book. Plants which form the nucleus of this collection came from M. Haworth-Booth's nursery some fifteen years ago. Gradually, through the auspices of the National Council for the Conservation of Plants and Gardens (NCCPG), and as a result of the collection holders' travels and research, more plants have been added. The aim is to include all the species in cultivation, as well as a large, selected number of correctly named cultivars. Confirmation of names is constantly being sought. Where there is serious doubt the shrub is left unnamed. There are other collections of hydrangeas, not registered with the NCCPG, of which the most extensive are probably those in Kew and Wakehurst Place, at Savill Gardens, Windsor, at Hillier's Arboretum, and at Wisley. Regional collections are being established in France, and Australia has two National Collections. Many private gardens which open to the public are careful with their naming and thus provide further useful sources of information. A list of gardens, open to the public and having a good display of hydrangeas, is included on page 168.

This book is written with two purposes in mind: firstly to promote a genus whose attributes are not generally appreciated. Hydrangeas are easy to grow, colourful over a long period (dozens are often still in flower in Lakeland, Cumbria, in November); they are hardy, long-lived and, when carefully sited, quite beautiful. They should be more widely grown. All aspects of their care and cultivation are covered.

The second intention is to provide a source of ready reference, so that more varieties can be recognized and less familiar forms can increase in popularity. The selection for inclusion, especially among the numerous cultivars of *H. macrophylla*, has been based on two main principles:

a The plant should have obvious merits (all plants which have received an AGM in the 1992 reassessment are included) and as clear a personal identity as possible, to aid recognition.
b The plant should be available. This is not guaranteed, but the majority can be traced through *The Plant Finder*. There are exceptions to this as explained in the Preface to the 2nd edition.

All the plants described in detail have been confirmed from more than one source, and have been grown by the authors. The names given are as accurate as constant search and comparison can make them. We quote from M. Haworth-Booth as he puts it so well:

Wise friends told me that it was really a hopeless task, but that it would be helpful if I could at least gather together and tabulate all the widely scattered previously written data on the hydrangeas and present them in a nice handy little book at a reasonable price!

M. Haworth-Booth proved, fifty years ago, that it was by no means a hopeless task. Inspired by his pioneering, this book is now offered in the hope that its descriptions, methods and colour illustrations will enable the reader to identify, care for and enjoy a much neglected but delightful group of shrubs.

Lacecap Hydrangeas

1 H.m. 'Beauté Vendômoise'
2 H.m. 'Lanarth White'
3 H.m. 'Möwe'
4 H.m. 'Veitchii'
5 H.m. 'Rotschwanz'
6 H.s. 'Grayswood'
7 H.m. 'Blue Wave'
8 H.m. 'Lilacina'
9 H.m. 'Libelle'

1 The Genus Hydrangea

This book is about the genus *Hydrangea* which is usually classed in the family *Saxifragaceae*. This family also includes, among others, *Deutzia* and *Philadelphus*.

The Name 'Hydrangea'

The widely accepted opinion is that the name derives from two Greek words; 'hydor' meaning water, and 'angeon', a vessel for storing dry or liquid substances. The vessel is supposedly shaped like the seed capsule (*Fig. 1*). The seed capsule could indeed be envisaged as a vessel, yet the Greek vase 'hydria' (water vessel) bears no similarity to the shape of the hydrangea seed pod. Nor do hydrangeas require more water than any other vigorous deciduous flowering shrub, so why refer to water? Another idea is that the derivation refers to the mythical monster Hydra, known for its many snake-like heads. The capsule could indeed be likened to this. So, it remains to the reader to decide, as he must also make up his mind whether to say 'hydr-aingea' or 'hydr-angea'. The choice is open.

Hydrangea Fossils

In the early and middle parts of the Tertiary period, temperate forests covered much of the northern hemisphere, extending as far north as Manchuria, Greenland and Alaska. Fossil finds show that hydrangeas grew in these forests.

La Motte (1952) lists hydrangea fossil finds in Eocene times (40–70 million years ago) in Alaska, California and Oregon; from

Oligocene (25–40 million years ago) in Colorado, Oregon and California; and from Miocene time (12–25 million years ago) in Oregon and Washington States.

Hu and Chaney (1940) record hydrangea fossils dating from the Miocene period, found in the Shantung province of China where forests were similar to those of Japan and Korea now.

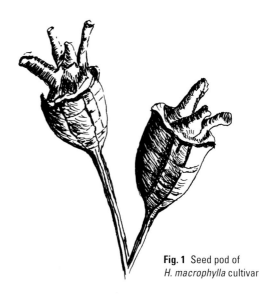

Fig. 1 Seed pod of *H. macrophylla* cultivar

Natural Distribution

Hydrangeas grow naturally in eastern Asia, in eastern North America and towards the western seaboards of Central and South America. The main occurrence, in eastern Asia, is in the temperate zones of Tibet, central and southern China, Japan, Philippines, Taiwan, Java and Sumatra. In the warmer latitudes the plants grow at higher altitudes where temperate conditions prevail. In North America the only two species which occur are *Hydrangea arborescens*, which grows in the Appalachian Mountains, and *H. quercifolia*, which is found in the Piedmont region of south-eastern USA. The hydrangeas which are found in Central and South America are all evergreen climbers. Once again, they grow in cooler mountainous parts of these sub-tropical regions. One of these climbing species, *H. integrifolia*, also grows in the Philippines and Taiwan.

Introduction into Cultivation

The very first hydrangea to be introduced into England was the American plant *H. arborescens*, which came from Pennsylvania in 1736. In the Orient, hydrangeas had doubtless been growing in gardens of China and Japan long before any records were kept, but the first to reach Europe was that brought from China by one of Joseph Banks's plant-hunting protégés. This, a globose-headed plant, was presented to Kew in 1798, where Banks was involved in helping to establish a centre for botanical studies. The plant, first called *H. hortensis*, was later renamed 'Sir Joseph Banks'. A similar plant was introduced into France at the same period.

Within Japan, the popularity of hydrangeas as garden plants increased during the seventeenth and eighteenth centuries. Since, however, Japan was closed to foreigners from 1639 to 1856, access to Japanese plants was restricted. The establishment of the Dutch East India Company's trading post on the island of Deshima, in Nagasaki Bay, nevertheless provided a base for some intrepid planthunters among the Europeans posted there. In particular, in 1775 the Swedish doctor and botanist Carl Peter Thunberg, and in 1826 Philip Franz von Siebold, a Bavarian eye specialist, spent some years on Deshima. In the few visits they were able to make to the Japanese mainland, plants were collected, seeds gathered and grown, and descriptions made. Thunberg, in his *Flora Japonica*, 1784, described plants as *Viburnums*, which were later, in 1830, transferred by Seringe to the genus *Hydrangea*. Von Siebold, in his *Flora Japonica*, 1840, described several Japanese species of *Hydrangea*.

Subsequently, seeds and plants of these Japanese species gradually reached Europe. *H. macrophylla*, *H. involucrata*, *H. paniculata* and *H. petiolaris* were all introduced. In the later nineteenth century, *H. anomala*, *H. aspera* and *H. heteromalla* were brought back from Nepal by Nathaniel Wallich and F. Buchanan-Hamilton. It was not until the early twentieth century that the evergreen climbing hydrangeas began to arrive in Britain from Central and South America.

Reclassifying and renaming has been a feature of the history of hydrangeas, especially of the most popular *macrophylla* species, and M. Haworth-Booth gives much detail as well as his opinions on the subject in his *The Hydrangeas*. Some of the problems and peculiarities of this species are discussed in a separate section on page 35.

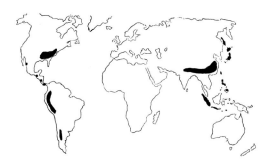

Fig. 2 The natural distribution of Hydrangea

General Description

The genus comprises flowering shrubs, small trees and climbing plants. The shrubs vary in size from dwarf specimens to huge bushes, several metres in height and width. All prefer moist and temperature conditions and the climatic conditions govern, to some extent, the dimensions achieved.

Dr McClintock divides the genus into two sections. The first, called Hydrangea, comprises eleven deciduous species, all of which are in cultivation and are described in this book. The second section, Cornidia, contains twelve evergreen self-supporting climbers. These are as yet less familiar, but three which are in cultivation, *H. integrifolia*, *H. seemannii*, and *H. serratifolia* are described.

Flowers

The flowers are a conspicuous feature of hydrangeas, being freely borne, long-lasting and often highly decorative. The inflorescence or flower head is made up of many florets. The overall shape of the flower head in the species is either a rounded or flat-topped corymb (*Fig. 3*) or a panicle (*Fig. 4*).

The Genus Hydrangea
(showing the species included in this book)

Section 1 Hydrangea

SUB-SECTION	SPECIES	SUB-SPECIES	CULTIVAR
		(example)	(example)
Americanae	*arborescens*		'Annabelle'
	quercifolia		'Snowflake'
Asperae	*aspera*	*sargentiana*	
	involucrata		'Hortensis'
	sikokiana		
Calyptranthe	*anomala*	*petiolaris*	
Heteromallae	*heteromalla*		'Bretschneideri'
	paniculata		'Unique'
Macrophyllae	*macrophylla*	*macrophylla*	'Altona' (mophead)
		macrophylla	'Lilacina' (lacecap)
		serrata	'Diadem' (lacecap)
Petalanthe	*hirta*		
	scandens	*scandens*	

Section 2 Cornidia

Monosegia	*integrifolia*		
	seemannii		
Polysegia	*serratifolia*		

The inflorescence usually comprises two different kinds of flowers:

a The tiny fertile 'true' flowers which are either grouped together in large numbers in the centre of the corymb, or distributed throughout the inflorescence; they can, in some species, make up the entire flower head. These fertile flowers supply the various insects with nectar and are fertilized in the process. To quote Pilatowski (1982): 'The compound cyme presents a stable platform on which the insects rummage for nectar. The dense inflorescence makes a good landing for various unspecified insects.'

b The decorative and conspicuous sterile flowers which are in fact enlarged sepals. These are either distributed around the margin of the corymb, as in *Fig. 3*, or are distributed throughout the panicle as in *Fig. 4*. The function of these sterile flowers is probably to attract insects to the plant.

The precise shape of the rounded flower cluster varies with the species, as does the proportion of fertile to sterile flowers.

Fig. 4 Panicle

Fig. 3 Composite lacecap type of corymb

The third hydrangea flower shape (*Fig. 5*) does not represent one of the species, but must be mentioned here because of its familiarity. Indeed, this globose flower head is what many people understand by the name 'hydrangea'. It occurs occasionally in the wild as a sport of both *H. arborescens* and *H. macrophylla*, and because of its attractive appearance, has been extensively cultivated. It is composed almost entirely of sterile florets, which hide among the few, if any, fertile flowers. This form of *H. macrophylla*, in particular, was developed extensively in Europe during the late nineteenth and early twentieth centuries and has become known there under the French name 'hortensia'. This term does not come readily to the English tongue, so the globose-headed flower is sometimes called in Britain, with more affection than aesthetic sense, a 'mophead'. A really good name for this flower type has not been found.

Fig. 5 Globose head of *H. macrophylla* cultivar

Another cultivated form of *H. macrophylla* resembles the species, in having a flat or slightly domed corymb with marginal sterile or ray flowers. This was called a 'lacecap' by M. Haworth-Booth, and the term has been commonly accepted in Britain.

Flower Colour

The colour of the fertile flowers in the species can be white, pink, blue or lilac. The predominant colour of the sterile flowers is white or creamy white, although pale shades of pink, blue, lilac and occasionally, as in *H. scandens* and *H. serratifolia*, yellow do occur. It is in the cultivated varieties that stronger colours appear.

Leaves

The leaves are usually ovate or elliptic and are opposite – that is, they arise from the leaf stems in pairs, with one leaf on the opposite side of the stem from the other. Occasionally, as with *H. paniculata*, the leaves are ternate, i.e. they arise from the stem in groups of three.

In two species, *H. quercifolia* and *H. sikokiana*, the leaves are pinnately lobed. The leaf margin is usually serrate but can, rarely, be entire. The surface is glossy, smooth, matt or hairy, according to the species.

It does not require a botanist to distinguish between the leaves of the species in cultivation – with a little practice a gardener can do this as the characteristics are easy to recognize. The illustrations on pages 17–21 are full-sized reproductions of actual leaves, and in Chapter 6 the illustrations of leaves and sepals are half the true size.

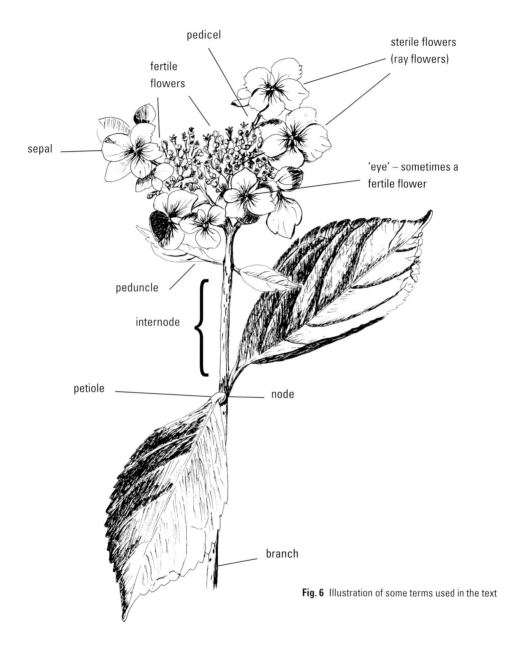

pedicel

sterile flowers
(ray flowers)

fertile
flowers

sepal

'eye' – sometimes a
fertile flower

peduncle

internode

petiole

node

branch

Fig. 6 Illustration of some terms used in the text

Fig. 7 Leaves of the hydrangea species

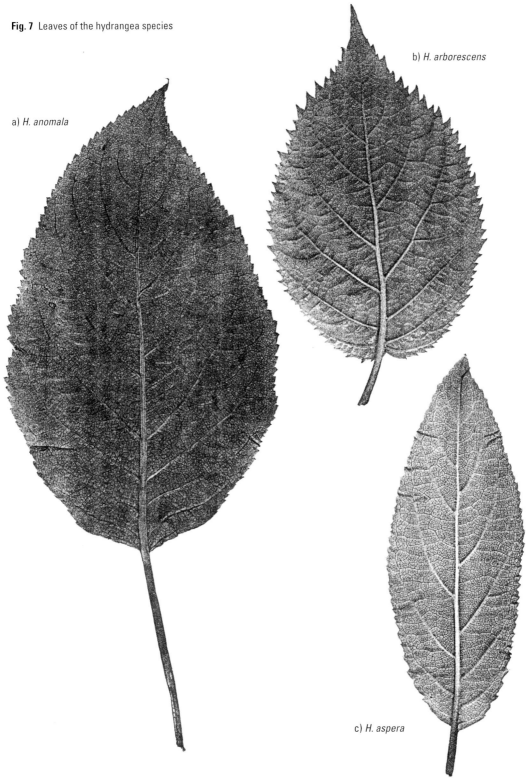

a) *H. anomala*

b) *H. arborescens*

c) *H. aspera*

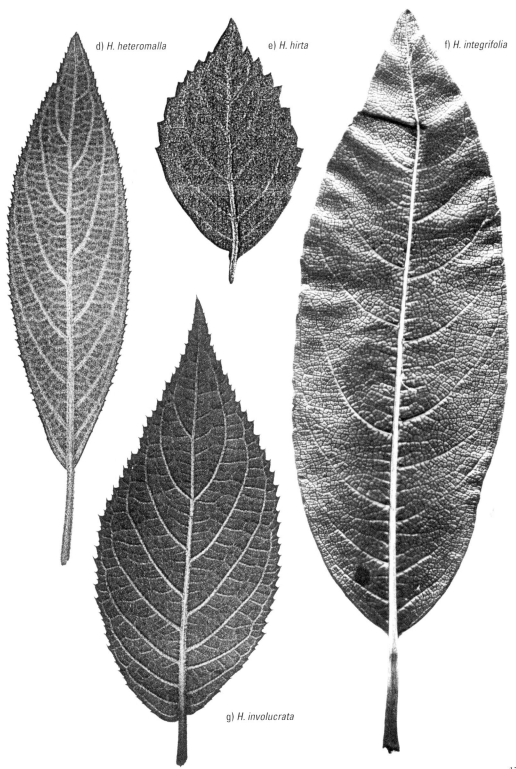

d) *H. heteromalla*

e) *H. hirta*

f) *H. integrifolia*

g) *H. involucrata*

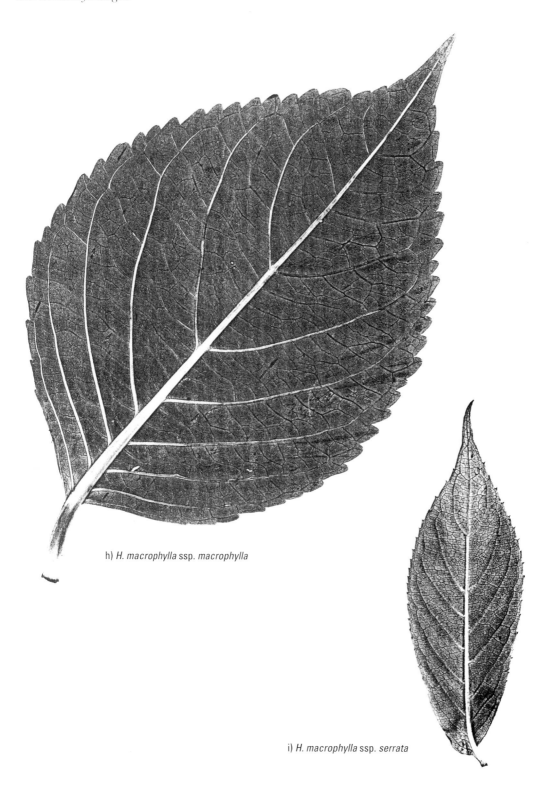

h) *H. macrophylla* ssp. *macrophylla*

i) *H. macrophylla* ssp. *serrata*

j) *H. paniculata*

k) *H. quercifolia*

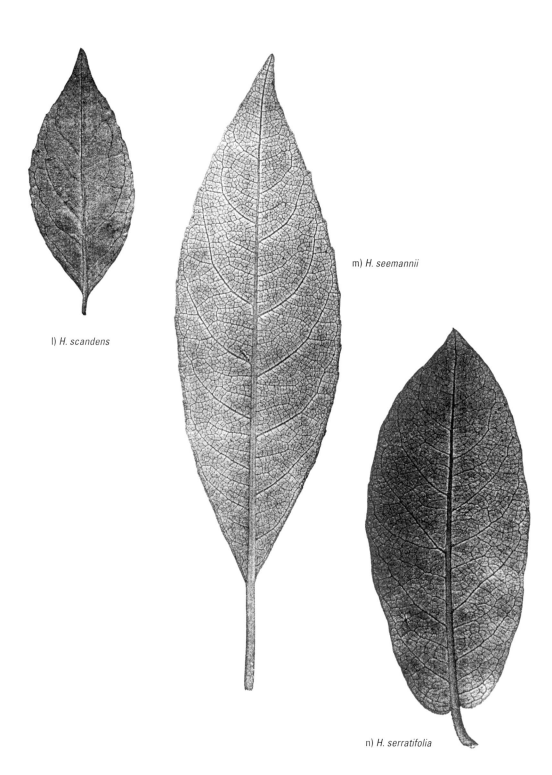

l) *H. scandens*

m) *H. seemannii*

n) *H. serratifolia*

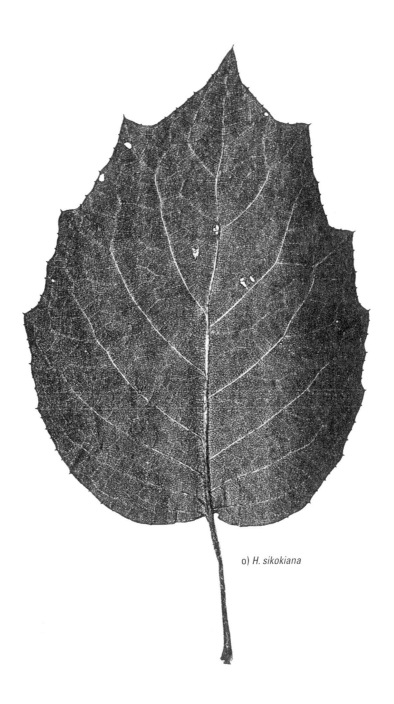

o) *H. sikokiana*

Species in Cultivation

(arranged alphabetically)

H. anomala D. Don

Collected by Wallich in Nepal in the early
1820s, described and named by D. Don in
1825, this plant was introduced into Britain
in the later 1830s, and by Thomas Hogg
into the USA in 1865. The only scandent
member of the section Hydrangea, it is
found in Japan, Korea, east Himalayas and
in central China. It inhabits woods, mixed
forests and mountain ravines and its
features remain fairly constant throughout
these areas. Hardiness Zone 5.

This is a woody, self-clinging deciduous
climber, which can attain a height of 12 m
(40 ft) or more. In its natural habitat, it is
not only a spectacular tree climber but can

Fig. 10 *Hydrangea anomala*

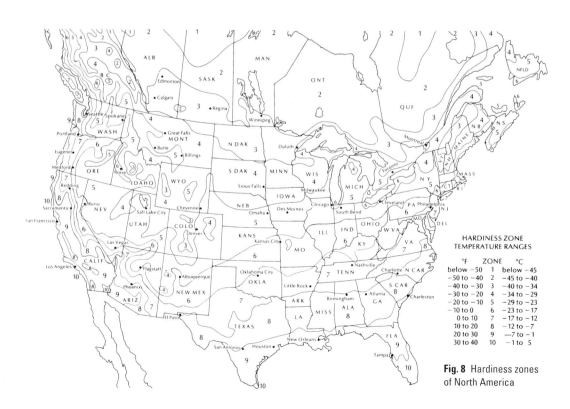

°F	ZONE	°C
below −50	1	below −45
−50 to −40	2	−45 to −40
−40 to −30	3	−40 to −34
−30 to −20	4	−34 to −29
−20 to −10	5	−29 to −23
−10 to 0	6	−23 to −17
0 to 10	7	−17 to −12
10 to 20	8	−12 to −7
20 to 30	9	−7 to −1
30 to 40	10	−1 to 5

HARDINESS ZONE
TEMPERATURE RANGES

Fig. 8 Hardiness zones
of North America

scramble over rocks, forming dense ground cover.

The inflorescence, which appears in June – earlier than most hydrangeas, is 15–20 cm (6–8 in) across and fairly flat. The very numerous central fertile flowers are creamy white, as are the few marginal sterile ones, the latter being held on long pedicels. A particular botanical characteristic of this species is that the petals are united and when they fall, do so as a cap.

The leaves are light-green, ovate/elliptic, 6–15 cm (1½ –6 in) long, 4–10 cm (1½–4 in) wide, shortly acuminate at the tip and cordate at the base. The leaf edge is coarsely serrate, and the surfaces are

smooth, apart from a few downy tufts in vein axils on the lower surface.

The bark is reddish-brown and shreds in strands from the older wood.

McClintock divides this species into two subspecies: *H. anomala* ssp. *anomala*, from the Asiatic mainland, and *H. anomala* ssp. *petiolaris*, from Japan and Taiwan. It is the latter plant, often listed as *H. petiolaris*, which is familiarly known as 'the climbing hydrangea'. It is readily and widely grown, being hardier and more vigorous than *H.* ssp. *anomala*. It is described on page 81.

H. arborescens L.
A native of eastern USA, introduced into Britain (1736) by P. Collinson. It shows

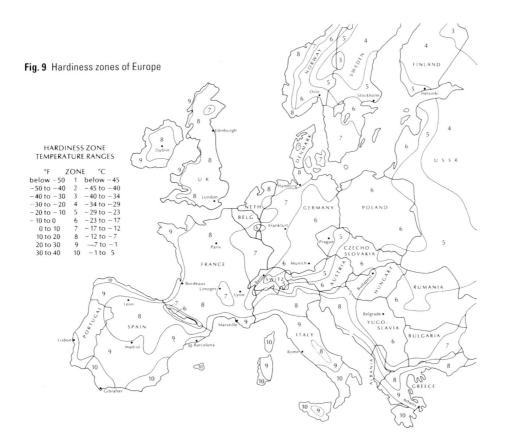

Fig. 9 Hardiness zones of Europe

HARDINESS ZONE
TEMPERATURE RANGES

°F	ZONE	°C
below −50	1	below −45
−50 to −40	2	−45 to −40
−40 to −30	3	−40 to −34
−30 to −20	4	−34 to −29
−20 to −10	5	−29 to −23
−10 to 0	6	−23 to −17
0 to 10	7	−17 to −12
10 to 20	8	−12 to −7
20 to 30	9	−7 to −1
30 to 40	10	−1 to 5

considerable variation throughout the regions where it occurs and is hardier than many hydrangeas. Hardiness Zone 4/5.

A small open, erect deciduous shrub, occasionally up to 3 m (10 ft), but normally around 1 m (3 ft), high.

The inflorescence is a fairly flat corymb, 5–15 cm (2–6 in) across. It comprises numerous small, whitish, fertile flowers and may or may not include a few large sterile flowers on long pedicels. Flowering time is from July to September.

The leaves are dark green above and paler beneath; ovate, with acute to acuminate tips and sometimes cordate at the base; 6–17 cm (2½–7 in) long by 2½–12 cm (1–5 in) wide. The margins are serrate, and the upper surface smooth while the lower surface is variably hairy.

According to McClintock (1957), this species is subdivided into three subspecies:

H. arborescens ssp. *arborescens*, *H. arborescens* ssp. *discolor* and *H. arborescens* ssp. *radiata*. As a result of extensive experimental work, these subspecies have been considered worthy of full species recognition by Pilatowski (1980) and have been named by him: *H. arborescens*, *H. cinerea* and *H. radiata*.

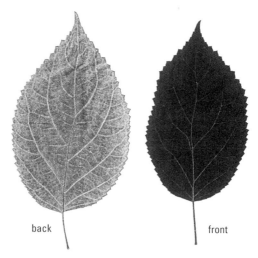

back   front

Fig. 12 Leaf of *Hydrangea arborescens* ssp. *discolor* (McClintock)

Fig. 11 *Hydrangea arborescens* ssp. *arborescens*

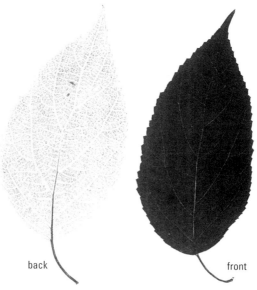

back   front

Fig. 13 Leaf of *Hydrangea arborescens* ssp. *radiata* (McClintock)

For the gardener, a quick way of distinguishing between the three subspecies (or species, if following Pilatowski) is by looking at the reverse side of the leaf. In *H. arborescens* ssp. *arborescens* the leaves are green beneath; in *H. arborescens* ssp. *discolor* (McClintock) the reverse of the leaf is grey; and in *H. arborescens* ssp. *radiata* (McClintock) the back of the leaf is white. This latter is a striking feature of the plant. In each case the differences in colour are caused by the differences in the type and form of hairs on the reverse of the leaf.

Again of interest to the gardener is the fact that this species and its cultivars flower on the new season's wood, and are therefore frost-hardy. *H. paniculata* has the same habit and these two species can therefore be grown where other species, such as *H. macrophylla*, would be subject to frost damage. *H. arborescens* also tolerates light shade and some degree of drought.

Another feature of this species' growth is that it sends out suckers. By this vegetative means the plant readily reproduces itself, and large plantings can quickly arise from a single shrub.

The species *H. arborescens*, for all its merits, is not a particularly attractive plant, but the cultivars *H. arborescens* 'Annabelle', and *H. arborescens* 'Grandiflora' with as many virtues, are beautiful shrubs and are described on pages 82, 83. In its native N. America, many more cultivars of *H. arborescens* are now available.

H. aspera D. Don

Described in 1825 by D. Don in a collection from Nepal and introduced to Britain in the early 1900s. This species, native to the east Himalayas, west and central China, Taiwan, Java and Sumatra, shows considerable variation over the wide range of its habitats. Hardiness Zone 7.

The shrub or small tree can be 1–4 m (3–10 ft) in height.

The inflorescence is slightly convex, up to 30 cm (12 in) across. Numerous fertile flowers, white, pink or lilac, are surrounded by white to pink sterile flowers, usually with four sepals, toothed or entire.

Both stems and leaves are hairy, the upper surface of the leaves being sparsely covered and the hairs on the lower surface varying in kind and quantity with the plant's location. Leaves vary in the range 5–35 cm (2–14 in) long and 1½–15 cm (½–6 in) wide, mostly lanceolate to ovate and greyish/green with fine serrations.

There are several variants of this species and they are highly decorative and valuable to the gardener, especially to those with above average planting space. They flower after midsummer, they tolerate chalky soil, some drought, and varying degrees of shade. Their flower colour does not alter with soil pH.

Fig. 14 *Hydrangea aspera*

The following are described and illustrated in this book:

H. aspera 'Macrophylla'	page 85
H. aspera 'Mauvette'	page 85
H. aspera 'Villosa'	page 88
H. aspera ssp. *sargentiana*	page 87

H. heteromalla D. Don

Collected by Wallich in the early 1800s and named by D. Don in 1825, *H. heteromalla* was introduced into cultivation in the early 1880s.

This species occurs over a wide area, ranging through the Himalayas and western and northern China, in mixed forests and open spaces. Hardiness Zone 6/7.

It is a deciduous shrub or small tree, usually growing to 3 m (10 ft) but can be up to 7 m (24 ft).

The inflorescence is an open corymb up to 30 cm (12 in) across. The numerous white, fertile flowers are surrounded by white sterile flowers, composed of four sepals and measuring up to 3 cm (1 in) across.

The young branches are hairy but in the second year they have brown bark, sometimes close and sometimes peeling. The leaves are ovate, 10–20 cm (4–8 in) long, 3–14 cm (1–5 in) wide, with very fine bristly serrations.

The upper leaf surface is a smooth dull green and the lower surface is variably covered with hairs. The petioles are red.

H. heteromalla, a native of temperate to sub-tropical zones, grows best where it has plenty of space; if crowded, it tends to get leggy.

Some of the forms or cultivars of this species can make a handsome feature for the larger garden as they flower generously from late June to August. The following are included in this book:

H. heteromalla 'Bretschneideri'
H. heteromalla 'Jermyn's Lace'
H. heteromalla 'Snow Cap'   } pp.89-90
H. heteromalla 'Wilsonii'
H. heteromalla 'Xanthoneura'
H. heteromalla 'Yalung Ridge'

H. hirta (Thunb.) Siebold

This species, named *Viburnum hirtum* by Thunberg in 1784, and transferred to *Hydrangea* by Siebold in 1828, is found in the mountainous districts of Honshu, Japan, and in Okinawa, Ryukyu Islands. Hardiness Zone 7.

It is a deciduous shrub and grows to a maximum of 2 m (7 ft).

The inflorescence is unusual in having only fertile flowers, which form flat corymbs 2–10 cm (0.75–4 in) wide, and appear early

Fig. 15 *Hydrangea heteromalla*

Fig. 16 *Hydrangea hirta*

Fig. 17 *Hydrangea integrifolia*

in the year. Flower colour is usually blue but can also be white or pink, and, on the Japanese plants, the flowers are scented.

The leaves are obovate to elliptic with a short acuminate tip, slight hairy on both surfaces, 3–10 cm (1–4 in) long and 2½–7 cm (1–3 in) wide. The leaf margin is a characteristic feature of this species, being likened to the leaf of a nettle, and having coarse serrations 3–8 mm (⅛–⅜ in) deep.

There is a substantial planting of this species in Savill Gardens, Windsor, England and the shrub is also growing well in the National Collection in Cumbria. It could be more widely grown, as it is not demanding, interesting and different.

H. integrifolia Hayata
This is a member of the section Cornidia, subsection Monosegia. It alone grows in the East, in Taiwan and Philippine Islands, while all other hydrangeas in this section grow in the Americas. Hardiness Zone 9.

It is a vigorous self-supporting evergreen climber, adhering easily to walls or trees and covering considerable areas. When in bud, the inflorescence is enclosed in bracts.

These fall leaving a scar on the stem. The mass of white fertile flowers emerges, surrounded by a sparse peripheral garland of white sterile flowers. The evergreen leaves are elliptic, 5–18 cm (2–7 in) long and 4–7 cm (1½–2½ in) wide. They are mid green, glossy both above and below and have entire borders.

The plant is similar to *H. seemannii*, described later, but is far removed geographically, the latter coming from Mexico. Both grow easily in Britain needing a sunny exposure to flower well.

H. involucrata Sieb.
A small deciduous shrub, usually less than 1 m (3 ft) high, found in Honshu, Japan and introduced in the early 1900s. It grows in woods and mixed forests, from sea level to 1,500 m (5,000 ft). Hardiness Zone 7.

The flower buds are spherical and enclosed in six downy bracts which fall when the inflorescence opens, leaving scars on the stem. The emerging corymb, 8–15 cm (3–6 in) across, has numerous fertile flowers, pink or lilac or blue, and a small, variable number of ray flowers, white or very pale pink or blue, appearing from August to October.

The leaves are a dull green, 7–15 cm (3–6 in) long by 2½–6 cm (1–2½ in) wide, elliptic to ovate with acuminate tips. The margins have very fine bristly hairs and the surfaces have appressed hairs, giving a rough texture.

This modest plant, although not widely grown, is of considerable garden value with its interesting buds and long flowering period. Its size makes it suitable for the front of a mixed border, where its deep-blue fertile flowers and white ray flowers give good effect. Several planted together would make an attractive feature, and the fact that it flowers late, in August, is an extra bonus. However, it is not especially hardy, often losing its top growth in a hard winter, although new shoots usually appear

Fig. 19 *Hydrangea involucrata*: six weeks later

from the base in the next season. It is thus best grown in milder areas or in a somewhat sheltered site.

The cultivar *H. involucrata* 'Hortensis' is attractive, and is described on page 90. Other variants of this species are grown in Japan, and would be welcome in western gardens.

H. macrophylla (Thunb.) Ser.
This is the species from which the majority of familiar cultivated hydrangeas derive.

The wild plant occurs in the eastern Himalayas, in north-east Burma and western China, but mostly in Japan and Korea. It is a deciduous shrub up to 4 m (15 ft) tall. Hardiness Zone 5/6.

The inflorescence is a much-branched corymb, of which the central fertile flowers are white and the sterile flowers white or blue, either entire or serrate. Leaves are ovate to elliptic to obovate, with acute or acuminate tips, 5½–19 cm (2–7½ in) long

Fig. 18 *Hydrangea involucrata*: flowers emerging from bracts

and 2½–13 cm (1–5 in) wide. Leaf length is 1½–4 times the width. Margins are serrated and the texture varies from thick to thin.

Dr McClintock describes four subspecies, two of which occur rarely on the Asiatic mainland. The other two, the most common and best known, are found in Japan and are the progenitors of garden hydrangeas. These Japanese plants are:

A **H. macrophylla ssp. macrophylla**
Synonyms: *H. macrophylla* f.*normalis* (Wils)
H. maritima (Haworth-Booth)
H. macrophylla (used for simplicity in this book)

This subspecies is only found in a few coastal areas of central Honshu. It is versatile, easily cultivated and adaptable. Its flowers can change colour according to the pH and mineral content of the soil, so it

Fig. 20 *Hydrangea macrophylla* ssp. *macrophylla*

lends itself to experiment. It is a vigorous plant, 1–3 m (3–10 ft) high, with glossy serrated leaves, thick and somewhat fleshy in texture, their length being approx. 1½ times greater than their width. The inflorescence of the native plant is composed of both fertile and sterile flowers, i.e. it is of 'lacecap' form.

The history of this species is complex. Although the globe or mophead hydrangea had been cultivated in China and Japan for centuries, and had been introduced into Europe in 1789, its origin remained for long a mystery. It was not until 1917 that Wilson located the native plant growing on coastal areas of central Honshu, and realized that it was the progenitor of the familiar mophead hydrangeas. The mopheads were merely an 'anomalous condition' of the wild form, the only significant difference being that the wild form had few sterile florets and the cultivated form, many. This opinion was accepted by McClintock, but Haworth-Booth differed in thinking that the mopheads were of hybrid origin.

With its origins in a warm, temperate, maritime climate, free from extremes, these are the conditions that *H. macrophylla* prefers. More detail on this subject is given in the chapter on cultivation, pages 45–64.

There are now over five hundred cultivars of this species, both mopheads and lacecaps, some of the best and most readily available of which are described in Chapter 6.

B **H. macrophylla ssp. serrata (Thunb.) Mak.**
Synonym: *H. Serrata* (used for simplicity in this book)

This is the second subspecies recognized by McClintock. It is found in the four islands of

Fig. 21 *Hydrangea macrophylla* ssp *serrata*

Japan, and in Quelpart Island of Korea, often but not always in mountainous areas. It is referred to by the Japanese as the 'mountain hydrangea'. Hardiness Zone 6.

It is a small deciduous upright shrub, seldom exceeding 1½ m (5 ft) high.

The inflorescence is a flat-topped or slightly convex corymb, 5–10 cm (2–4 in) across, with sterile flowers almost always present. The fertile flowers may be pink or blue and the sterile ones may be pink, blue or white, with entire or serrated margins.

The leaves are ovate, to lanceolate, to elliptic – 5–15 cm (2–6 in) long, 3–6 cm (1–2½ in) wide, with acute or acuminate tips. The leaf length is 1½ to 4 times the width. The texture is thin (as opposed to the thicker and rather lush texture of *H. m.* ssp. *macrophylla* leaves), more or less pubescent and dull in appearance.

This subspecies is sometimes quoted as being less hardy than *H. m.* ssp. *macrophylla* but this has not been the authors' experience. *H. m.* ssp. *serrata* is of smaller stature, and has slender more woody stems and less lush growth, but this does not make it less hardy. It prefers to be cool, but can withstand drought better than *H. m.* ssp. *macrophylla*. In its native habitat, in the mountains of Japan, it grows in open places in the cooler north, but in the warmer south it often takes to the woods for shelter.

Many cultivars of this species change flower colour with the pH and mineral content of the soil, as do the cultivars of *H. m.* ssp. *macrophylla*. There is one group within *H. m.* ssp. *serrata*, however, in which the sterile flowers open white, then, in sunlight, change through pink to various shades of red. They never display a hint of blue, no matter what composition the soil may have. These and other cultivars of *H. m.* ssp. *serrata* are described on pages 137–150.

H. paniculata Sieb. AM 1964
This species, introduced by Siebold in the 1860s, is a native of China and Japan and shows little significant variation throughout the regions where it occurs.

It is a deciduous shrub or tree, up to 7 m (24 ft) high in favoured places. Its natural habitat is in woods and open places, up to heights of 1,200 m (4,000 ft). It is adaptable, as the climates where it grows range from cool temperate to sub-tropical, but it can withstand low winter temperatures. Hardiness Zone 3/4.

The inflorescence is a much-branched pyramidal panicle and is the only Asiatic hydrangea to bear an inflorescence of this shape. It is 15–20 cm (6–8 in) long and 10–13 cm (4–5 in) wide at the base, and is

Fig. 22 *Hydrangea paniculata*

frosts. This makes them an attractive proposition in areas which would be too cold for other hydrangeas. They do have a slight disadvantage however. Because they grow so fast their stems tend to be brittle. This, combined with the fact that they carry large flower heads, makes them subject to wind damage. This problem, however, is quite easily overcome by careful positioning, and is outweighed by the species' attributes – strikingly beautiful, easy to grow and frost-hardy.

Several cultivars of *H. paniculata* are described on pages 151–157.

H. quercifolia Bartr. AGM 1992 (H4)
Found in south-east USA and introduced to Britain in 1803, this species is one of only two in the genus to have pinnate leaves. Hardiness Zone 5.

It is an open deciduous shrub growing 1–2 m (3–7 ft) high. The inflorescence is an open panicle 15–225 cm (6–10 in) long and up to 12 cm (5 in) in diameter at the base.

composed mainly of whitish fertile flowers with only a few white/pinkish sterile florets. The lowermost flowers open in sequence before the upper.

The mid-green leaves are either opposite or ternate, ovate to elliptic, 7–15 cm (3–6 in) long, (3½–7 cm (1½–3 in) wide, with acute or acuminate tip. The edges are finely toothed. Some bristly hairs appear on the upper surface, and more on the veins of the lower surface.

The wild form of this species is not commonly grown, but the cultivar *H. paniculata* 'Grandiflora', with its few sterile flowers is, especially in eastern USA, where it is known as the 'PG hydrangea'. Many cultivars are now available and are becoming increasingly popular, not surprising as they are very decorative. They also have the great advantage that, because they flower on the current season's wood, they bloom late in the season (with the exception of *H. paniculata* 'Praecox'), and are therefore not subject to late spring

Fig. 23 *Hydrangea quercifolia*

The numerous white sterile flowers with long pedicels and dense clusters of white fertile flowers bloom from July to September.

The leaves are 8–25 cm (3–10 in) long and 5–17 cm (2–7 in) wide, usually five-lobed and resembling an oak leaf. The leaf margins are variably serrated, the upper surface is rugose and the lower pubescent, as are the petioles and young branches. The colour of the leaves, which is light to mid-green early in the year, darkens and then turns to shades of gold and crimson in the autumn, when the plant makes a splendid and eye-catching feature.

This species is readily available and is specially prized for the attractive autumn colouring of its leaves, as well as for its white panicles. In the warmth of native south-east USA it grows vigorously and produces large inflorescences on erect stems. Cooler conditions hamper its development, producing smaller flower heads and weaker stems. It is, nevertheless, a distinctive plant for western parts of the British Isles, and in gardens where some shelter can be given. It does well in Devon and Cornwall; good specimens have been seen in a walled garden in Yorkshire, and several are flourishing on a sheltered hillside in Cumbria.

Some excellent cultivars have been developed, and are described on pages 158–160.

H. scandens (L.f) Seringe 1830

A deciduous shrub, up to 4 m (13 ft) tall, found in south Japan and east Asia. Introduced to Britain in 1878 by M. Leichtlin, and then grown in the temperate house at Kew. Hardiness Zone 9 according to Krussman (1985), but seen growing out-of-doors in southern England.

Fig. 24 *Hydrangea scandens*

The inflorescence is a lax compound cluster, 2–18 cm (³/₄–7 in) across. Fertile flowers may be either few or many, yellow or blue, and the sterile flowers may be white, yellow or blue, turning red or yellow as they age. They have slightly serrated sepals, and are held on long pedicels.

Leaves are ovate/elliptic/lanceolate, 2–18 cm (³/₄–7 in) long by 1–8 cm (¹/₂–3 in) wide, smooth, or hairy in the vicinity of the veins.

McClintock divides this species into four subspecies, two of which, ssp. *scandens* and ssp. *liukiuensis* are found in Japan, and the other two of which, ssp. *kwangtungensis* and ssp. *chinensis*, are found on the east Asian mainland.

Although not widely grown in Europe, several plants of *H. scandens* ssp. *scandens* have been seen by the authors, and this subspecies is now stocked in a few nurseries. The fact that the ray flowers show a yellow colour is so unusual for a hydrangea, that the species might well become more popular. Attractive variations are to be seen in Japan, with stronger shades of yellow (Yamamoto, 1985).

H. scandens ssp. *chinensis* shows considerable variations throughout its range in eastern Asia, and McClintock gives a long list of synonyms for it.

H. seemannii Riley

This vigorous evergreen climber is one of the section Cornidia of the genus *Hydrangea* and is found in Mexico. Here it grows in the Sierra Madre Occidental at heights of 2,000–2,600 m (6,500–8,500 ft), where, in spite of the altitude, the low latitude ensures warm temperatures. Hardiness Zone 9.

The inflorescence, a single and terminal corymb, is contained in pale-green/cream bracts at the bud stage. These open and fall to release the inflorescence, which is tightly compressed, but which gradually expands to display a flower head of somewhat untidy outline. Numerous white fertile flowers are surrounded by a rough, irregular circle of several white sterile flowers with overlapping sepals.

Fig. 25 *Hydrangea seemannii:* bud enclosed in bracts

Fig. 27 *Hydrangea seemannii:* flowers developing

Fig. 26 *Hydrangea seemannii:* flowers emerging

Fig. 28 *Hydrangea seemannii:* inflorescence fully open

The leaves are elliptic, 5–20 cm (2–8 in) long, 1½–6 cm (½–2½ in) wide. They are dark green, smooth above rather like laurel, and have slight, very shallow serrations.

This species, described in 1924, is not included in McClintock's list of cultivated hydrangeas of 1956 because it had not been introduced by that date. It is mentioned by Nevling (1964) as being held in only a few collections. Neil Treseder reports having been sent seeds in 1973 which produced good plants, but still had not shown flowers in 1988. Our own experience concurs with that of Neil Treseder, in that the plant grows well and makes excellent ground cover as well as climbing with vigour, but flowers are slow to appear. When it does flower the blooms are rather more attractive than those of the similar *H. serratifolia*, so it is hoped that, in time, this will become a popular addition to the few flowering evergreen climbers.

H. serratifolia Hooker and Arnott

This evergreen climber, another of the section Cornidia, was introduced into Britain by H.F. Comber in 1927. It is a native of Chile and Argentina, and found at altitudes of 800–1,500 m (2,500–4,500 ft), thus in a colder environment than the other climbing hydrangeas described. Hardiness Zone 9.

Clinging by adventitious roots, it climbs on rocks and up tall trees, and can achieve a height of over 30 m (100 ft), so its vigour is something to be taken into consideration when planting.

The all-fertile inflorescence, up to 10 cm (4 in) across, is usually pale cream but can be deep yellow. In the bud stage each corymb is enclosed by several creamy yellow bracts, each forming an attractive globose

Fig. 29 *Hydrangea serratifolia*: flowers emerging

Fig. 30 *Hydrangea serratifolia*: some flowers fully open shape. As the bud opens, the bracts fall and the flowers with their generally long stamens emerge, usually in June.

The leaves, 5–15 cm (2–6 in) long and 2½–7 cm (1–3 in) wide, are elliptic with acute tips. They are smooth and glossy above and smooth below, and are rather similar to laurel. The outline of the leaf, however, belies the name *H. serratifolia*, as the leaves are almost always entire. The earlier name of *H. integerrima*, meaning entire, would seem more appropriate, but following the rules of botanical nomenclature, the name *H. serratifolia* takes preference.

All in all, this is a useful garden plant. It is one of few evergreen, flowering climbers, is self-supporting, and with its glossy leaves, its unusual spherical buds and its creamy flowers, has much to recommend it, especially to those with the space to do it justice.

It has been seen growing well in the Royal Botanic Garden, Edinburgh, and in Logan Garden, Dumfries and Galloway, Scotland, as well as in the Van Dusen Garden, Vancouver, Canada.

H. sikokiana Maximowicz

Found in the mountainous districts of the islands of Honshu, Kyushu and Shikoko, Japan, this shrub grows to approximately 2 m (6 ft). Hardiness Zone 6.

The inflorescence is a many-branched compound cluster, of indeterminate shape. The white fertile flowers are numerous. The sterile flowers, though few, are always present, around the periphery of the corymb. They have four orbicular sepals, white fading to cream, and measure 1–3 cm (½–1 in) in diameter. The flowers appear early to mid-season.

Fig. 31 *Hydrangea sikokiana*

The leaves are pinnately lobed, as are those of *H. quercifolia*, and these are the only two species in the genus with lobed leaves. The leaves of *H. sikokiana* measure 8–20 cm (3–8 in) long by 8–20 cm (3–8 in) wide, and are hairy along the veins on both surfaces. Petioles are long – up to 18 cm (7 in). According to a Japanese writer (Yamamoto, 1985) the cut leaf smells of melon.

Only one plant of this species has been seen by the authors, but it was growing well in southern England in semi-shade. Another is reputed to be growing well in a National Collection near the coast of Ayrshire, Scotland. It is unusual, decorative and hardy and could well be more widely cultivated.

Some Problems and Peculiarities of *Hydrangea macrophylla*

Naming the species

Confusion started a long time ago. It seems likely that plants growing in Japanese gardens, some of them imported from China, had acquired names before Western botanists became interested. Perhaps the language barrier prevented names from being transferred or understood. The plant-finders' urge to identify and classify was strong, however, so names were given and opinions varied. A few of the names which have emerged over the years, and which the reader may encounter, are shown below. Although not an exhaustive list of synonyms for *H. macrophylla*, it is sufficient to illustrate the potential for confusion:

a *Viburnum macrophylla* and *Viburnum serrata*

These names were used by the Swedish doctor, Thunberg, in his *Flora Japonica* of 1784, for plants he had grown from seed obtained from mainland Japan. These plants are today known respectively as *Hydrangea macrophylla* and *Hydrangea serrata*, the transfer to the genus *Hydrangea* being made by Seringe in 1830.

b *Hortensia*

This generic name was given by the French botanist, de Jussieu, in 1789.

c *Hydrangea opuloides*

This specific name was given by Lamarck, in 1789, to a plant cultivated in Mauritius.

d *Hydrangea hortensis*

Sir James Smith gave this name, in 1792, to the plant given to Kew, England. under the auspices of Joseph Banks in 1789. The plant, a mophead, was reminiscent of *Hydrangea arborescens*, from USA, identified by Linnaeus in 1753.

e *Hydrangea hortensia*

This was the name used by Siebold, in 1829, to describe a plant found in Japanese gardens which was very similar to *H. hortensis* named by Smith.

f *Hydrangea* 'Otaksa'

Siebold and Zuccarini used this name in their *Flora Japonica* (1839) for a plant which closely resembles those already mentioned in *d* and *e* above.

g *H. japonica, H. acuminata, H. thunbergii*

These were given by Siebold and Zuccarini to plants which had been observed in cultivation in Japan in the 1820s. The names were taken by Haworth-Booth as being recognized distinct species, but McClintock disagrees, saying that they are most probably forms of *H. macrophylla* ssp. *serrata*.

h *Hydrangea hortensis* 'Otaksa'

Ebel, in his *Hydrangea et Hortensia* of 1934, used this name to designate a plant introduced to France around 1860. This was a strong-growing mophead reminiscent of Thunberg's plant, and from it, Lemoine, one of the great French nurserymen, produced the cultivar *H.* 'Otaksa Monstrosa' in 1894.

i *Hydrangea* 'Azisai'

The word 'azisai' is Japanese for hydrangea. The Japanese use it for plants native to Japan; but for species and cultivars from elsewhere, they use the name 'Hydrangea'.

The name 'Azisai' was used by Siebold and Zuccarini for a lacetop type plant grown in Japan, and the name is still used for a plant in present-day cultivation.

j *Hydrangea maritima*

This name was given by Haworth-Booth, in 1950, to the plant identified by Wilson in 1917, and called by him *H. macrophylla* var. *normalis*, and called by McClintock *H. macrophylla* ssp. *macrophylla*. It is a lacetop form.

The proliferation of names may be due partly to the wide span of variability within the species, particularly of the eye-catching changes in the inflorescence. The proportion and arrangement of fertile and sterile flowers varies greatly. This also happens in other hydrangea species, such as *H. arborescens*, but is more marked in *H. macrophylla*. The flower colour in this species ranges from white, through all shades of pink, lilac and blue. There is a large planting of *H. macrophylla* in Kew Gardens, and the colourful display there epitomizes this characteristic, with each shrub slightly different and flower colours varying within the same plant. Sports are quite common. Sterile flowers can have serrated or entire sepal edges, both on the same flower head, or sepal edges can change as the flower matures. Leaf size and shape vary, not only from one shrub to another, but within the same plant. This marked capacity for change must present problems even to the most dedicated taxonomist.

Development of cultivars

Some of these features, especially the form and colour of flower heads, have naturally been exploited by breeders. Early varieties were introduced to Europe from Japan. Some, such as *H. m.* 'Mariesii', *H. m.* 'Rosea', *H. m.* 'Otaksa' and *H. serrata* 'Rosalba', were the ancestors of plants still popular today. During the early 1900s, famous nurserymen Lemoine, Mouillère and Cayeux in France, Veitch in England, Schadendorff and Wintergalen in Germany, to name but a few, bred a wide range of colourful and decorative plants from early introductions. Sadly some records were lost in the devastation of the Second World War, notably those of Cayeux and Mouillère, but many plants are still with us.

The plants developed in this productive era were selected to obtain particular results of stamina, resistance to pests or special colour effects. The majority were for the 'pot trade', i.e. for growing in pots

as presents for Easter and Mother's Day, and for indoor decoration for municipal offices, entrance foyers or sporting events. Hortensias were considered preferable and lacecaps were mostly discarded. Large numbers of cultivars evolved – over five hundred are known. Haworth-Booth thought in 1955 that 'the breeding of the old type Hortensias (mopheads) has nearly reached stagnation – almost every conceivable combination of the available genes has given birth'. Inevitably, there are similarities between the cultivars, and distinctions are often drawn with a very fine line. Given the capacity for change in colour and form already described, the differences between two flower heads from one plant may well be greater than that between two flowers from supposedly different cultivars. Also, even with the best care, labelling is never perfect, and name errors can arise. Once the identity of a hydrangea cultivar is lost, re-establishing it is difficult, if not impossible, due to the ephemeral nature of the flower features.

The fact that hydrangeas are easy to propagate allows confusion to spread rapidly. A cutting taken from a friend's garden may grow into a totally different-coloured plant in one's own garden, and may also change again as it matures. The chameleon hydrangea is a challenge to any keeper of garden records.

'Teller' hydrangeas

The word 'Teller' is the German for 'plate' and, in this context, refers to the flat-headed hydrangea flower known in Britain as a lacecap. Lacecaps were not appreciated by early European breeders, although some excellent plants did, and still do, exist. After the enthusiasm for plant breeding in the early part of the twentieth century, war years interrupted progress.

After the Second World War, however, some good cultivars were produced in Wädenswil, Switzerland. Among these were *H. m.* 'Hörnli' and *H. m.* 'Tödi'. Further research at this centre resulted, by 1964, in the so-called 'Teller' series of lacecaps. These were bred for strength, compact growth and beauty in form and colour of sepals. Their hardiness in gardens is yet to be established, but certainly some are totally successful in both northern and southern England.

The plants have Swiss/German names of birds. These names should either have been retained when the plants were exported, or could easily have been translated. Sadly, neither has happened, and in British nurseries they are often found merely as 'Teller Red', 'Teller White' or 'Teller Blue'. Fortunately, one or two specialist firms are promoting these plants with the correct names. There are twenty-six different cultivars in the series, so that yet again the differences are sometimes slight, but even half that number, under correct or translated names, would be welcome, for they are beautiful plants.

The second section of this book contains the detailed plant descriptions. It was difficult to decide which of the Tellers to include as almost all of them are growing well in Cumbria. The following, however, have been selected: *H. macrophylla* Bläuling, Blaumeise, Libelle, Möwe, Mousmée, Pfau and Rotschwanz.

In some regions with more 'continental' type climate, Tellers have been reported to be damaged by early autumn or late spring frosts. Our own experience, and that of other growers in UK, has shown them to be every bit as hardy as the majority of cultivars of *H. macrophylla*.

Japanese plants

In the land where several hydrangea species are native, including the popular *H. macrophylla*, breeding has taken place intermittently over centuries. Perhaps because they grow so freely there hydrangeas have been taken for granted in Japan. However, up-to-date plant catalogues, and lectures on hydrangeas at major flower shows in Japan indicate present-day interest. There are many plants which are not known in Europe and America, and which are exceptionally beautiful. Different colours, varying sepal shapes, double flowers and two-coloured sepals are illustrated, and 'bonsai' hydrangeas are being developed. Very gradually, some of these plants are becoming available in Europe and USA. It is to be hoped that this trend continues and that original names are retained. Japanese names are not difficult to pronounce and future confusion would be avoided.

Garden hardiness

Plants growing on the islands of Japan enjoy a maritime climate, except in mountainous areas. Parts of mainland Europe experience more continental climatic influence, with much greater extremes of temperature. For this reason, the early hydrangeas introduced to Europe were treated as delicate and grown in pots. Thus the reputation of hydrangeas as attractive pot plants developed, both in Europe and in USA. In Britain, the climate is similarly maritime, and the vogue for pot plants not quite so strong; so hydrangeas have become familiar, or even commonplace, as garden plants.

Such reputations die hard. It is necessary to consider the climate, the aspect and the individual plant before deciding whether it will flourish out-of-doors. Cultivars of *H. macrophylla* grow well in most parts of

Britain, and also in the maritime areas of France, Germany and the Low Countries. The *Revue Horticole*, in 1946, referred to Biarritz as 'ville des hortensias', of which Angers, where one of the French Regional Collections now flourishes, 'should not be jealous!'. In Madeira, hydrangeas are so prolific that they are used as hedges. The plants also do well in the lake areas of northern Italy, and in many other parts of Europe where the temperature range is moderate. In USA, eastern, south-eastern and north-western states are suitable for growing a range of hydrangea species; and even as far inland as St Louis, Missouri, a collection is being formed. Wonderful displays can be seen around the coastal areas of British Columbia and into Canada, and in many parts of Australia and New Zealand.

The establishment of National Collections in Britain, Regional Collections in France, North American Plant Preservation Council Collections, and Ornamental Plant Collections in Australia, has done much to foster interest in particular genera, and all these organizations include hydrangeas in their lists. *H. macrophylla* may have its problems, but none which cannot be overcome with good horticultural practice. Reginald Kay, in the *RHS Journal*, April 1969, writes: 'It seems to be the fate of many groups of plants to experience maximum periods of popularity followed by a general waning of interest, to a time when they almost disappear from cultivation.' There would seem to be a resurgence of popularity for hydrangeas (which usually means cultivars of *H. macrophylla*), and this time they are becoming widely appreciated as garden plants.

2 Hydrangeas in Gardens

A 'garden' can be anything from a small, suburban plot, or even a city roof-top, to an estate of many acres. Within the boundaries, wide or narrow, some gardeners accept an existing layout, while others impose their own ideas, and a row of similar houses often has a great variety of gardens. Among this diversity of plots, hydrangeas are widely grown, but not always with sufficient discrimination to benefit the garden or show the plant to its best advantage.

A brief resumé of the different hydrangeas available may be helpful at this point.

Hydrangea species are generally less decorative than the cultivars which have been derived from them. They can be obtained from specialist nurseries, but most are grown more for interest than for appearance.

The commonly grown cultivars are those of *Hydrangea macrophylla*, and their size, mostly around $1\frac{1}{2}$ m (4–5 ft) in height and width, makes them suitable for many different gardens. Of these cultivars, mopheads are more numerous than lacecaps, but there is also quite a choice among the lacecaps, and their delicate form has a charm of its own. Originally they appeared mostly in pastel shades, but new varieties have bolder colours, to match those of the more flamboyant mopheads. Where *H. macrophylla* cultivars are grown, flower colour will be influenced by the soil (see Chapter 3), and those gardening on alkaline soil may find it impossible to get blue flowers. One of the subspecies of *H. macrophylla*, is *H. serrata*, and the cultivars

of this group, nearly all lacecaps, are most attractive, some adding to their elegant display with good autumn colouring which is independent of soil type.

Cultivars have been developed from some of the other hydrangea species, many of which, although less familiar, are worthy of consideration and inclusion in appropriate gardens. Space is always a controlling factor, and some of the cultivars of *H. aspera* and *H. heteromalla* can become large shrubs or small trees. *H. aspera* 'Villosa', a most beautiful shrub, can grow very large, but *H. aspera* 'Mauvette' would suit a medium-sized garden. *H. arborescens* 'Annabelle' grows to about $1\frac{1}{2}$ m (4–5 ft), as do *H. quercifolia* 'Snow Queen' and *H. quercifolia* 'Snowflake', in cooler northern latitudes, while *H. involucrata* 'Hortensis' is a small and attractive plant. From *H. paniculata* have been developed some excellent cultivars, which can grow to large shrubs and make splendid feature plants. Alternatively, they can be pruned as desired to produce smaller shrubs, in which case larger flower heads will result.

Lastly, the climbers: three evergreen species are available, *H. serratifolia*, *H. seemannii* and *H. integrifolia*, which are vigorous, but flower better in warmer areas. The deciduous climber, *H. anomala petiolaris* is easily grown, although it dislikes too much sun. Once established, it makes a good wall plant, giving early summer flower and autumn leaf colour.

Such then is the broad outline of the range, and Chapter 6 supplies detailed descriptions of many hydrangeas. In this present chapter some specific indications are given of how the different types can be incorporated in various locations.

In the smallest of gardens – maybe a balcony, a town-house terrace or a basement 'area', a hydrangea in a tub would look well and, given care with feeding and watering, would give many months of colour. A special advantage of container growing is that the soil pH can more easily be controlled and hence the colour of the flower influenced. Some of the smaller cultivars of *H. macrophylla* would be suitable. *H. m.* 'Pia', which is a dwarf; *H. m.* 'Ami Pasquier', 'Ave Maria', 'Hörnli', 'Tovelit', 'Westfalen', none of which exceed 1 m (3 ft) in height, would look well. *H. serrata* 'Diadem', a lovely lacecap, would suit a large pot or half a barrel, as it grows slowly to a maximum of around a metre (3–4 ft), and is decorative for a very long season.

Against a house wall is definitely a favourite place for hydrangeas – the warmth and shelter of the house seems to bring out the best in them. A west or north-west facing wall is ideal, as it will not get too hot and will protect the plant from cold east winds. One suggestion might be *H. serrata* 'Preziosa' which flourishes in the extra protection; and its attributes could be enjoyed at the close quarters they merit. *H. macrophylla* 'Mme E. Mouillère' also gives a long and splendid display in this setting, where the beautiful white mopheads are sheltered from the hottest sun. Many of the other *H. macrophylla* cultivars could benefit from this position – it is mostly a question of personal selection. *H. involucrata* 'Hortensis' would be another choice as it needs some extra protection; it has a delicate and beautiful flower which repays close inspection. It can also withstand the alkaline soil which often occurs near house walls.

Underplanted with snowdrops and later small spring bulbs, any of these could make a trouble-free arrangement, attractive from spring to autumn.

The majority of gardens in Britain are probably around 0.05 hectare ($\frac{1}{8}$ acre) and in such a plot there may well be room for one or two hydrangeas. Indeed, some should be included, for their attributes of flowering both late and long are particularly appreciated where the number of plants has to be limited. In a mixed border, or in a shrub area, a mophead could give a bold accent of colour, particularly welcome late in the season. An advantage of a modest-sized garden is that each plant gets more individual attention, and many hydrangeas have features which can only be appreciated when seen close up. They can otherwise be too readily dismissed as 'just a hydrangea'.

Some of the smaller *H. macrophylla* cultivars which should be considered are: 'Alpenglühen', a good red even down to pH 6.5, and a well-formed flower; 'Amethyst', with its double florets; 'Ayesha', the colour of whose unusual-shaped sepals is closely related to the soil; 'Brunette' – if a plant can be found – is striking with dark leaves; 'Gentian Dome' and 'Pfau' should not be omitted by those on acid soil, for their colour is eye-catching; 'Soeur Thérèse' is a delicate white; 'Nigra' has attractive flowers as well as dark stems; the variegated leaves of 'Quadricolor' add interest, while one of the Teller lacecaps such as 'Blaumeise' or 'Rotschwanz' gives strong colour and elegant shape. For overall merit, *H. serrata* 'Blue Bird' would be hard to beat for colour, length of flowering, hardiness and grace.

Remembering that colour will be related to the soil, a few of these suggested plants –

or others in Chapter 6 – would enhance the average garden.

The larger garden offers more scope. Larger varieties can be used and the season extended by selecting some early flowering cultivars as well as some later ones. Examples of early flowerers are *H. serrata* 'Blue Deckle', the well-known *H. macrophylla* 'Générale Vicomtesse de Vibraye' and the lovely white *H. macrophylla* 'Veitchii'. Among particularly good later ones are *H. macrophylla* 'Blue Wave', 'Lilacina', 'Mariesii' and 'Sea Foam', all of which often carry blooms into November, in English Lakeland. Both *H. s.* 'Tiara' and *H. m.* 'All Summer Beauty' have long flowering seasons.

With more space there is also more choice in the arrangement of plants. As with the smaller garden, single hydrangeas are an asset in mixed borders, or in a shrub area. Hydrangeas could also be planted in a bed devoted solely to them, and this would give interest from late June to November. Single plants of several different cultivars give a multi-colour effect, which is interesting if the bed can be viewed at close quarters and the individual plants enjoyed. Impact from a distance is better achieved, however, when two or more of one cultivar are planted together. A 'hydrangea bed' is not an attractive sight in winter. It would be enhanced, perhaps, by the inclusion of a flowering cherry or a *Hamamelis* (which would give some welcome shade). An ideal arrangement is to form a backdrop of evergreen shrubs which flower earlier in the year and, in acid soil areas, rhododendrons are the obvious choice. This combination, together with an underplanting of small spring bulbs or even a carpet of the lovely blue *Omphalodes*, would give a trouble-free area with colour for the greater part of the year.

In alkaline soils, evergreens which flower at a season to complement the hydrangeas could be selected from among such shrubs as berberis, choisya, mahonia and viburnum. Many of these would make ideal companions in a border.

Positioning to serve as a garden feature or accent is another role for hydrangeas. Some are sufficiently showy over many months to justify planting alone, in a bed cut into a lawn: for instance *H. macrophylla* 'Altona' is ideal for this. It grows to approximately $1^1/_2$ m (5 ft) high and wide, and is robust and decorative from mid-summer to late autumn. The deep-red colouring of the flowers in September and October is quite dramatic, when many other shrubs are fading. Feature planting would also be appropriate for the *H. paniculata* cultivars. *H. paniculata* 'Grandiflora' is the best known, but there are now many other excellent cultivars, all of which make an impact with their striking conical flower heads. *H. paniculata* 'Unique' is very showy for several months, ending its season by turning deep pink, while *H. paniculata* 'Tardiva', with open white panicles, remains decorative often until November. Shelter from strong winds is needed as the long stems are brittle when laden with blooms, but the shrubs are frost-resistant and very easy to grow. *H. arborescens* 'Annabelle' is another eye-catching shrub, with large white globose heads. It also has a long season, and withstands frost and drought better than most, so has much to recommend it. It will sucker and grow quite fast, but the impatient gardener could plant several together, and quickly obtain a striking feature.

A sloping site is attractive for planting hydrangeas, as they show to advantage when viewed from above. Either interspersed with other shrubs, or 'block planted', they make strong patches of colour. Some of the mopheads with really large blooms, such as *H. macrophylla* 'All Summer Beauty', 'Mousseline', and 'Hamburg', or vigorous flowerers like 'Joseph Banks', 'Frillibet' or 'Merritt's Supreme', would display well on such a site. Some extra attention to feeding, mulching and watering is recommended because nutrients can readily be leached out on a slope, and the benefit of rain can be quickly lost by sharp drainage. Awareness of these facts, and sensible gardening practice, are all that is needed.

A large garden may have large trees, and thus be able to supply the semi-shade conditions which are especially suited to some hydrangeas. Provided that the plants do not have to compete with trees for food and water, some light-coloured blooms such as those of the lacecaps *H. macrophylla* 'Libelle', 'Beauté Vendomoise' or 'Tokyo Delight' would grow well under tall trees. *H. serrata* cultivars prefer to stay cool, so 'Rosalba' or 'Grayswood' would suit dappled shade. The beautiful cultivars of *H. quercifolia*, 'Snowflake', 'Snow Queen' and 'Harmony', would all like the protection given by trees, but they really need all the warmth they can get, so would have to face into the sun.

It may be desirable to include one or more of the larger hydrangeas, depending on the size of the garden. *H. aspera* 'Villosa' grows to a very large shrub, but is quite lovely, keeping its colouring of pale-pink ray flowers around a centre of lilac/blue regardless of soil pH. Given the space, this too would make an excellent feature plant, as would *H. a.* 'Kawakami' or *H. a.* 'Peter Chappell'. Even bigger, and really for a large place in semi-shade, is *H. aspera sargentiana*. It is rather gaunt, but with its huge leaves and flowers provides a good

background for smaller, shade-loving plants. The *heteromalla* species need a large garden, and are strikingly beautiful in early summer, especially if their light flowers can be seen against a background of evergreens. Some also give a display of yellow autumn foliage.

Walls add another dimension to any garden, and the deciduous climber, *H. anomala petiolaris*, can be grown where it will not get too hot – a north-facing wall is ideal. It takes a little time to 'get its feet down', but then climbs quickly and supports itself, flowering in July with lovely golden leaves in autumn. It can also be grown up a tree trunk, or to cover an old stump or shed and will be a mass of stems in the winter. The three evergreen climbing hydrangeas now available, *H. serratifolia*, *H. seemannii* and *H. integrifolia* grow vigorously and are also self-supporting, covering rapidly with very strong growth once established. Their flowers are interesting, with globose buds opening to white lacy blooms, but their season is short and they require a sheltered garden position to flower well. They merit inclusion, however, where space allows, for climbing evergreen flowering shrubs are not numerous and they do make a good talking point!

The extent to which any plant is used in a garden is a matter of personal choice as well as suitability. It will have become apparent, however, that hydrangeas have a wide range in habit, size, colour and flowering time. Their considerable potential can be exploited to best advantage by those with large gardens.

The planting and management of a garden of an acre or more will be of a different order from that of a small plot, and its scope will be wide. Hydrangeas could really come into their own in such a garden, particularly if the soil is slightly acid so that all *H. macrophylla* colours can be displayed.

Many of these large gardens are open to the public, with the interest often in the spring, centred on azaleas and rhododendrons. The season could easily be extended well into the autumn, by the inclusion of large plantings of hydrangeas forming the classic combination already mentioned. The soil requirements are similar; the flowering seasons follow each other; even the foliage is complementary, the light green of the hydrangea leaves forming an attractive contrast to the dark glossiness of the evergreens. Large sweeps, twenty or more plants of one variety such as *H. serrata* 'Diadem' or *H. serrata* 'Blue Bird', would be effective, giving trouble-free colour from July to October. Some of the colourful 'Tellers', such as *H. m.* 'Möwe' or *H. m.* 'Blaumeise' would be magnificent. Recently in Britain, some large gardens have been extending the area devoted to hydrangeas, so it would seem that the popularity of the genus is increasing. Bold planting is to be recommended.

Features such as woodland, and maybe even a valley with a stream, open up planting possibilities, and the woodland scene could be extended with drifts of white or pastel-flowered cultivars glowing in the semi-shade. The larger species, *H. aspera* and *H. heteromalla*, would also be more suitable here, planted individually among other taller trees. Along the banks of a stream drifts of *H. macrophylla* look spectacular, either multi-coloured or in blocks of single colour, and if some dip into the water, so much the better. Bodnant Garden in North Wales has such a planting, as have some of the gardens in sheltered inlets on the south Cornish coast, and on the Isle of Skye, off the coast of western Scotland.

In areas with frost problems, the two species already suggested, *H. arborescens* and *H. paniculata*, will give good displays, even in the face of late frosts. Savill Garden, Windsor, tends to have 'frost pockets' – areas where low temperatures persist. The generous plantings of *H. paniculata* cultivars in this garden look magnificent, and are unaffected by the cold in spring. Similarly, *H. arborescens* 'Grandiflora' makes a splendid show in a garden where the 'temperate' climate does not quite live up to its name.

Those hydrangeas that need some extra warmth, such as *H. quercifolia* cultivars would be at home within a walled garden. The evergreen climbing species mentioned would also be suitable here, and would have every encouragement to flower well.

The areas where hydrangeas have escaped into the wild are on a greater scale. This can be seen in Cornwall, and in Brittany, where they grow beside roads and in churchyards, and in the Azores, where the plants form a decorative and trouble-free screen, dense and efficient.

3 Cultivation

There is nothing difficult about growing hydrangeas – they are robust, thrive in many different parts of the world where there is a temperate climate and will even withstand a fair degree of neglect. They can be found looking dull and commonplace in the odd corner of many a garden, yet seldom is a dead hydrangea seen. They can, however, do better than merely struggle for survival. Their likes and dislikes are few, but provided attention is paid to their modest requirements, they will offer a long-lasting, colourful display for many years.

Site

If a hydrangea has been planted in a position where it does not thrive, do not despair – it can be moved, provided it can be lifted. A hydrangea's root ball is, in most cases, quite compact and the plant comes out of the ground with a good quantity of soil adhering to its roots. This enables transplanting to be accomplished with a minimum check to growth (see page 55). A shrub more than six or seven years old, however, would be awkward to lift intact from one site to another because of its weight. It is wiser to examine the factors which will help to get the planting position right first time.

Space
Hydrangeas have a long life span. In Cumbria there are many shrubs over fifty years old which are still thriving. It is essential, therefore, to have some idea of the size to which they can grow before choosing a site. Size varies with species,

and there can be further variations among the cultivars within a species. Indications of approximate sizes of cultivars are given with the individual descriptions in Chapter 6, and maximum sizes are mentioned in the descriptions of species (Chapter 2). It may be useful here to summarize the sizes of the cultivated species, putting them into four groups:

a   The climbers: *H. anomala*, *H. seemannii*, *H. serratifolia* and *H. integrifolia* are vigorous once they have got their roots down, and it really is no use planting them where only one or two square yards of house wall need covering. They can cover the side of a house or the length of a large garden wall, according to how they are trained. They can and will expand to fill the space available. They can equally climb up a tree trunk or tumble down a steep bank, forming good ground cover.

b   *H. aspera*, *H. heteromalla*, *H. paniculata* and *H. scandens* can all be large shrubs or small trees. Heights of up to 7 m (20 ft) are quoted in the wild, but in cultivation 2–3 m (7–10 ft) is normal.

c   *H. arborescens* and *H. macrophylla* can be from 1–4 m (3–14 ft) tall, but are readily contained by pruning. An average garden shrub is around $1\frac{1}{2}$–2 m (5–7 ft) tall.

d   *H. hirta*, *H. involucrata*, *H. quercifolia* and *H. sikokiana* are all normally 1–2 m (3–7 ft).

These figures are only general guidelines. Some cultivars of *H. macrophylla*, for example, if left unattended, can self-layer vigorously and thus produce a huge bush.

The habit of suckering, shared by *H. aspera sargentiana*, *H. involucrata* 'Hortensis' and *H. arborescens* and its cultivars, enables the plant to spread without human intervention, as is evidenced by the road-side colonization of *H. arborescens* in parts of the Appalachian Mountain area of south-eastern USA. Alternatively, a plant's spread may be restricted by careful and selective pruning, so that it can be contained in a smaller space yet still give abundant bloom.

Rate of growth is of importance to the gardener, although it is not easy to generalize on the subject. Hydrangeas grow quite fast – a small cutting of *H. macrophylla* cultivar can become a shrub 1 m (3 ft) high within three years, after which time growth is more a matter of consolidation than just increasing height and width. It may take up to ten years for maximum effect, but flowers should appear on a two-to-three-year-old plant, and most garden centres sell shrubs which are of flowering size. A climber may take a couple of years to get established, but it will then cover rapidly, spreading a square metre (square yard) or more a year.

Sun and shade

Most hydrangeas are natural woodland plants, yet this is not always taken into consideration when choosing a site. The high cover of tall woodland trees gives dappled shade which is ideal. In such a setting the hydrangeas flower well, but the blooms are protected from strong sunlight. While early-morning and late-afternoon sun do no harm, hours of midday sun can bleach the flowers and finally scorch them, so that they turn an unattractive brown colour. Shrubs grown in a woodland site not only keep their flowers well and true to colour, but the colours seem almost luminescent in the semi-shade. Moreover,

both flowers and leaves last longer into the winter when under some tree cover, and can still be seen shining out on a dull winter day. Edge of woodland, too, is ideal especially if some evergreens are included, as the trees give not only shade and protection but also a backcloth for the various coloured blooms.

Aspect is not a simple subject, however. Dappled shade, which undeniably suits hydrangeas, is not always easy to achieve. A tree canopy which produces dense shade will also prevent sufficient precipitation from reaching the shrubs below. They will then fail to thrive because of the shortage of moisture, light and food, and smaller flowers on a small, starved bush will result. Too much sun also can be damaging, but even here one cannot generalize, for in northern England and Scotland, the fewer hours of sunshine and the lower angle of the sun will allow greater exposure without the flowers spoiling. All these factors need to be taken into consideration.

As well as assessing the balance of sun and shade, care should also be given to the individual plant's habits; not all hydrangeas react to the elements in the same way. Cultivars of *H. aspera*, for example, prefer some tree cover, while cultivars of *H. paniculata*, whose brittle stems are at risk in strong winds, nevertheless flourish in full sun. *H. arborescens* cultivars are hardy and withstand cold, heat and drought better than other species, while *H. quercifolia* likes warmth. Cultivars of *H. macrophylla* ssp. *serrata*, most of which originate in the mountains of Japan, prefer some shade, or a cool temperate climate, given which they are very robust.

The numerous cultivars of *H. macrophylla* (the familiar mopheads and lacecaps) show many variations in their response to sun. On the whole, the lacecaps withstand hot sun better than hortensias, although their colours are less intense. *H. m.* 'Lanarth White', for example, a lovely white lacecap, fares well in an open position, and does not readily scorch. The white mopheads, however, require some shade to protect them. *H. m.* 'Mme E. Mouillère', an old-established white mophead but still one of the best, gives a splendid display all summer if grown against a north-facing wall. Those hortensias that come into flower early, blooming in June and July, are subjected to the sun at its highest, and are more readily scorched. Later flowerers, and occasional autumn blooms, developing when the sun-power is less, can provide a freshness of colour which prolongs the season. Blue hortensias seem to suffer more conspicuously from scorching than pink or red ones, but such a generalization is risky. *H. m.* 'Gentian Dome' resists scorching better than *H. m.* 'Maréchal Foch', both excellent deep blues, on soil of pH 6.5 or less. Mention of other responses will be found under the individual plant descriptions (Chapter 6).

Proximity to the sea means greater humidity, which reduces the damaging effects of the sun. Mopheads and lacecaps flourish in these conditions, for they are naturally littoral plants. In Britain, where the warming effect of the Gulf Stream is felt on the western shores, superb hydrangeas can be seen as far north as the Isle of Skye. Some compensation, then, for living where cloud and mist is common – hydrangeas will flourish! Among plants which particularly benefit from these conditions are *H. m.* 'Sea Foam', 'Joseph Banks' and 'Ayesha'. Britain's north-east coasts are subject to cold winds, and are thus less hospitable to hydrangeas.

Not all of us, however, live near the sea, nor do we have areas of woodland, so how can we best satisfy the hydrangea's need for shelter? Most gardens have some shade, and, in more northerly latitudes, it is only the hottest midday sun from which protection is needed. A wall, fence or hedge may be the answer, with a north-, east- or west-facing bed being preferable to a south-facing one. The shadow of one large tree may be all that is needed to cut out the hottest sun – sometimes, a neighbour's tree does just that. The foot of a house wall, facing north, east or west is traditionally a good place for hydrangeas, provided that care is taken with soil preparation, feeding and watering. Evergreen shrubs can give excellent protection, as well as providing a pleasing backcloth to the hydrangeas. Some evergreens, such as rhododendrons and pieris, have similar requirements to hydrangeas and complement them by flowering at a different season. In alkaline soils, varieties of holly, mahonia and eleagnus, to quote but a few, would make good companions and provide the necessary shelter.

Wind

The majority of hydrangeas flower on the wood produced during the previous year. Flower buds are carried through the winter and will begin to develop, often rather too early, in the spring, ready for flowering in later summer and autumn. They are at their most tender in April and May and can be completely destroyed by searing cold winds. More flower buds can be formed later in the year, but these will not be ready to produce blooms in the same season. So, although the plant will not die – it takes a lot to kill a hydrangea – a whole season's flowers can be lost.

The winds most likely to create this sad cycle of events come from the north and east in the British Isles, so it is from these directions that some protection should be given, if possible, when considering planting positions. Very strong warm winds from the south and west, while they may snap off a few flower heads, do not cause shrivelling of the buds and leaves – the hurricanes in Britain of autumn 1987 and spring 1990, which felled so many trees, had little effect on hydrangeas. Hydrangeas will grow on the western side of the British Isles with less protection than they would need on the east. Should winds pose such a problem that shelter does have to be provided, this is best done by trees, hedges or evergreen shrubs – or failing these, by a latticed fence. Any of these will filter the wind and reduce its speed, whereas walls or solid fences can create turbulence without lowering wind velocity.

Frost

Frost resistance varies with the species, as is indicated by the hardiness zones included with the species' descriptions. These zones refer to survival level of the plant, rather than acting as a guide to the conditions in which it should flourish. Many other local factors can and do affect the plant's success, and good gardening practice can defy the limits prescribed by hardiness zone boundaries.

The hardiest hydrangeas, with respect purely to temperature, are *H. arborescens* and *H. paniculata*. The reason for this has already been mentioned – flowers are borne on the new wood, so buds do not appear until all danger of frost has passed. The growing season is thus short and vigorous, and takes place during the warmest time of year. For those who fear their climate is too cold for hydrangeas, these plants are recommended.

The deciduous climbing hydrangea *H. petiolaris* is hardy to −28.8° C (−20° F) as,

somewhat surprisingly, is *H. quercifolia* – but for the latter to produce a good display of flowers warm summers are needed. These conditions prevail in parts of south-eastern USA, where *H. quercifolia* is native.

H. macrophylla is rated Hardiness Zone 5/6, a little less robust than *H. petiolaris* and *H. quercifolia*. Certainly in Britain, most of which is Hardiness Zone 8, a plant of *H. macrophylla* is unlikely to be killed by frost, but its buds and leaves can be severely damaged by unseasonably low temperatures. An exceptionally prolonged and early frost in the autumn will not only turn the flower heads an immediate and unbecoming brown colour, but will also damage large lengths of stem before they have had time to ripen fully. As the buds for the following year's flowers are already formed on these stems, they too will be destroyed and a season's floral display lost. Young shrubs are more susceptible to this problem than older, more mature plants. Early-flowering cultivars, whose buds for the following year also form early, are more likely to escape unscathed as they will be more advanced. Similarly, a late spring frost can shrivel opening leaves, and if severe, can also damage flower buds. Recovery can be complete (see page 59, on pruning), but should this cycle be repeated annually, it might be a good idea to consider growing another species or even another genus – or moving the hydrangea!

H. heteromalla likes temperatures similar to *H. macrophylla*, but comes into flower a little earlier and is an excellent summer shrub in Britain. *H. sikokiana* is little grown but is quite hardy at Zone 6. *H. aspera* would prefer a little more warmth, and some of its derivatives can suffer badly from frost in late spring in Britain, as can *H. involucrata*; but given a favoured spot, they will thrive and flourish. *H. scandens* and *H. hirta* have been seen growing well in several parts of Britain. The evergreen climbers *H. seemannii*, *H. serratifolia* and *H. integrifolia* rated at Hardiness Zone 9, certainly do grow at much colder temperatures, but it cannot be said that they flower freely – they really need more sun to give their best.

It should be emphasized that local variations can affect conditions, even when the hardiness rating indicates that all should be well. Some gardens harbour 'frost pockets' – areas, often at the foot of a slope, where cold air gathers and does not escape, perhaps because it cannot rise over a surrounding hedge or wall. Temperatures in such a location may be considerably lower than on the more exposed hill slope.

The hardiness ratings, however, which are based solely on temperature, should be considered as 'flexible guidelines' (*RHS Dictionary of Gardening*), and sometimes act as a challenge to the gardener.

Moisture

Hydrangeas have a reputation for being thirsty plants. The interaction between sun and water, however, is of more significance than the effect of water alone. Hydrangeas are good indicators of any imbalance between these two influences and, on the whole, light plays a bigger part than moisture in the control of growth. The shrubs will certainly grow well where there is high humidity – whether this arises from lake or stream, from rainfall or from moist sea breezes. D. Bartrum (1958) even suggests hydrangeas as good plants for water gardens. So, once again, the west and south-west of the British Isles have the advantage. In drier parts of the country more care will have to be taken to supply the necessary humidity.

It is necessary to be discriminating in deciding when to water. Sometimes, on a warm day, drooping leaves will give the impression of a distressed and very thirsty plant. Closer examination, however, will reveal that the soil is quite moist. The explanation of the malaise is overexposure to hot sun. This can create such rapid transpiration from the large foliage area that the leaves temporarily droop. Once the temperature drops they will recover. If they are still drooping at the end of a long, hot day, they will recover overnight. They appear to suffer no lasting ill effect from this transitory setback.

When plants in a shady position show similar signs of distress the situation is more serious. This is a sure indication that the soil is too dry, and measures have to be taken to correct it. The obvious course of applying water is effective. It is remarkable just how quickly the leaves become turgid when the plant is given a good draught of water. More long-term care should include checking on the condition of the soil, to which it may be necessary to add more compost or leaf mould to increase water retention; mulching may also be a wise course. Another possibility is that the shrub is growing under a tree which, while providing welcome shade, is also taking priority when rainfall is limited. Young plants, in particular, always require close attention in times of water shortage as their root system is shallow and small and they may easily die.

Rain showers may lure the gardener into a false sense of security. In a prolonged dry spell the occasional shower is of little value, and vigilant attention to watering should not be relaxed. Watering artificially should always be done thoroughly, even if it means doing it less frequently. A good soaking once a week is more beneficial than a little drop given daily.

Soil texture

Hydrangeas will grow in almost any soil, but they will grow better if the soil does not dry out frequently. A rich loam is therefore more suitable than light sand, but the latter can be satisfactory if sufficient well-rotted garden compost, leaf mould, bark or animal manure is added. Chalky or stony soils, too, need to have the humus content increased to improve water retention. Heavy clay, which fluctuates from being boggy in wet weather to being as hard as a rock in drought, requires working and the addition of all possible composted material; it is then a very fertile soil with improved texture. While a boggy, stagnant place would not be a suitable planting site, hydrangeas are so adaptable that they would grow in very wet soil provided that it drained well. They have been seen by the authors growing magnificently on the banks of a stream in a sloping, peaty garden on the Isle of Skye, and in sheltered inlets beside streams in Cornwall.

Peat has not been included in the soil texture improvers mentioned above. The incorporation of peat would certainly lighten a heavy soil, and it helps to improve drainage and aeration. However, this is now considered an extravagant use for peat, and in the cause of conservation, other more economic products can be used with equally good effect. Both garden waste and household vegetable refuse can be composted, even more quickly and effectively with the addition of either ammonium sulphate or a proprietary activator. Leaf mould is another excellent product where there is a sufficient supply of fallen deciduous leaves, and their relatively slow decomposition can also be hastened by the addition of a herbal activator, or by the addition of ammonium sulphate. Farmyard or stable manure adds

not only organic material and a recycled version of the minerals already in the garden soil, as does ordinary garden compost, but manure has the extra advantage of other materials which were part of the animals' diet. The manure will be mixed with either straw, bark or sawdust and can be put on the garden in the later autumn, or left in a pile, covered in black plastic sheeting, to decompose before applying in the spring.

Yet another source of natural product is a sawmill. Shredded bark can often be obtained there for little or no charge, while many gardeners are now acquiring their own shredders. The shredded material, be it small branches, twigs or woody herbaceous prunings, provides a mulch which can be used directly on the soil (in which case, some ammonium sulphate should be added in the spring), or it can be composted before application. Even shredded newspaper can be used, if incorporated in the garden compost heap until it, like the rest of the waste material, breaks down to a form in which it is easy to handle and beneficial to the soil.

These are some of the many materials which can be used to improve soil texture, thereby enabling it to retain the necessary moisture. Some of them may also add nutrients and minerals. This, and the relation of soil to the colour of hydrangea flowers, will be discussed in the next section.

Mention should be made of the use of 'coir', the inner pith of coconut fibre, as a peat alternative. It is standing up well to tests and becoming widely used in composts for plant propagation. It would possibly serve well also as a garden-soil improver, but would be much more expensive than the materials mentioned above.

The final choice of a planting site to meet these needs is a challenge to the gardener. The chances are that a hydrangea would look just right where there is maximum exposure to a north wind, or sandy soil or a frost pocket – but that's gardening!

Soil and Colour Change

However little is known about hydrangeas, one fact tends to stick in people's minds: the flowers have a habit of changing colour. Hardly surprising that this is remembered, for it is unusual plant behaviour. Roses, azaleas, camellias, any shrub that comes to mind, all produce the same-coloured flowers each year, and it would be a great surprise if they did not. Hydrangeas are different!

The flowers of several species of hydrangea show some colour variation, throughout the regions in which they occur. However, it is with *H. macrophylla* ssp. *macrophylla*, and its cultivars, the familiar mopheads and lacecaps, that the more dramatic colour changes occur: a plant can produce pink flowers one year, lilac ones the next and blue the year after. Also, one shrub can display different-coloured flower heads; one flower head can be composed of different-coloured florets, and these can change colour within the season. White cultivars tend to stay white, but even here the tiny fertile flowers (which form the centre of a lacecap head) can vary between pink and blue.

The colour changes among hydrangea flowers were first recorded in the late eighteenth century (Chenery, 1937), and the idea gradually emerged that the fluctuations were related to the soil. Throughout the nineteenth century, various attempts were made to influence or control these variations. Red seemed to predominate, and the search was invariably for a good blue colour. Experiments were made with soils from different regions, and a variety of substances added to the soil to note the effect on flower colour. Among the many minerals and salts tried, compounds of iron and aluminium gradually emerged as likely candidates for influencing colour change.

Understandably, some mystique has grown up around this strange phenomenon. As well as the addition of chemicals, rusty nails have been buried near the plants, teapots emptied over them and even magic incantations made at the time of the full moon, in attempts to achieve colour changes! Through trial and error and controlled experiment, however, the following conclusions have emerged.

To obtain good blue flowers it is necessary to have:

a. acid soil
The acidity and alkalinity of the soil is measured in terms of pH. Soils in temperate climates with moderate rainfall, such as Britain, are rarely more alkaline than pH 8.0, or more acid than pH 4.5. A soil of pH 6.5–7.0 is the level at which there is a maximum general availability of plant foods (Gill, 1988). PH 6.5 is sufficiently acid to allow hydrangeas to develop blue flowers, although a lower pH will encourage more intense blues.

An easily used kit for testing soil pH can be purchased at most garden centres. It is possible to arrange a professional pH test and simple soil analysis for a modest charge.

It is not easy to increase soil acidity, and in an area where, for example, there is much chalk or limestone in the soil, it is unlikely that a stable long-term low pH value could be achieved. It would be virtually impossible to grow hydrangeas with blue flowers in such soil. Starting from a neutral soil, however, around pH 7.0, it is possible to increase the acidity by the addition of sulphur. The application of 125–250 g of sulphur per square metre (4–8 oz per square yard) should lower the pH by 0.5 unit. In addition, the incorporation of some acid peat would help to increase the acidity. So, for those gardens with soil which is neutral or only slightly acid, it is possible to lower the pH so that blue hydrangeas can be grown.

b. aluminium

It has also been established that a hydrangea plant needs to absorb aluminium in order to maintain blue flowers. The sepals of blue flowers contain ten times more aluminium than pink ones (Chenery, 1937). More recent studies (Asen, Stuart, Siegelman, 1959) have indicated that potassium and molybdenum, and possibly several other substances, may also be essential for maximum blue coloration, but it is agreed that aluminium is the principal requirement. There is usually aluminium present in the soil, but it has to be in a form of a soluble salt which can be absorbed by the plant. This can only happen in acid soil, as in alkaline soil the aluminium forms an insoluble compound which the plant cannot absorb.

Should soil analysis indicate a lack of aluminium, it can be added in the form of aluminium sulphate. This is the 'blueing compound' recommended by nurseries to those who wish to achieve blue-flowered hydrangeas. It should be applied with caution as an excess of aluminium damages the plant's roots. A solution of 1½–3 g of aluminium sulphate to a litre of water

(or ¼ oz–½ oz per gallon) should be applied to two/three-year-old plants throughout the growing season, or the commercial 'blueing' compound used according to instructions.

Another product which could be used with advantage for 'blueing' of hydrangeas is potassium aluminium sulphate, also called potash alum or even just alum. Unfortunately, it is not easy to obtain. Should it be found, however, it has the advantage over ordinary aluminium sulphate in that it is released slowly in the soil, and thus need be applied less frequently. The potassium contained in this potash alum is also an additional aid to the production of blue flowers (Asen, Stuart, Specht, 1960). Potash alum should be applied in a solution of 4 g per litre (0.66 oz per gallon).

Having endeavoured to see that the soil is acid and that it contains available aluminium, attention must also be paid to the type of fertilizer used. The balance of chemicals in the soil is critical for hydrangea flower colour. Still considering the case of blue flowers, a fertilizer low in phosphorus and high in potassium is needed, while the nitrogen content should be in the form of nitrates rather than ammonium (Halevy, 1985). An NPK ratio of 25/5/30 is recommended (Weiler, 1980). Superphosphates should be avoided, and little if any bone-meal used in planting.

Such, then, are the requirements for the production of blue hydrangeas, but what of the reds and pinks? Their needs are more easily met. They will tolerate a slightly acid soil of pH 6.5, and will produce good colour in soils of pH 7.0 to 7.5. This degree of alkalinity, if not naturally occurring, can be achieved by the addition of lime to the soil or by watering with lime solution twice yearly. Excessive alkalinity is to be avoided as it can cause chlorosis – the plant cannot absorb sufficient iron and shows yellowing of the leaves. Fertilizer for red-flowering hydrangeas should have an NPK ratio of 25/10/10.

Though the reasons for the development of both red and blue flowers on hydrangea plants have been discussed, some puzzling aspects of this tantalizing subject remain: one is the development of different, or even mixed, colours all on the same shrub. It is already obvious that hydrangeas act as very sensitive indicators to the pH of the soil, and even as pointers to the presence or absence of some minerals. The explanation of the mixed colours may be that the soil pH and the mineral content varies within the area covered by the shrub's roots. Vessels within the plant carry nutrients direct from individual roots up into the flowers and leaves – there is no general 'pooling' of the nutrients absorbed by the roots. Thus individual flowers, or even parts of flowers, may vary in colour.

Another strange phenomenon often occurs when a *H. macrophylla* cultivar (and this applies especially to young plants) is moved – from pot to open ground, or from one part of the garden to another. There is frequently, if not always, a colour swing towards the red. This occurs regardless of the pH of the soil into which the plant is moved. So, a pale pink will go a deeper pink, a pale blue flower may turn mauve and a deep blue may quite possibly go pink. If the 'new' soil is acidic, the blue content of the colour will gradually return, probably by the second flowering season. This has been observed by the authors who can only explain it by assuming that the plant, while re-establishing its roots, does not initially absorb the available aluminium. This behaviour certainly adds to identification problems.

Flower colour alone obviously cannot be used to identify a cultivar of *H. macrophylla*. Unfortunately, many of them resemble each other closely in other physical characteristics, such as flower size, sepal shape, leaf shape and colour, so how is certain recognition to be achieved?

Work is being done in France by Hélène Bertrand, at the École Nationale d'Ingénieurs des Travaux et du Paysage in Angers. The object of this procedure is to establish the identity of new cultivars, by comparison with existing plants. This is done in order to ascertain that they *are* in fact new, before they receive a Certificat d'Obtention Végétale (plant breeders' rights).

Some confirmed plants are used as a base line, and these are planted out in 'terre de bruyère' – an impoverished, leached, acid, heath peat, pH 4.4, lacking in available aluminium. The flower colours of these plants, as they grow in this soil, are carefully measured with the RHS colour charts. Any other significant physical characteristics, such as shape of leaves and sepals, flowering time and vigour, are recorded. All other hydrangeas which come for name confirmation are planted in the identical soil, and their details kept. Flower colours are carefully noted, but a wait of two years, sometimes even three, is allowed before true comparison of colour can be made with the confirmed established plants. Due to the absence of aluminium in the soil, none of the plants so far described show blue colouring, in spite of the low pH, but the varying shades of pink and red are meticulously recorded. This interesting project should put the subject on a more scientific basis and help to solve some of the identification problems of *H. macrophylla* cultivars.

It might be concluded, from all the discussion so far, that any cultivar of *Hydrangea macrophylla* can have its colour changed, given the appropriate conditions. It is not quite as simple as that. Whites continue to be mainly white, no matter what the soil (apart from the small fertile flowers which do vary). On alkaline soil, where reds and pinks flourish, it is rare to see a blue hydrangea. On slightly acid soils, a good mixture of colours can coexist. A splendid example of this was seen in 1990 at Rosewarne, in Cornwall, where some 130 different cultivars, planted thirty-five years earlier in a soil of pH 6.5, were still displaying as wide a range of colours as hydrangeas can produce. On more strongly acid soils, there would be an increasing number of strong blues and some, but few, reds. Clearly, some cultivars of *H. macrophylla* are more prone than others to this colour variability. The fact that there are some innate preferences within the individual plants has to be accepted, and not every mophead or lacecap will change its colour in response to a gardener's alchemy.

The cultivars of *H. macrophylla* which will give red or pink colouring on alkaline soil are numerous. A few examples are *H. mm.* 'Harry's Red' (bright red), 'Deutschland' (deep pink) and 'Floralia' (paler pink). These and many others are described in Chapter 6.

There are a few plants which display red colour even on acid soils. An outstanding one is *H. serrata* 'Preziosa', which changes through a series of deep pinks and reds to end, usually, in deepest red in the autumn although in one or two gardens of slightly acid soil (pH 6.5) the autumn colour of this plant has shown a slightly purple hue. Within the serrata group are several plants which never show a hint of blue, and many of these give lovely dark reds in the autumn. Examples here are *H. serrata* 'Grayswood' and *H. serrata* 'Beni Gaku'. Among mopheads, *H. m.* 'Alpenglühen' is one which maintains its red coloration on acid soil, and another, *H. m.* 'Altona', gives a particularly splendid display of red and bronze in the autumn.

Plants which will give blue colouring on acid soil are known to the trade as 'good bluers'. It must be remembered that they also require a low level of phosphate to give their best colouring. These include such varieties as *H. mm.* 'Gentian Dome' and 'Maréchal Foch', both deep blues, 'Générale Vicomtesse de Vibraye', a good pale blue, and *H. serrata* 'Diadem' and *H. serrata* 'Blue Deckle', two lovely blue lacecaps.

Not everyone, however, will want to alter their plants. The colours which hydrangeas produce naturally in their garden may be satisfying and acceptable. The blooms will certainly be long-lasting. Should colour changes occur gradually, during the season, or as the plant adapts to garden soil, or even because varying nutrients are supplied by the gardener, this too can be fascinating and decorative. The changes produced by the application of chemicals may well be transitory and, as with drugs and humans, repeated care and application may be necessary. The reader who wants to play safe should plant a white hortensia, or try one of the species other than *H. macrophylla*, for it is necessary to remember that only this species has the habit of dramatic colour changes. The more daring can try a pink or a blue cultivar of *H. macrophylla*, and see what happens. There are hydrangeas to suit most tastes and most gardens – above all they should be planted and enjoyed.

Planting

Having chosen a hydrangea, taken its various requirements into consideration and decided on the best position, the next step is to plant it. This operation will be described in detail, as it is important to get it right.

The ideal season is either late spring, after the danger of frosts, or autumn, but container-grown shrubs can be planted out at any time when the soil is workable. Never plant in periods of frost, drought or cold winds. The ground should preferably be friable and moist after rain.

First prepare the planting hole. The size will have to be estimated, but the aim should be to prepare a hole twice the area and twice the depth of the plant's root ball. Having taken out the soil, lay it aside, fork over the bottom of the hole and then fetch the shrub. It will either be in a pot or in open ground, and should be watered in preparation for planting out. It should have a good, compact, root ball, retaining plenty of the original soil. The roots of a pot-grown plant may have become restricted, and if so they need to be teased out very gently. This, done, try the plant for size in the prepared hole – the top of the root ball should eventually be just below ground level. Lift out the plant, adjust the soil level if necessary, allowing space to put some well-rotted manure or compost in the bottom of the hole. Replace the plant and spread its roots out as evenly as possible. Fill the cavity with the remaining soil to which some peat or leaf mould has become added to aid water retention. A handful of bone-meal can be included, which will help development but may initially encourage pink rather than blue flowers. Once the hole is filled, tread lightly round the plant in a circle beyond the spread of the branches to form a shallow moat. Then water thoroughly, and when the water has soaked away, level the soil. Check during the next few days for signs of wilting. Should this occur, water copiously. It is a good idea to add a layer of mulch round the plant to help retain water, add nutrients and suppress weeds.

The process just described applies equally to the removal of an established hydrangea from one part of the garden to another. No harm will be done provided the shrub is not too heavy to lift. A layer of strong, plastic sheeting may be helpful to slide it to its new site.

When planting in grass, leave a circle of bare earth around the shrub, so that its roots do not have competition from those of the grass. This bare earth can be covered with chipped bark, or even with the cuttings from the surrounding grass, provided a little ammonium sulphate is added to aid decomposition. As the size of the shrub increases, enlarge the area of bare soil so that it extends to the spread of the leaves. When you are planting on a bank or sloping site, moisture retention around the roots can be helped by placing large stones or even cut logs upended, in a semi-circle on the slope below the shrub, about 50 cm (1 ft 8in) away from the stem. Within this arc, soil level can be raised to create a platform or ledge which will help to prevent rapid run-off of moisture.

A hydrangea will live a long time – it is worth giving it a good start with careful planting.

Feeding and Mulching

Hydrangeas are hardy and long-lived shrubs which do not demand a lot of attention or special feeding. They will, however, benefit from good garden care and practice, and will reward with a better display of flowers. Longevity, too, has its problems. Since they are long-term residents in one plot in the soil, the plants will benefit from some added nourishment to maintain their vigour.

Shrubs are usually purchased in containers or moved from nursery beds when they are two to three years old. At this stage, they should be growing vigorously on several good strong shoots arising from the base. After planting out, a feed of any good general fertilizer should be given, and the application of this twice yearly afterwards is all that is needed. Alternatively, some liquid, balanced fertilizer can be given in the recommended dose, at the same time as watering. Such soluble or liquid fertilizers have the advantage that there is a wide range of formulations available for different soil types and requirements. Thus it would be easy to choose a low phosphate/high potassium formula if feeding for blue hydrangea flowers.

As important as feeding, and in fact another method of supplying nutrients, is mulching. There is no mystique surrounding organic methods of gardening – plants will grow perfectly well given water and inorganic foods. The benefits of using available organic matter in the form of a mulch, however, are numerous:

a The materials, such as garden compost and leaf-mould, are available for the expenditure of only a little time and effort, and might otherwise be wasted.

b A mulch is particularly important to hydrangeas as it helps to combat one of the few conditions they dislike – the drying out of their roots.

c A surface mulch not only helps retain moisture in the soil but also tends to maintain a more even soil temperature. These factors both facilitate the activities of soil organisms.

d Nutrients are supplied to the plant from the mulch. It is only fair to say that they will be supplied more slowly than if they were given directly by an inorganic fertilizer, but it is a decorative garden shrub being considered, not a food crop – there is no hurry. Also, compost or leaf mould made in a garden can only supply those nutrients which came from that garden, and a soil deficiency could be perpetuated. This may need occasional correction by the supplement of specific fertilizer.

e A mulch acts as a weed suppressor, provided it is added to a clean soil.

f The application of a mulch does not require much special knowledge to administer, and can do little harm. It will certainly do some good!

The materials which can be used for mulching are similar to those mentioned in connection with soil texture. They are leaf mould, garden compost, pulverized bark, peat, farmyard manure, even grass cuttings if properly used.

All these, except peat, are best used when they have been thoroughly rotted down. Should they be used unrotted, they will take from the soil the nitrogen they require to decompose; this will then be denied to the plant which is being mulched. Nitrogen can be added as a replacement in the form of ammonium sulphate, at the rate of approx. 100 g to the square metre (3–4 oz per sq/yd) and this is essential if partially decomposed material has been used. Grass cuttings are often available in quantity, and they can be used directly as a mulch for convenience, but the ammonium sulphate must be added too. Even if you have no scruples about the use of peat it is expensive and, if used alone, tends to dry out on the surface of the beds – it is best mixed with one of the other materials as available.

Mulch should be applied in the spring, when the ground has had some time to warm up but weeds have not yet started to grow. The exact time will depend on the area and the weather. More mulch can be added throughout the season if necessary, to keep a permanent cover. Around shrubs, a thickness of approximately 7 cm (3 in) is ideal. Provided there is sufficient mulching material, it should be spread over the whole planting area, but if there is not enough for this it is better to put the correct depth just around the shrubs, rather than spread it thinly over a larger area.

Mulching need not be particularly demanding, yet it is beneficial to the plants, cuts down the weeding and, once time for thorough composting has been allowed, finds a use for garden and household waste.

Pruning

The urge to prune is strong in some gardeners and many misguided actions are taken with hydrangeas. NO pruning is, in this case, better than wrong pruning. Provided they are fed and watered, hydrangeas will grow and flower if they are never pruned at all. They may grow too large, they may become a bit straggly and they may produce few and smaller flowers, but they will still make a show of colour. It is only when an eager but ill-informed gardener with itchy secateurs intervenes, that flowering, and even growth, may be impeded. Correct pruning, however, can help the plant and rectify some mishaps. It is best, then, that the right time and place for pruning is understood, so that the display is improved and not depleted.

The first and most obvious form of pruning of *H. macrophylla* cultivars, which is a routine cosmetic operation, is dead-heading. It is generally thought that the dead flower heads of hortensias protect the buds of next year's flowers which have formed along the supporting stem. For this reason, these flower heads are commonly left on the plant during the winter. The idea may have some foundation, although the lacecap flower heads generally get blown away in the winter, and their new flower buds do not seem to suffer. Remaining dead flower heads have, nevertheless, to be removed or they will mar the new summer's display. Each stem should be cut back to just above the uppermost pair of new buds, taking great care to avoid damaging any green shoots, as these provide the new season's flowers. Spring to early summer is the time for this operation, when all danger of frost is past – this can be as late as mid-May in some parts of Britain. Gardeners have to make their own decisions as to the likelihood of further frosts.

An extension of this 'spring cleaning' of lacecaps and mopheads is necessary if an early autumn frost has damaged unripe shoots and their buds, leaving an untidy mass of bare stems. In late April/early May these dead stems have to be removed, cutting down to where new, vigorous growth is appearing. Some stems, not showing any rejuvenation, may have to be removed at ground level. New season's growth will appear in plenty from the base of the plant. Later in the year, it is best to remove some of these new, soft shoots to allow sun and air to ripen the remaining growth. No flowers will be carried on the current year's stems, but the following year should see good blooms once again.

Another pruning task, sometimes made necessary by a combination of weather

Fig. 32 Replacement pruning

a) Mature shrub in winter

b) Old branches for removal

c) After removal

d) New growth will appear in spring

eccentricities, is the removal of leaves which have been shrivelled or browned by frost. A mild winter and early spring, encouraging early growth, followed by sudden late frosts, can cause havoc. The brown leaves have to be rubbed or cut off, sometimes together with a portion of the stem. This is a sad and tedious job, but the shrubs look much better for their trim. The number of flowers in the current season will inevitably be reduced, but hydrangeas have a great capacity for survival, even in the face of climatic adversity.

In the normal course of events a young hydrangea will scarcely need any pruning beyond dead-heading, except perhaps the trimming of a branch which spoils the shape or symmetry of the bush. It must always be remembered that whenever any part of a branch is removed, it takes away with it the flowers for a season. New shoots will break out from below the cut, but these will not bear flowers for their first year. All pruning of young shrubs should be done after the danger of frost has passed, in the spring.

Older shrubs, beyond five or six years, can take more extensive pruning if desired. A safe rule to keep a plant in good shape and vigour, and to control its size, is to remove annually about a third of all main shoots at ground level. Those selected for removal should be the oldest, most gnarled wood. Their removal allows light to the centre of the bush, which encourages ripening of the wood, and new growth will break out from the base. This practice, known as replacement pruning, should be carried out in mild weather during January or February, as at that time there are no vulnerable new shoots that might accidentally get damaged during the operation (*see Fig. 32*).

More drastic pruning is necessary if a shrub has become grossly oversized for its site, or has been severely damaged by late spring frosts. Once it is fairly certain that frosts have finished for the year, *all* stems should be cut off at 45 cm (1½ ft) from the ground (*see Fig. 33*). There will be no flowers for a season, but new growth will be prolific throughout the following summer. Not all the new shoots need to be retained. Some selection can be done, thinning out at ground level, so that by the autumn the rejuvenated bush has a good framework of branches. Flowers should appear again the following season. It should be stressed, however, that this practice, of cutting down all stems, should only be adopted if the plant is either irretrievably damaged by frost, has become grossly oversized or has grown straggly from too little light and considerable neglect. The stems which develop readily enough after such severe pruning tend to be somewhat floppy, and the bush takes time to re-establish good firm growth.

Having now described several different circumstances in which some pruning is beneficial, it would be worth emphasizing what is to be avoided. The cosmetic annual pruning should not take place until after the last frosts, late spring or early summer being the correct times. Autumn pruning is to be avoided. 'Growth follows the knife' is a true maxim, and new shoots will arise below any cuts made. These shoots need time to ripen and harden before frosts attack them, so pruning in the autumn would encourage growth which could still be tender when the first frost occurs. Prune hydrangeas in late spring to early summer – which, in Britain, means late April to early May – and be on the safe side.

The foregoing descriptions of pruning apply to all hydrangeas except the climbers and the two species *H. arborescens* and *H. paniculata*. These two species, and their more commonly grown cultivars, produce their flowers on the current year's wood. This habit enables them to withstand late-spring frosts. All other species and their cultivars flower on wood grown the previous year. *H. arborescens* and *H. paniculata*, therefore, require pruning differently.

H. arborescens and its cultivars can be hard pruned to about 30 cm (1 ft) from the ground every year and they will flower well, producing large blooms. These, however, are often too heavy for the fresh supple stems which support them and the flower heads tend to flop. They can of course be supported, but an alternative is to prune much less severely. Remove only the previous season's flowers, cutting above a node, in February/March. Smaller flowers will result but they will have firmer stems. Should the shrub get too large, then an intermediate strategy is suggested. Starting at the outside of the shrub, cut the outer layer of stems to 30 cm (1 ft). Circling the bush, leave the next layer at about 60 cm (2 ft) from the ground and so on until the centre is reached. A well-rounded bush

a) Neglected or
damaged shrub
in spring

Fig. 33 Treatment of an oversized or severely frost-damaged shrub

b) After pruning

will result and less support should be needed by this method.

H. paniculata cultivars can be treated in two ways: the first method is for the previous year's wood to be pruned back to leave only two buds at the base of each stem. This is done in winter (February or March in Britain), and within the same season new shoots bearing large panicles of flower will result. Occasionally, to control the bush size, a whole branch can be removed. The fewer the number of shoots allowed to grow, the larger will be the panicles. Some people consider this method to be similar to docking a dog's tail, and prefer the alternative method, that is to leave them totally unpruned, so that a large bush of smaller flowers will develop. These flowers, too, may bend their stems a little, but if one has the space for this natural development, the shrub is a fine sight. A spectacular display of pruned *H. paniculata* cultivars can be seen in Savill Gardens, Windsor, England and unpruned ones in Kalmthout Arboretum, Belgium.

Climbing hydrangeas require very little pruning. *H. petiolaris* takes a while to become established, but is then self-supporting and independent. The most likely pruning, eventually, will be to restrict

its vigour, to contain it within the space available. It is a good plan to remove the dead flower heads, fairly close to the main stems, to encourage future flowers.

The evergreen climbers, *H. seemannii*, *H. serratifolia* and *H. integrifolia* also grow strongly after a slow start, and then probably need restraint rather than encouragement. When grown on a wall they will need cutting back so that they clothe the wall and do not project too far forward. Their lower stems, if left to their own devices, often self-layer and are thus a source of new plants. To flower well these plants need exposure to sun.

These suggestions for pruning hydrangeas show that it is not a complicated task, and, if done carefully, is beneficial. Otherwise, it is best avoided altogether.

Pests and Diseases

Hydrangeas are hardy plants and once they are established in the garden, have few enemies or ailments. The greatest hazards are frost and searing cold winds in the late spring, and precautionary measures against these have already been discussed. Deer and rabbits, which can cause havoc in rural gardens, avoid *H. macrophylla* but all other species are vulnerable to their ravages. Man himself, by faulty siting of a shrub, by over-enthusiastic pruning or by careless cultivation, is likely to cause more harm than the few pests or diseases which affect garden hydrangeas. Plants raised under glass may have more problems, but these are not within the scope of this book.

The following do sometimes attack hydrangeas in the garden:

Aphids	which cause the leaves to curl, damage flowers and can spread viral diseases.
Capsid bugs	which make small, ragged holes in leaves and damage flowers.
Scale insects	which form brown scales on the underside of leaves, usually along veins.
Thrips	which cause discoloration of leaves and flowers.
Vine weevils	which eat irregular notches out of the leaf edges.
Whitefly	which gather on the underside of leaves and make a sticky residue.

The range of chemicals permissible to the amateur gardener has changed considerably with increasing vigilance for safety. It is necessary to identify the problem and then search assiduously for the appropriate deterrent. Good garden centres will offer advice and the RHS has excellent advisory leaflets available to members on application. All permitted deterrents describe in detail the uses for which they are prescribed and the small print should be read with care. In addition, there are still some old, tried and tested substances, such as Liquid Derris, which can be readily bought and is acceptable to organic gardeners. Frequent spraying with this can

often obviate the need for further treatment, but persistent pests may need specific pesticide application. Good garden practice and hygiene are the best permanent aids.

It bears repeating that, although these pests may attack hydrangeas, an established plant will usually shrug off such an invasion and remain virtually unharmed. Greater care has to be taken if plants less than two years old should be affected.

Slugs and snails in particular love young hydrangeas, and it is essential to maintain some effective form of deterrent against these pests when young plants are put outside. Garden hygiene again must be meticulous in the planting area, and unfailing use made of whatever form of slug and snail warfare the reader prefers. On larger shrubs, snails have been found several feet from the ground, without there being any visible signs of damage.

Few diseases affect hydrangeas but some of the mildews can be troublesome. During propagation, when held under glass, grey mould (botrytis) can occur. This is identified by brown, dead patches of tissue on leaves or stems, sometimes followed by grey/white fluffy mould when cool and humid. All affected parts should be removed and burned and a specific spray used if necessary. Good ventilation is essential for hydrangeas so greenhouses and cold frames should always allow air circulation, even in cold weather. Watering should be kept to a minimum in winter.

Hydrangeas can be affected by powdery mildew, especially if stressed by dry soil during the growing season. This can happen to plants grown entirely in containers. A greenish-white powdery coating appears on leaves, stems and buds. Affected parts may become distorted and the plant weakened.

Preventive measures are thorough mulching, regular watering in dry summer spells and pruning out of old wood to allow air circulation to the shrub. Treatment is by a fungicide recommended for the disease. Dead and discarded plant debris should be burned or destroyed but not composted.

Hydrangea ring spot, appearing on short flower stalks and causing leaf distortion and fewer and smaller flowers, can occur, as can mycoplasma, which causes the flowers to remain green. These are both viral diseases, difficult to treat, and in the unlikely event of their occurrence it is best to destroy the affected plant before the problem spreads.

Honey fungus

Grown out-of-doors, hydrangeas are in general robust and disease-resistant plants. There is, however, one enemy to which they can succumb with alarming rapidity, and that is honey fungus (*Armillaria mellea*). The authors speak here from personal experience of the attack and, hopefully, the successful defence of plants that were in their care.

Honey fungus is so named because it does produce honey-coloured fruiting bodies (or toadstools).These may be noticed, but they can easily be damaged by walking among the plants, and could be overlooked. The greater danger is underground. The fungus exists as a saprophyte, living on dead wood such as rotting tree roots in the ground. From this source, black boot-lace-type structures (rhizomorphs) with barbed tips, extend through the soil at a rate of 10–15 cm (4–6 in) per year, until they reach a live root. These black strands give the fungus its other common name of 'boot-lace fungus'. The pointed tips can penetrate living root tissue, and then the fungus lives as a parasite on the host plant. A white fungal layer forms beneath the bark of the host, around the collar at or below ground

Fig. 34 Piece of rotting cherry wood, showing invasion by honey fungus

level. From this base the fungus proceeds to strangle the host, preventing the flow of supplies of water and nutrients. The host dies, the fungus reverts to its saprophytic existence, and the cycle begins again, as the fungus lives on the dead tissue of its victim. Rhizomorphs can, and will, extend from one food source to another, with both dead and live tissue acting as host.

The first symptom of this disease in hydrangeas is usually the sudden deterioration of a shrub which appeared quite healthy. Part of the plant may show distress in the form of drooping leaves, similar to the effect of drought, but restricted to one or two stems. Watering does not alleviate the symptom, and soon the flowers also droop. Removal of the affected branches does not halt the spread, and within weeks, or possibly even days, the whole shrub succumbs.

Examination of the main stems just below the soil level will probably reveal a white fungal film under the bark. Thus suspicions are confirmed, and the diagnosis will be confirmed by digging into the surrounding soil and finding the typical boot-lace rhizomorphs. To be absolutely sure, samples of roots can be sent for analysis.

Prevention and cure

Honey fungus is a common parasite where there is any source of rotting wood, such as old tree stumps, roots left in the ground after tree removal, even old fence posts. So, although many hydrangeas like the shelter of a high tree canopy, and although edge of woodland is often a suitable setting, one should if possible avoid areas where trees are known to have been felled. Such ideals, however, cannot always be achieved, and it is impossible to know, when planting, if there is a source of honey fungus nearby. The spread of the fungus is erratic and unpredictable, and while some plants may be affected, most escape. One has to go forward in faith.

The best preventive measure is to take good care of the plants. Any shrub under stress through adverse growing conditions is more likely to succumb. So, good mulching and feeding, and watering when necessary, as well as careful choice of site, will increase resistance.

Cure is more difficult. An affected plant must be dug up and burned, taking care to include all roots; this is easy with hydrangeas as they have a compact root ball. It is preferable to remove the surrounding soil, including all visible rhizomorphs, and replace with clean soil. The source of infection, the rotting wood, needs to be located and, if possible, removed and burned.

Trenching around other threatened plants in the area is helpful as rhizomorphs may be exposed and can then be severed. Trenching should be as deep as possible, without damaging roots of the very plants which are to be protected – not an easy task! Ideally, the trenches should be refilled with fresh, clean soil and the old soil discarded.

There is one course of action worth taking, before burning an affected hydrangea. Should there be any branch still in good form, once the disease has been identified and the bush condemned, take cuttings from that good stem. There is no reason why they should not thrive, and if they do, they will not carry the disease with them. Strangulation is not transmissible!

The shrubs mentioned earlier, had originally been planted, of necessity, in an area of poor soil on a steep bank, so they had been subjected to stress. When honey fungus attacked, the suggested procedures were followed, and the remaining shrubs pruned hard, to encourage root growth and reduce flowering for a season. Finally, they were well fed and mulched. So far, there has been no recurrence of the malaise.

In general, good garden hygiene and care of the plants is the best form of defence against this, as against most diseases.

4 Propagation

Once hydrangeas are established in a good position in the garden and are flowering well with the little attention they need, the chances are that the desire will come to produce more of the same! It is a compliment to any gardener to be asked for a cutting.

Fortunately, hydrangeas are some of the easiest shrubs to reproduce, and tentative gardeners are encouraged to experiment with this genus as a high rate of success is likely. New plants can be raised from cuttings taken over a range of months, as well as from seed, by layering and in some cases, from suckers. The various methods are described here in detail, and, in Chapter 6, any special preferences for one method over another is noted in the individual plant descriptions.

Softwood and Semi-ripe Cuttings

a) Taking cuttings

Cuttings of *H. arborescens* and *H. paniculata* should be taken early, before the end of June, because these two species and their cultivars have a different growth cycle. Cuttings of all other hydrangeas can be taken at any time from April to October in Britain. The earlier ones would be classified as softwood and the later ones as semi-ripe. Both are treated in exactly the same way initially and both will be equally successful; but the after-care of the rooted cuttings will be different according to the season.

The first step is to check your stock of pots, compost, plastic bags, ties and labels.

If using round pots, a 7½ cm (3 in) pot will hold one cutting and an 11 cm (4½ in) pot will hold four. With square pots, a 7 cm (2½ in) one will take one cutting while a 9½ cm (4 in) pot will hold four. It is immaterial which are used, provided there are transparent plastic bags ready into which the chosen pots will fit comfortably.

The compost used should be free-draining yet moisture-retentive and free of nutrients. A 50/50 mix of moist moss peat, with either sharp sand, fine grit or perlite, is suitable.

Having seen that all necessary materials are available it is time to take the cuttings from the parent plant. The preferred time is in the early morning, when the leaves are turgid and the plant is not under stress from the sun. A non-flowering side shoot is best, although a tip of a stem will serve. Take cuttings 10–15 cm (4–6 in) long, severing them from the plant with a knife or secateurs. (*Fig. 35a.*) Put them immediately into a plastic bag, seal this with a tie and label it. Keep this in the shade, if necessary, while other cuttings are to be taken.

Should it be necessary to delay potting up the cuttings for hours, or perhaps even days, both the following emergency methods have been found to be effective. Firstly, if a refrigerator or cold box is available (not a freezer), the sealed bag of cuttings can be kept in this as long as it necessary – they have been known to last perfectly for a week or more, lying in their bag on the shelf of a domestic refrigerator. Alternatively, the cuttings can be removed from the bag, and kept in a glass of water like cut flowers in as cool and shady a place as possible. Should any of the cuttings wilt, this is probably due to an air-lock in the stem. Cut off about 1 cm (¹/₂ in) from the bottom of the stem, totally immerse the cutting in water for an hour, or even overnight, and then replace in the glass of water. This should sort the problem. Provided they are kept as cool as possible at all times, this process can be continued for several days, but careful supervision is necessary.

The sooner potting-up can be done, however, the better. Decide which pots are going to be used and fill them loosely to the top with the chosen compost. Do not press down.

Prepare the cuttings by severing the stem cleanly with a sharp knife, just below a leaf joint. Remove the pair of leaves at this node, until only two pairs of leaves and a tip bud remain. Should these leaves be large, cut the lower pair in half to reduce the transpiration (*Fig. 35b*), then simply poke the cuttings gently but firmly into the prepared pot of compost. In a pot that takes four cuttings, place the cuttings close to the edges or corners of the pot; but when planting only one cutting, position it centrally. Then water the pot with a fine rose on the can (*Fig. 35c*) – the level of compost will drop as the pot drains but the cutting will be well supported without the need for any further pressing down (*Fig. 35d*). When the pots have had time to drain place each one in a plastic bag large enough to contain it and its cuttings without difficulty or constraint, and without the leaves touching each other. Seal the bag with a plastic tie which can also hold the essential label with name, source and date (if the label is kept in the pot inside the plastic bag, it will be impossible to read the label when the bag mists up with

condensation). It's amazing how easy it is to forget what a cutting is and where it came from. When preparing cuttings from several different plants at the same time, great care must be exercised to keep the labels together with their respective cuttings at each stage – the safest way is to prepare one pot of cuttings at a time, through to the 'plastic bag with label attached' stage (*Figs 35a–e*).

Particular mention must be made of those species which have 'hairy' leaves – namely *H. aspera*, *H. involucrata* and *H. sikokiana*. These hairy-leaved plants will rot if water accumulates on the surface of their leaves. It is best, therefore, to pot these cuttings immediately after they have been taken from the parent plant, for they will not tolerate the total immersion mentioned as a rescue operation for most hydrangea cuttings. Neither will they like the humid atmosphere in a closed plastic bag while roots develop. It has been found, however, that they will root satisfactorily if the bag is only partially closed, allowing some ventilation (*Fig. 37b*). These cuttings require careful supervision, and propagation from hardwood cuttings or by layering (both described later) are possible alternatives.

When all the required cuttings have been potted up, place all the bags, labelled and with pots inside them, in a place where they will get maximum light but no direct sun. A cold greenhouse built against the north wall of a house is ideal, but any part of the garden where shade from direct sun is guaranteed will serve. A north-facing house windowsill is satisfactory at this stage. Cuttings can develop roots in approximately three to four weeks, although sometimes they take a little longer. During this period they should be checked to see if any leaves have fallen off (in which case these should be removed),

Fig. 35 Softwood cuttings

a) Cutting taken from parent plant

b) Prepared cutting

c) Watering into rooting compost

d) Ready to go into plastic bag

e) Cutting enclosed: method for most hydrangeas

f) Bag is only partly closed: for hydrangeas with hairy leaves

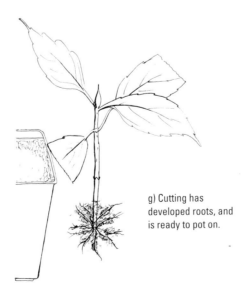

g) Cutting has developed roots, and is ready to pot on.

or for drooping or signs of rot. Such problems are rare with hydrangeas, but a little extra water, or a spray with an appropriate product to combat fungal mould, may be necessary on occasions.

Cuttings taken late in the year, may need a little more protection than the garden can provide, and a greenhouse, house windowsill or heated propagator maintained at around 15° C (60° F) will provide satisfactory conditions for rooting. A Dewpoint propagator is ideal for larger numbers.

b) Potting on
The establishment of a root system is essential before potting on. Three to four weeks after taking cuttings, open up the bag and have a look. Occasionally, roots are visible, protruding at the bottom of the pot or sometimes even at the surface of the soil. Usually, however, it is necessary to test. Hold the pot in one hand and with the other hand, give the cutting a gentle pull. If a good root system has developed, the plant will resist the pull, but if it comes away easily, it is not ready and should be carefully replaced for another week or so. Actual inspection of the cutting, by removing it carefully from the pot, using a very small trowel or a spoon, will do no harm – it can be replaced if no roots have developed, or potted on if roots are visible. It has been found that quite a small root development is sufficient to allow progress to the next stage.

Each rooted cutting should be potted on in an individual 7½ cm (3 in) pot, using a proprietary potting compost or a home-made one of one-third each of sifted peat, sifted good loam and fine grit/coarse sand, together with a little fertilizer. After potting on and watering (remembering a label for each pot) a little extra care is needed for a few days, as this is the most vulnerable stage. Keep the cuttings on a shady windowsill, or in a cold greenhouse or cold frame, but avoid direct sun. Some extra watering may be needed, and spraying with water is also helpful. Should they be placed in a sheltered area of the garden, snails and slugs will surely find these tender delicacies, so some effective deterrent must be used around the pots. Given care at this crucial time, the cuttings should grow and flourish.

Once the 7½ cm (3 in) pot is filled the plants should be potted on to the next suitably sized pot, depending on rate of growth – probably 13 cm (5 in). These can stand outside in a shady place provided protection from slugs and snails is given. Feeding with half-strength liquid feed monthly will be necessary and then removal to a cold frame or cold greenhouse before the first frost. They should lose their leaves during winter and these should be gathered as they fall. No feeding is necessary during winter and minimal watering only if they have become noticeably dry. Next spring, nearly a year after taking the cuttings, a further potting on is required and feeding should begin again.

When the frosts are over – and that may not be until the end of May – a decision has to be made. In favoured areas they could be planted out into nursery beds provided great vigilance is given. The safer method, allowing the plant to develop more woody tissue and thus ability to resist frost, is to continue pot-growing for another year. The same procedure should be followed – potting on as needed, standing in the shade, feeding and watering in summer, giving cold frame or cold greenhouse protection in winter with plenty of ventilation but no feeding and minimal watering. The second spring, after the last frost, the plants can be planted in the ground with confidence.

c) Growing on

Whatever location is chosen – garden or pot – particular attention has to be given to avoid the plants becoming tall and 'leggy': the growing tips must be 'stopped'. Flowers are not desirable on young plants (however much the gardener would like to see a bloom on his new cuttings), as it is best that the plant's energy should go to root growth. Flowering tips should therefore be pinched out, to leave only one or two nodes, and strong, stocky plants will result.

Getting hydrangea cuttings to root is not difficult, and potting on is straightforward. It is the after-care which requires special attention – sometimes more than is realized. This consists of gentle weaning, relating each development stage to the season and to the available equipment and conditions; thereby, a cutting is given a careful balance of protection and encouragement, enabling it to become a strong, independent plant. The philosophy followed in a good nursery caring for small children can be paralleled in a nursery raising small plants!

It should be emphasized that the methods described here are those found to be satisfactory by the amateur gardener. Commercially, it is necessary to get the maximum yield of cuttings from stock plants, so smaller pieces of stem – one node, or a tip with an inch of stem – are used. The gardener can do likewise if he wishes – it will take a little longer to achieve a large plant. Heated propagation units and mist are employed commercially, and the gardener with such equipment can achieve excellent results.

Hardwood Cuttings

Since soft and semi-ripe cuttings of hydrangeas root so easily, there is perhaps less requirement to follow the longer process (necessary for some other shrubs) of taking hardwood cuttings. However, there may be circumstances when hardwood cuttings are more convenient: they are taken late in the year, so it is still possible to make good an earlier omission to propagate; the difficulties sometimes encountered with hairy-leaved plants, are overcome; hardwood cuttings are easily parcelled up and posted.

Hardwood cuttings are 20–30 cm (8–12 in) lengths of the current year's growth of stem, taken from the plant in the late autumn/early winter, after the leaves have fallen. Make the lower cut a horizontal one, taken just below a node, and trim the upper end of the cutting at an angle. This makes it possible to identify which is the top and which is the bottom, and the sloping top cut encourages rain to run off the exposed surface. Since the cuttings will stay out in the garden until they are rooted, choose a sheltered spot which will not need to be disturbed. With a spade, make a furrow in the soil, approx. 20 cm (8 in) deep, with one vertical side. Put some sharp sand in the bottom of this trench. Take each cutting in turn, barely touch its base with fresh hormone rooting compound, shake off any surplus and then insert the cutting vertically in the trench so that it rests on the sand. Insert the cuttings to two-thirds of their length, so that one-third protrudes above ground level, and position them at intervals of approx. 10 cm (4 in) along the trench. When all have been positioned, fill the trench with soil, firming it gently with the foot so that the cuttings remain upright and are not loose. Water thoroughly. No further care is needed, except to check from time to time that the cuttings are still firmly in position. Rooting will take until the following autumn, when it will be time to plant out those which have developed good roots.

Fig. 36 Hardwood cuttings, maintained at 15° C (60° F)

b) February

a) November

c) March: ready for potting on

The percentage of success with this traditional method of taking hardwood cuttings of hydrangeas is not always high, and an alternative sometimes works better. The cuttings are prepared in exactly the same way, but are inserted, five or six to a pot, in rooting compost (50/50 peat and grit or sand) instead of in the soil (see Fig 36). This pot can then be kept in a cold greenhouse until rooting occurs, which should be by the next summer. An even further extension of this method, and one which speeds it up even more, is to keep the potted cuttings on a house windowsill or in a heated propagator at approx. 15° C (60° F), giving sufficient water to keep them just moist. When growth appears from some of the nodes, check the cutting to ensure that roots have in fact developed. This being the case, the rooted cuttings should be individually potted on and kept cool and frost-free until planting out in a nursery bed in early summer.

These modifications show that hydrangeas respond to almost all methods of propagation, and it is worth having a try at almost any time of the year.

Fig. 37 Section through Jiffy Pot, showing the bud and roots developing

Buds

Following on from hardwood cuttings, another method was discovered almost by chance by Norman Yock in Oregon, USA.

When gathering hardwood cuttings of *H. macrophylla* cultivars, they were trimmed, as has been described, and the tips of the stems discarded on the ground. Later, these tips were found, rooted and growing, so the idea developed of making use of them for producing yet more plants.

The method now used is to break off just the bud, at the tip of a shoot, and simply to insert this, to one-third of its depth, in a small pot of compost (*see Fig. 39*). No special conditions are needed, but kept moist, light and warm, around 15° C (60° F), these buds root quite quickly once their dormancy has broken and they begin to unfurl. They then need feeding, as they have little reserve, and can be potted on when sufficient root has formed. The use of Jiffy 7 Pots obviates the need to disturb the roots when potting on, and is commercial practice.

This procedure has only recently been tried, but appears to be working well.

Layering

As they grow larger, the branches around the outside of the hydrangea bushes will bow down near to, or perhaps actually touch, the ground. This habit can be turned to advantage in the production of more new plants. Where a branch is already touching the ground, this is the point of contact at which a new plant can develop. Should no branch touch the soil, choose one which nearly does so and bend it gently into a curve, the lowest point of which can lie comfortably just below soil level. It is best if this critical point of contact coincides with a node. At this contact point, the branch needs to have its under-surface damaged – a fingernail scratch will do, or a knife can be used, to expose the cambium layer from which roots will develop. Make a small depression in the soil, see that no stones or weeds are in the way, even put in a handful of peat or compost, and then lay the damaged part of the curved branch in the prepared spot. Cover it over with soil and put a stone on top, heavy enough to hold the branch in position without it moving. Put a label in the ground beside the stone – it is easy to forget, and one stone looks much like another. Now leave it entirely alone for at least six months, but better still for a year. A new plant will form, with its roots under the stone. It can be separated from the parent plant by severing, on the side towards the parent plant, the branch which has joined it like an umbilical cord. The new 'layered' plant can then be lifted and planted elsewhere.

This method produces strong young plants, identical to the parent, with minimum effort from the gardener. It is useful for those shrubs, such as *H. aspera* 'Villosa', which are more difficult to propagate from cuttings.

Self-layering

A shrub can bend its own branches down to such an extent that, if they are left undisturbed by over-zealous 'weeders', new plants are created, as described under 'layering', without any help from the gardener. These can be severed from the original shrub, moved and replanted elsewhere in the garden. They can also be left where they develop, of course, and thus a very large area will eventually be covered with the same type of plant. One shrub which is particularly adept at this process is *H. macrophylla* 'Générale Vicomtesse de Vibraye', and large plantings of this can be quite dramatic where space allows such a display.

Suckering

Some hydrangeas, and in particular *H. arborescens*, *H. aspera sargentiana* and *H. involucrata* 'Hortensis', are prone to sucker, i.e. they send off new growth below ground spontaneously, and these underground shoots start to grow into subsidiary plants around the periphery of the original shrub. Once again, a large area can become covered with identical plants which may, or may not, be what is wanted. In south-east USA, where *H. arborescens* is native, extensive plantings are utilized to cover roadside verges. Should the new plants not be required where they arise, they too can, like layerings or self-layerings, be severed and transplanted.

H. sargentiana and *H. involucrata* 'Hortensis' are not the easiest hydrangeas to propagate from softwood cuttings, so their suckering habit can be used to advantage when additional plants are wanted.

One other variation on the self-propagating theme is that adopted by the Japanese. The stems of *H. paniculata* are used in Japan for supplying 'neri' or 'nori', a glutinous substance used in the making of Japanese handmade paper – 'washi'. To increase the crop of *H. paniculata*, stem tips, still attached to the plant, are bent over and pushed, tip down, into the ground. New plants arise from this point. This method has not yet been tried by the authors, but there is no reason to doubt that the versatile hydrangea will succeed.

Seed

The previous methods of propagation described are all asexual, vegetative methods which give rise to new plants genetically identical to their parents. For a gardener wishing to be certain of reproducing plants of a known species or cultivar an asexual method must be used.

Hydrangeas can, however, be grown from seed and this is particularly important for the breeder seeking to change the genetic makeup of a plant in order to produce different characteristics. It can also be an interesting exercise for the gardener, especially one with a number of plants which could have been cross-pollinated by insects. The seed then collected is open pollinated.

Most hydrangeas have a mixture of sterile and fertile flowers, although there are some 'mopheads' where there do not appear to be any fertile flowers. The seed capsules on fertile flowers which have been

pollinated will ripen about 2–3 months after the inflorescence has died – in the UK this is about the middle of December.

The dust-like brown seed can be harvested by inverting the dead inflorescence in a paper bag and storing in a warm, dry place such as a boiler room for a few days. As the seed capsules dry and open, the seed will fall into the paper bag and a gentle shake will dislodge the remainder. Seed gathered in this way will not require further cleaning. The collected seed can then be sown fresh or stored dry in the refrigerator until required.

The seed should be sown in pans on to the surface of a good quality seed compost such as John Innes which has previously been watered. There is no need to cover the seeds; indeed, some species such as *H. quercifolia* have a photo-requirement in order to germinate. The pans should then be covered with a sheet of glass or placed in a seed propagation case. The temperatures required for germination should relate to the climatic conditions where the plant originated. Those which originate in warm areas, such as *H. macrophylla*, *H. serrata*, *H. quercifolia* and *H. arborescens* will germinate in 10 to 14 days at a temperature of 22° C (70° F). Similarly, the evergreen climbers *H. integrifolia*, *H. heteromalla* and *H. aspera* which come from cooler areas can be sown fresh and placed in the cold frame throughout the winter and will germinate in the spring. Seeds from *H. anomala* require cold treatment and should be chilled for 30–60 days at 5° C (40° F) after sowing before being placed in a cold frame.

The seedlings should be pricked out when they are large enough to handle and can at this stage be susceptible to attack from slugs. They should be potted on, fed and held in a cold frame until some of the stems have become lignified – perhaps two seasons. They can then be planted out in the garden. The first seed-grown plants will flower in the second season and most will have flowered by the third season. The most desirable forms can then be retained and propagated vegetatively if wished.

Division

Sometimes, when moving a large *H. macrophylla* cultivar, the plant falls apart during the operation. It has been found that, provided that each section has good roots, planting the separate pieces is totally successful. So, the easiest of all propagation methods – that of simple division – is also available to the gardener growing the ever versatile hydrangea.

The method of propagation chosen will depend on the availability both of plant material and of the gardener's time. Since the choice is wide and success is probable, hydrangea propagation is a satisfying occupation. Reproducing a cultivar of which the name has been researched and confirmed, is of benefit also to the total concept of plant conservation.

5 Other Aspects of Hydrangeas

Pot Plants

Since their introduction into Europe over two hundred years ago, hydrangeas have been grown mostly as pot plants. Naturally enough, most of the literature also relates to the potted plant. In this book, however, orientated as it is to hydrangeas in the garden, it is sufficient to mention that the pot-plant trade continues to flourish. Hydrangeas excel as striking plants for indoor decoration, especially in public places such as hotel foyers and concert platforms. Grown in pots, they give many weeks of colour indoors and continue to make very popular and acceptable gifts, especially in Europe and the USA. Some spectacular (and very expensive) specimens can be found in those garden centres which also specialize in plants for the house or for conservatories. Such plants can, of course, be planted in the garden after their season of indoor adornment is over. The resulting shrub will not necessarily, however, reproduce exactly the effect of the forced plant.

Cut Fresh Flowers

Grown as garden shrubs, hydrangeas offer late-season attraction to the cut-flower arranger. One or two heads can give accent in a mixed display, and they are invaluable in large-scale arrangements. However, they are not the easiest flowers to handle, for, only a few hours after picking, they can droop disastrously, each individual floret going limp and shrivelled. Precautions can be taken to combat this:

1. Remove all leaves, keeping just the stem and flower head.
2. Immediately after picking, totally immerse the whole flower, stem and head, in water. Leave for one to two hours. This 'conditioning' is a good insurance. Lift and use the flowers as required, gently shaking off the surplus water. The procedure can be repeated should the flowers wilt later.
3. Another method for reviving a drooping flower (similar to that described in page 65): cut about 2–3 cm (1 in) off the base of the stem, before replacing it in the vase. The problem, which may have been an airlock in the stem, is thus removed.
4. The use of cold water which has previously been boiled is recommended, having less air in it.
5. Short stems are best, and a container which allows the greater part of the stem to remain immersed.
6. Oasis does not make a very satisfactory medium for supporting hydrangeas and chicken wire is preferable, and as deep a container as possible.
7. Should very large, heavy heads be desired (and these are often readily available on the plant) they can be wired quite easily to help support the weight.

Provided these precautions are taken, as appropriate, fresh hydrangeas can be colourful and indeed dramatic subjects for floral art.

Dried Flowers

It is probably as dried flowers that hydrangeas are most appreciated by the flower arranger. They dry easily and well, and produce long-lasting blooms in a wonderful range of soft, muted colours. The heads, which are larger than those of many other plants, are most effective mixed with flowers of contrasting shapes and textures, but a simple bowl of dried, mixed hydrangeas also has appeal as the colours are so unusual.

Timing is critical when drying hydrangeas. Choose a dry day towards the end of the flowering season. (In Britain this will probably be in October.) It is no use gathering them when it has been raining – the blooms must be dry when picked, or they will quickly rot. Touch is the only sure way of telling if a bloom is ready to be picked for the drying process. To select, squeeze the flower head gently, using the whole hand with finger tips extended. If it feels 'crisp' rather than 'soft', it is ready. Watch, however, for florets hidden beneath the crisp ones – if these are still soft, wait a few more days.

Take the chosen flowers indoors and prepare them carefully. Remove all leaves. Also, with a small pair of scissors, cut out any florets which are brown or damaged, to prevent any rot spreading to the rest of the flower head.

The flowers are now ready for drying. They need to be kept in a dark, dry and preferably warm place. Light will cause the colours to bleach, and warm air will hasten the drying process. Even better is a current of air, but this is not always easy to find. A dry cupboard is satisfactory, or a dry airing cupboard (not one used for damp clothes). An attic or dry dark store room will serve the purpose, but a garage will be open to the atmosphere, and too damp. Whichever place is chosen, some means must be found of storing the flowers until they are dry. They must have

enough space for air to circulate and, as they are fragile, they need to be protected from knocks. They can be stood in a vase (without any water), but each vase can hold only a few. Another way is to suspend the blooms upside down, tying fine string round each stem and then looping this over a hook, or attaching it to a wire coat hanger. Hooks could be on a beam, or the underside of a shelf – anywhere which will allow the inverted flowers to hang freely.

The drying process should take two to three weeks, depending on the conditions available. When ready, the heads will be very crisp and the stems hard. They can be used in a range of displays, and the type of Oasis made for dried flowers is an ideal supporting material. The flower heads can be sprayed with gold or silver paint, if desired, to add glamour to Christmas decorations. Dried hydrangeas will last for months or even years, although they will very gradually lose a little colour – and will certainly gather dust. They are so easy to dry, however, that it is a pleasure to prepare fresh ones each year.

Many hydrangeas dry well. Some are mentioned in Chapter 6 – among especially successful ones are *H. macrophylla* 'Altona', 'Général Vicomtesse de Vibraye', 'Lilacina', 'Maréchal Foch', 'Veitchii' and *H. serrata* 'Grayswood', as well as some of the cultivars of *H. aspera*. This collection alone would give a wonderful range of colours.

Individual sepals and florets can be pressed and dried satisfactorily for use in pressed-flower pictures. The range of colours, once again, is most attractive, and fading when exposed to light is only a very slow process.

Well Dressing

An unexpected use for fresh hydrangeas is found in Derbyshire, where well dressing has been carried out in one form or another since pagan times. Although the early Christian church expressly forbade the worship of fountains in AD 960 and St Anselm was still condemning this form of idolatry in AD 1102, the custom was revived during the Black Death of 1348–1349 and again in the great drought of 1615. The village of Tissington was the centre in ancient times (Christian, 1987). Nowadays, over thirty villages, with several wells to each village, compete with each other in dressing wells usually, but not always, to a religious theme. New designs are prepared for each well every year. On the Saturday before the well dressing, there is a village fête with processions, bands, decorated carts complete with the village queen, princess and rosebuds (children up to the age of about seven).Besides each well is a collecting box, the proceeds of which are given to charity. On the Sunday, the decorated wells are blessed by vicars of local parishes.

The villages have their celebrations during weekends from mid-May to late August. Only natural materials may be used, and because of the span of date, the flowers vary according to what is available. Hydrangeas are used at wells in Bonsall, Pilsey and Tissington, while at Bradwell the three wells are dressed almost entirely with hydrangeas. After the villagers have scoured local gardens for supplies, they are obliged to buy hydrangeas from elsewhere. A week or so before assembling the picture, specific orders are sent to suppliers indicating the colour and number of hydrangeas heads required. The sepals must be of uniform size, and not too large, to avoid giving the impression of filling the space too cheaply. The heads are gathered as near as possible to the time they are to be used. No stalks are needed, so only selected flower heads are picked and immediately submerged in water. They are removed from the water and transferred to plastic sacks for delivery to the villages. There they are pulled to pieces, to provide thousands of separate sepals. Meanwhile, large wooden frames, about an inch thick, have been soaking in the local stream or pond for several days. These are lifted out, and clay from the previous year mixed with salt to prevent premature drying out, is smoothed on to the frames.

The paper with the chosen design is then laid on top of the clay. A bodkin or tailor's pricking wheel is used to transfer every detail to the clay, and then the paper is removed. Black knitting wool or small beans or peppercorns are used to define the outline on the clay. Infilling begins with natural materials which will last, such as bits of bark, lichen etc. used to represent paths, roads, walls and rocks. Lastly the flowers, representing the more colourful parts of the design. Starting from the bottom, petals/sepals are pressed gently into the clay following the design, each row overlapping the one below like slates on a roof to help shed the rain. Hydrangea sepals of all colours are used in vast numbers. A colour copy of the design is pinned up to help the Dressers select the right colours. The task takes several days to complete and is very tiring but still satisfying. The finished frames are placed round the well where they remain for about a week for all to see. Each well is the responsibility of a different organization and the village is socially united.

Paper-making

Another unexpected use for hydrangeas is paper-making. *H. paniculata* provides a glue-like material called 'nori' (or 'neri'), which is an integral part of the production of quality hand-made paper in Japan (Hughes, 1982). This plant is readily found in Hokkaido, and is known as Nori-utsugi. It grows rapidly, as has already been described, producing new stems each year to bear the current year's flowers. These stems are gathered, their bark is stripped off and stored in a phenolic preservative solution. When required for paper-making, the bark is removed from the preservative, washed and crushed on a flat stone. It is then placed in water and left for a few hours, when a clear viscous mucilage is formed.

This glue-like mucilage is nori (neri), and is added to the fibres from which the paper is to be made. It has several attributes: it holds the fibres in suspension and aids alignment while the hand-made sheets are formed; it helps to separate the prepared sheets and it increases their strength, allowing thin paper to be produced. Other plants, such as hollyhock, rose mallow and okra, are also used to provide nori, from their roots. The nori from the stems of *H. paniculata* is used for the making of high-quality paper with a textured surface.

Adverse Effects of Hydrangeas

There have been some recorded cases, mentioned by C.R. Lovell (1993), of contact dermatitis being caused from handling *Hydrangea macrophylla* cultivars. The known cases are few, and were treatable with medical advice, or preventable by wearing gloves. Those suffering were members of the floral or horticultural trade. The Collection holders, who handle all kinds of hydrangeas, have not had any personal adverse reactions, nor have they heard directly of anyone suffering from this problem. However, should any reader

know of such a reaction, the authors would like to know of it.

Some hydrangeas have been found to contain varying amounts of the cyanogenic glycoside, hydrangin, especially in the flower buds, but also in the leaves (Hardin and Arena, 1969). Cyanide poisoning can result from eating these parts of the plant, although no fatalities have been recorded. Animals are more likely to eat the plants, and have been known to develop gastrointestinal symptoms. In one case cited (Spoerke and Smolinske, 1990), a family ate salad containing hydrangea buds and were ill, but this would not be a common item of diet.

The making of tea from hydrangea leaves is a custom in Japan, and will be described later (page 79). Although mainly a ceremonial procedure, it would hardly have been continued if illness resulted! It should be stressed that only certain hydrangeas contain hydrangin, and that in differing quantities. The Japanese cite six different hydrangeas which are used for tea-making, and these presumably are carefully selected because they are hydrangin-free. The indiscriminate making of tea from hydrangea leaves, or the consumption of any part of the plant, *should be avoided*.

Smoking the leaves of *H. paniculata* 'Grandiflora', which grows so freely in USA, has been known to cause illness instead of the hoped for 'high' (Turner and Szezawinski, 1991)! Again, the practice of smoking leaves of any hydrangea is not recommended. Yet one more use, in connection with smoking: the Ainu, tribes of fishermen and farmers, now few in number, living in Hokkaido, north Japan, made pipes from the branches of huge *H. paniculata* growing there (Sargent, 1894).

There have been some beneficial uses for hydrangeas. The Cherokee Indians used roots of *H. arborescens* for a variety of medicinal purposes, including the treatment of kidney stones, and the Chinese use dried hydrangea sepals to treat heat stroke and malaria (Jiaxi and Yue, 1988). These practices should, however, be treated with caution by the uninitiated.

Hana Matsuri

One of the national festivals in Japan is Hana Matsuri, the Flower Festival. This is held annually on 8 April, when the birthday of Gautama Buddha, the founder of Buddhism, is celebrated. The ceremony takes place in Buddhist temples all over Japan, and centres on a ritual known as Kambutsue, when a tiny statue of Buddha is anointed with sweet tea. The tea used for this act of devotion is made from hydrangea leaves. The miniature Buddha, made of bronze, is placed in the centre of an open lotus flower, and each person pours a little of the sweet tea (amacha) over the statue three times, from a small bamboo ladle. Often, the festivities also include processions, with the statue being carried through the streets on a cart, followed by children carrying flowers.

Several varieties of hydrangea are employed, all being classed as 'amacha' or 'sweet tea' hydrangeas. The leaves apparently have a sweet taste and were used as a sweetener before the use of sugar. These hydrangeas are found in the mountains of north and central Japan. Most have narrow leaves with a matt surface, similar to those of *H. serrata*. The flowers, lacecaps of great delicacy, may be white, pink or pale blue. There is one beautiful version with double flowers, and there is another with variegated leaves, which grows so fast that, even if cut to the ground, it can still supply an early crop of hydrangea tea for the next season. The sweetest tea is made from the long-leaf tea hydrangea, 'nagaba amacha', which grows in central Honshu.

This use of hydrangeas may seem unusual to us in the Western world, but what more natural in the land where so many of the genus originate?

6 Descriptions of Cultivars and Subspecies

H. anomala   page 81
H. arborescens   pages 82–3
H. aspera   pages 84–88
H. heteromalla   page 89–90
H. involucrata   page 91
H. macrophylla   pages 92–136
H. serrata   pages 137–150
H. paniculata   pages 151–157
H. quercifolia   pages 158–160

Reference Keys to Terms Used in Text

Flowering Times

Early: before mid-July
Mid: mid-July to mid-August
Late: after mid-August

Shrub Height

Dwarf: up to 50 cm (1 ft 8 in)
Small: 50 cm to 100 cm
          (1 ft 8 in to 3 ft 4 in)
Medium: 100 cm to 150 cm
          (3 ft 4 in to 5 ft)
Large: over 150 cm (5 ft)

Flower Head Diameter

Small: 7 cm to 15 cm (3 in to 6 in)
Medium: 15 cm to 19 cm (6 in to $7\frac{1}{2}$ in)
Large: over 19 cm ($7\frac{1}{2}$ in)

Reproductions of actual leaves and sepals are half life size. On each page the photographs and descriptive details are of the same cultivar, but not always the same location. The appropriate pH is given, for both description and photograph.

The symbols in brackets following the AGM date refer to the RHS hardiness categories. This is *not* the same scale as the USDA hardiness zone system referred to in Chapter 1 and illustrated on pages 22–23. The RHS categories used are as follows:

(H3) plants hardy outside in some regions or particular situations, or which, while usually grown outside in summer, need frost-free protection in winter
(H4) plants hardy throughout the British Isles

The category (H3/4) has been given by the RHS to cultivars of *Hydrangea macrophylla*, which, in some years and some locations, can lose their flowers for a season. This is discussed further in Chapter 3, pages 48–49. The RHS ratings are qualified by the statement: 'Where there is a question over the hardiness of a particular plant, the rating errs on the side of caution.'

H. anomala ssp. petiolaris

Syn. *H. petiolaris*. AGM 1992 (H4). Country of origin: Japan

This is the common deciduous climbing hydrangea reaching 16 m (50–60 ft) up into tall trees or against walls, where it adheres like ivy, with aerial roots. These do not appear until the shrub is near or against a vertical support, to which it does no harm. The flower heads, held well away from the support on long peduncles, open in June and are irregular in shape. If the season is very dry, the flowers do not last long, normally about three weeks. The eye-catching white ray florets are raised above the creamy/white fertile flowers in the centre, on long pedicels. The shrub is hardy, shade-tolerant and will grow on north-facing walls, but takes a while to get properly established. It is also useful on steep banks, where it will form dense foliage and therefore act as a good ground cover. It can be grown as a free-standing plant or trailed over a tree stump where it will form a mound. The shrub has bright-yellow autumn foliage, but this tends to be transient. It looks unsightly when not in leaf, but if carefully trained and pruned against a wall, the bare branches can be most decorative in the winter months.

Flower

Head Shape: irregular
Head Size: medium
Sterile Flowers: randomly around edge
Sepal Number: 4
Sepal Immature: cream
Sepal Mature: white
Fertile Flower Immature: creamy white
Fertile Flower Mature: creamy white
Peduncle: creamy green, long
Pedicel: cream, long
pH: 6.5

Leaf

Main Colour: mid-green
Autumn Colour: bright golden yellow
Edge Colour: yellowish
Texture: leathery
Back of Leaf: light green, smooth
Veins: very fine, dark on front, light central vein on back tufted with hairs
Curvature: tip down, edges
Branch: young, light green; brown peeling bark when older
Petiole: creamy green

Height: climber
Flowering Time: early

All images: *H. anomala* ssp. *petiolaris*, Windermere (pH 6.5)

H. arborescens 'Annabelle'

AM 1978. AGM 1992 (H4). Found in Anna, Illinois, USA.
Introduced to Great Britain 1907

A spectacular shrub with huge, white, drumstick flower heads
blooming from mid-July until late into the autumn. These
stand erect and are held on strong branches. When massed in
a bed they are an arresting sight. The size of the flower heads
can be easily controlled. Simply, the rule is the less the shrub
is pruned, the smaller the blooms. Enormous inflorescences
can be produced by pruning last year's growth to ground
level in the spring and feeding the shrub well. The bigger the
bloom, the more the stem will bend in rain. The individual
florets are white to cream. The leaves are thin and smooth,
with irregular wavy edges and prominent veins. The branches
are sometimes reddish. The shrub increases by underground
suckers, but not invasively. Being frost-hardy, because it
flowers on the current season's growth, and controllable in
size, it is well worth growing. It is tolerant of light shade and
is useful for lighting up the darker corners of the garden all
summer long.

Flower

Head Shape: convex to hemispherical
Head Size: large, dependent on pruning
Sterile Flowers: very small not overlapping
Sepal Number: 3–5
Sepal Immature: pale green to cream
Sepal Mature: white/cream, fine grey lines
Sepal Autumnal: pale green
Fertile Flower Immature: green
Fertile Flower Mature: greeny-white
Peduncle: plain green
Pedicel: creamy white
pH: 6.5

Leaf

Main Colour: mid-green
Edge Colour: as leaf
Texture: smooth
Back of Leaf: lighter green
Veins: obvious, recessed
Curvature: flat with wavy edges
Branch: plain green/reddish
Petiole: plain green turning brown

Height: medium to large but dependent on pruning
Flowering Time: early to late

H. arborescens 'Annabelle', Windermere (pH 6.5)

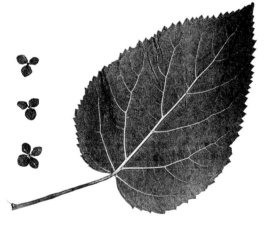

H. arborescens 'Grandiflora'

AM 1907. AGM 1992 (H4). Found wild in Ohio USA by E.H. Hill. Introduced to Great Britain 1907

Now widely cultivated, this plant needs space and time to fulfil its excellent potential. It increases by suckering to a large bush, and would make a good feature plant. It is criticized because the flower heads tend to flop on their slender stems. This does happen, and is noticeable on a small plant. On a large, well-developed shrub, however, the central flowers are held erect while the outer ones 'dip' rather than 'flop'. The result is a well-rounded bush, light and informal, with flowers right down to the ground – an attraction rather than a defect.

Despite its name, the flower heads are not exceptionally large – they do not rival those of *H. arborescens* 'Annabelle' – but are very numerous and somewhat irregular in shape. It is the individual florets which are large for this species. The sepals are also more pointed than those of *H. a.* 'Annabelle'. Of purest white, they bloom from July to early autumn.

Other benefits, beyond the multitude of blossoms and the long flowering period, include the hardiness of this plant. It withstands late frosts, and is resistant to periods of drought. A superb specimen was discovered in a garden in Kanab, Utah, USA, where the annual rainfall is around 30 cm (12 in), and temperatures often reach over 35° C (100° F). It was only watered twice weekly, in the hottest periods. A splendid plant.

Flower

Head Shape: flat/convex, irregular, lax
Head Size: small/medium
Sterile Flowers: flat, crowded, overlapping
Sepal Number: 3–5, mainly 4
Sepal Immature: lime green
Sepal Mature: white/palest cream
Sepal Autumnal: fading brown
Fertile Flower Immature: green
Fertile Flower Mature: cream
Peduncle: very pale green
Pedicel: cream
pH: 6.5

Leaf

Main Colour: yellowish green
Edge Colour: as leaf
Texture: matt
Back of Leaf: as front, lighter
Veins: central raised on back
Curvature: flat, some tips down
Branch: grey, green
Petiole: red above, green below

Height: large
Flowering Time: early to late

Above and below: *H. arborescens* 'Grandiflora', Snowqualmie Village, Washington, USA. (GL-H)

H. aspera 'Kawakami'

Introduced from Taiwan

A tall, open plant well provided with blooms. Late flowering like all *H. aspera*, it continues to produce new heads well into September. The fertile flowers are packed into the centre of the corymb and are the highlight of the display. Initially pale coral pink, their colour intensifies until they open when anthers and filaments make a striking show of deep mauve. A garnish of white sterile florets makes a decorative edging.

Needing space to do itself justice (ours is 6ft × 6ft, 180 cm × 180 cm after six years), this is a hardy, trouble-free, unusual and beautiful late summer shrub.

Above and below: *H. aspera* 'Kawakami', Windermere (pH 6.5)

Flower

Head Shape: domed lacecap
Head Size: medium
Sterile Flowers: rather few for head size
Sepal Number: 4
Sepal Immature: light pink
Sepal Mature: light pink, suffused deep pink
Sepal Autumnal: white
Fertile Flower Immature: pink
Fertile Flower Mature: deep mauve
Peduncle: pink, hairy
Pedicel: pink
pH: 6.5

Leaf

Main Colour: mid-green
Autumn Colour: yellowing
Edge Colour: browning with age
Texture: hairy, velvety feel
Back of Leaf: lighter green
Veins: cream
Curvature: flat, tips down with age
Branch: light brown, hairy
Petiole: light brown, hairy

Height: large
Flowering Time: late

H. aspera 'Macrophylla'

H. aspera var. macrophylla (McClintock)

AGM 1992 (H4). From Nanto and mountains to the north, Hupeh Province, China

Because of the wide range of habitats, there are many forms of this species, making identification difficult. *H. aspera* 'Macrophylla' is a shrub for the larger garden. The flowers emerge from a fat, rounded, hazelnut-shaped bud and expand to a flower head about 23 cm (9 in) diameter, being slightly convex, surrounded with ray flowers which are lower than the central mass of fertile flowers. The sepals are orbicular, overlap at the base and are coloured rose pink. The fertile flowers at the centre are blue/mauve, as are the fertile flowers of all members of this species, even in alkaline soils. The velvety leaves ask to be stroked. The leaves are pubescent with ciliate edges and have a central red vein which is brown on the reverse.

H. a. 'Mauvette' is another cultivar but differs in the following respects: the flower head is more domed and has more numerous ray flowers. These colour to a deep lilac, and often have slightly serrated sepals. The fertile flowers turn dark red in the autumn. The leaves are slightly smaller, the central veins on the front and reverse being red and the remaining veins white. It is possible to dry the flowers for winter decoration, but the red/lilac colouring fades immediately, leaving a bluey/grey flower. However, this is quite delightful and adds a certain lightness to dried floral arrangements. These are truly handsome shrubs when they are allowed to grow in plenty of space.

Flower

Head Shape: slightly convex
Head Size: medium to large
Sterile Flowers: many, overlapping
Sepal Number: 4
Sepal Immature: pale pink
Sepal Mature: rose pink
Sepal Autumnal: dull pink to brown
Fertile Flower Immature: pale blue/mauve
Fertile Flower Mature: deep blue
Peduncle: pinky red, rough, hairy
Pedicel: pinky-red, rough
pH: 6.5

Leaf

Main Colour: dull, dark green
Autumn Colour: going blotchy brown
Texture: pubescent, thick
Back of Leaf: paler than front
Veins: front central red, all on back brown
Curvature: mainly flat
Branch: reddish brown
Petiole: pinky brown, dull, hairy

Height: large
Flowering Time: mid to late

Above: *H. aspera* 'Mauvette', Spinners Garden, Lymington, Hants (pH 6.1)
Below: *H. aspera* 'Macrophylla', Levens Hall Garden, Kendal, Cumbria, England

H. aspera 'Peter Chappell'

Origin unknown – named by M. Foster as a tribute to Peter Chappell

H. aspera, with its forms and cultivars, is a rather neglected section of the hydrangea family. The plants are hardy, late flowering and extraordinarily decorative.

H. aspera 'Peter Chappell' is a large but compact shrub bearing white to cream lacecap inflorescences. White sterile florets with pink streaked sepals form a garland around the very numerous fertile flowers. These latter steal the show as when fully open they form a dense central cream mass to the flowerhead which is certainly eye-catching. The leaves are hairy on both surfaces. Withstanding drought quite well, best results are achieved in mulched, moisture retentive soil where flower colour is not related to soil pH. Flowering into autumn, it is good as a specimen plant or in a large border.

Flower

Head Shape: domed lacecap
Head Size: large
Sterile Flowers: 10–20
Sepal Number: 4
Sepal Immature: cream/pale pink
Sepal Mature: white
Sepal Autumnal: brown
Fertile Flower Immature: cream
Fertile Flower Mature: cream
Peduncle: pink, hairy
Pedicel: pink
pH: 6.5

Leaf

Main Colour: mid green
Autumn Colour: yellowing
Edge Colour: as leaf, browning later
Texture: velvety, hairy
Back of Leaf: light green
Veins: centre vein red on front
Curvature: flat
Branch: brown
Petiole: brown, hairy

Height: large
Flowering Time: mid-late

Above and below: *H. aspera* 'Peter Chappell', Windermere (pH 6.5)

H. aspera ssp. sargentiana

AM 1912. AGM 1992 (H4). From Hupeh Province, China

This unusual shrub requires space, lots of it, growing to 4 m (14 ft) high and 2 m (7 ft) wide, but can be rather leggy. The ray flowers, although decorative, seem disproportionately small for the size of the plant and flower head. These white, sterile flowers are fairly numerous and appear haphazardly round the edge of an amorphously shaped slightly domed corymb of fertile flowers. These are of a pale-blue/mauve colour when immature, opening to a mid-blue/mauve. The leaves can be huge with a texture like shark skin and are often over 25 cm (10 in) × 18 cm (7 in) in size. They sometimes appear to be attacked by pests but, on closer inspection, the dots are caused by pollen dropping on to the platelike leaves where it remains trapped on the pubescent surface. Both branches and petioles are covered in short bristly hairs, as are the pedicels. The shrub needs protection from wind, especially the cold searing sort. If subjected to a few degrees of frost, the leaves curl and droop and turn grey immediately. As the plant is greedy, it requires to be mulched regularly. It can be pruned to improve its shape, but when happily planted, it can increase itself by suckering and self-layering. This is an arresting shrub given space and attention, but is really only suitable for the larger garden.

Flower

Head Shape: slightly domed
Head Size: large
Sterile Flowers: many, on long pedicels
Sepal Number: 4
Sepal Immature: green
Sepal Mature: greeny/white
Sepal Autumnal: pale green
Fertile Flower Immature: pale blue/mauve
Fertile Flower Mature: mid-blue/mauve
Peduncle: green, coarse bristly hairs
Pedicel: pale green/pink, short hairs
pH: 6.5

Leaf

Main Colour: dull green
Edge Colour: as leaf
Texture: rough, hairy, like shark-skin
Back of Leaf: lighter green, bristly
Veins: central pink, brown on back
Curvature: almost flat, tip dips slightly
Branch: green, hairy
Petiole: very hairy, almost bristly

Height: large
Flowering Time: early to mid

Above: *H. a.* ssp. *sargentiana*, Levens Hall Garden. Below: *H. a.* ssp. *sargentiana*, Washington Park Arboretum

H. aspera 'Villosa'

Syn. *H. aspera* Villosa Group. AM 1950. AGM 1992 (H4).
Collected by E.H. Wilson 1908

This variety is highly variable, so it is necessary to obtain a good clone. It can grow to over 3 m (10 ft) high and 4½ m (15 ft) wide. The lacecap head has quite a dense central corymb of fertile flowers, adored by bees. The four rounded sepals have slightly serrated edges and are on long pedicels taking them 2½ cm (1 in) from the central group of fertile flowers. The flower colour of this shrub does not change with the pH value of the soil, but as it ages, the sepals reverse, the original upper surface turns a dull green and the reverse turns pink. Excellent at the base of a wall, it does prefer protection from wind, being slightly brittle. The leaves, which have pink veins on the underside, are smaller and less velvety than other *H. asperae*. Because the leaves are hairy, it is not so easy to strike from cuttings that dislike the enclosed atmosphere normally used, so hardwood cuttings are an alternative. It can also be increased by layering or if a good clone cannot be obtained, seed should be sown in December in the hope that a good variety can be produced. The flowers can be dried but the red colouring leaches out, leaving a pleasant grey/blue flower which can be attractive in dried flower arrangements. An aged shrub often has several branches starting at ground level. One of these can start splitting away from the main shrub at the junction with the ground. This branch should be removed entirely or, if not broken, it should be severely cut back to encourage new growth nearer the base.

Flower

Head Shape: convex
Head Size: medium
Sterile Flowers: slightly cupped and overlapping
Sepal Number: 4–5
Sepal Immature: pale pink
Sepal Mature: violet blue to pink
Sepal Autumnal: front light green, reverse deep pink
Fertile Flower Immature: blue
Fertile Flower Mature: deep blue/violet
Peduncle: deep pink, hairy
Pedicel: red, very long
pH: 6.5

Leaf

Main Colour: blue/green
Texture: rough, very fine hairs
Back of Leaf: silvery grey
Veins: very detailed on back
Curvature: bending backwards
Branch: red/brown, hairy, peels when older
Petiole: pink, hairy

Height: large
Flowering Time: mid to late

Above and below:
H. aspera 'Villosa',
Windermere (pH 6.5)

H. heteromalla 'Bretschneideri'

Syn. *H. heteromalla* Bretschneideri Group. AGM 1992 (H4).
From various sources in China

This species is very widely distributed in the Himalayas, China, Indo-China and Taiwan. Naturally there are many variations so identification of different forms can be difficult. Growing as shrubs or small trees, they have many branches starting at ground level and all have similar flowers – cream or white on opening and reversing to pink later in the season. They are hardy, extremely decorative, and of a convenient size – usually around 4½–6.0 m (15–20 ft) high. The early flower display, in June-July, is followed by additional colour as the florets reverse to pink, then drying to brown and remaining until the first frosts. Autumn leaves give an extra display of yellow colour.

H. heteromalla 'Bretschneideri' is a large shrub with flattened white lacecap inflorescences and identified by its peeling bark in maturity. Another form, given a clonal name because it is distinct, is *H. heteromalla* 'Snowcap'. It grows to around 2.4 m (8 ft) high and has very large flattened corymbs. These have a dense mass of fertile flowers and a garnish of white sterile florets. Another smaller named form is *H. heteromalla* 'Wilsonii' to be found in Ernest Wilson's memorial garden in Chipping Campden, Gloucestershire.

Flower

Head Shape: concave
Head Size: medium
Sterile Flowers: small, on long pedicels
Sepal Number: 4–5
Sepal Immature: yellowish white
Sepal Mature: creamy white
Sepal Autumnal: turns pink/red/green
Fertile Flower Immature: greeny white
Fertile Flower Mature: creamy white
Peduncle: green
Pedicel: very pale, green, hairy
pH: 6.5

Leaf

Main Colour: mid-green
Edge Colour: lighter
Texture: soft, leathery
Back of Leaf: light green, hairy
Veins: reverse prominent
Curvature: edges up and wavy
Branch: light green/white dots on young wood, peeling bark when older
Petiole: red

Height: large, treelike
Flowering Time: early

Left: *H. heteromalla* Logan Botanic Garden, Wigtownshire, Scotland
Above right: *H. heteromalla* 'Bretschneideri', Royal Botanic Garden, Edinburgh, Scotland (pH 6.5)
Below right: *H. heteromalla Wilsonii* , memorial garden, Gloucestershire, England

H. heteromalla 'Jermyn's Lace'

Provenance unknown. Named by Coomes and Hillier in *Hillier's Manual of Trees and Shrubs,* 2002

A striking example of a heteromalla showing what a splendidly decorative tree could be grown in small gardens. This is a well-rounded tree of about 4½ m (15 ft) high and similar width. It carries a generous display of corymbs making it an eye-catching sight in June to July. The dense mass of fertile flowers is surrounded by numerous large white/cream sterile florets, held on very long pedicels. As the season progresses, these florets become lime green, reverse to pink and droop in a most decorative fashion.

H. heteromalla xanthoneura is another variation which flowers slightly later, each inflorescence carrying a garland of sterile florets. This shrub was seen in Alsace in the Jardin des Alpines of Nancy University. Here at over 1000 metres (3000 ft) it formed a rounded large shrub growing and flowering well.

H. heteromalla 'Yalung Ridge' (Schilling) from Nepal has red petioles, carries an abundance of attractively shaped florets and again could grace many a garden.

The decorative value of these plants has been stressed. They are also hardy and available. They could and should be more widely grown where there is space.

Flower
Head Shape: flattened corymb
Head Size: medium-large
Sterile Flowers: numerous, on long pedicels
Sepal Number: 4
Sepal Immature: white/cream
Sepal Mature: cream reversing to pink and lime green
Sepal Autumnal: brown
Fertile Flower Immature: white/cream
Fertile Flower Mature: green/brown
Peduncle: green
Pedicel: pale green, long

Leaf
Main Colour: mid-green
Autumn Colour: yellow
Edge Colour: as leaf
Texture: velvety
Back of Leaf: lighter green
Veins: darker than leaf on front
Curvature: edges up
Branch: brown
Petiole: pink

Height: large
Flowering Time: early

Above left and right: *H. het.* 'Jermyn's Lace', The Sir Harold Hillier Garden and Arboretum. Soil just acid. (GL-H)
Below left: *H. het.* 'Xanthoneura'. Jardin des Alpines, Alsace
Below right: *H. het.* 'Yalung Ridge'. Savill Garden

H. involucrata 'Hortensis'

AGM 1992 (H4)

This is a most unlikely looking hydrangea. The shrub eventually reaches a height of about 120 cm (4 ft) after many years. The flowers are produced in racemes which tend to droop. These develop from nut-shaped buds enclosed in bracts. The immature flowers open white and the fertile flowers are apricot pink in colour. The flower head is very irregular, looking like coral, with numerous sepals to each floret. The leaves which are slender and pointed have bristly serrations and feel like suede; they often turn yellowish from the edges. It is easy to propagate from cuttings but it is difficult to maintain these through their first year. An easier method is to take advantage of the fact that it produces suckers. This species tolerates chalk soils. Once established, its attractive but unusual shape is an interesting and conversational item. The difficulty in propagation and the occasional discoloration of the leaves may be the reason for this lovely cultivar not being much more widely grown. It is not suitable for flower arranging nor for drying, but is a useful, indeed fascinating, front-of-border plant.

Flower
Head Shape: very lax, open branched
Head Size: medium
Sterile Flowers: in racemes
Sepal Number: numerous
Sepal Immature: enclosed in bract, opening white
Sepal Mature: apricot pink
Sepal Autumnal: cream with brown edges
Fertile Flower Immature: white
Fertile Flower Mature: cream/pink
Peduncle: cream
Pedicel: cream
pH: 6.5

Leaf
Main Colour: light green
Autumn Colour: brown edges
Edge Colour: often yellow blotches
Texture: downy, hairy
Back of Leaf: very hairy
Veins: faint and dark on front, conspicuous and light on back
Curvature: flat, tip down
Branch: pale green/pink, hairy
Petiole: light green/deep pink/red

Height: small to medium
Flowering Time: mid to late

H. involucrata 'Hortensis', Hidcote Manor Garden, Gloucestershire.

H. macrophylla 'All Summer Beauty'

One of the best growers in our garden in Cumbria and also highly prized in USA, this shrub really does live up to its name. It came to us from Holland but the provenance is unknown.

The well rounded bush stands out in the border as it is one of the first to come into bloom, withstanding well any late spring frosts. It displays a covering of medium-sized mopheads held close to the leaves. By July, the blooms are so numerous that the leaves are almost obscured. The show continues until the first frost with fresh flowers appearing well into the autumn, thus giving an exceptionally long flowering season.

On soil of pH 6.5, young blooms are a charming mix of cream and palest blue. These mature to an overall pale blue and fade to a lilac blue. Because of the continuing arrival of fresh flowers there is a constant mix of gentle shades. Leaves darken as the season progresses and many show dark red autumn colour.

Above and below: H. mac. 'All Summer Beauty', Windermere (pH 6.5)

Flower
Head Shape: well domed mophead
Head Size: medium
Sterile Flowers: tightly packed
Sepal Number: 3–5
Sepal Immature: pale blue edge, cream centre
Sepal Mature: light blue
Sepal Autumnal: lilac blue, some red marks
Fertile Flower Immature: blue
Fertile Flower Mature: blue
Peduncle: green flecked red
Pedicel: blue – deeper shade than flower
pH: 6.5

Leaf
Main Colour: mid green
Autumn Colour: many going dark red/brown
Edge Colour: as leaf
Texture: leathery
Back of Leaf: lighter green
Veins: light green
Curvature: edges up on young
Branch: green flecked red
Petiole: light green under, pink above

Height: medium
Flowering Time: early to mid-late

H. macrophylla 'Alpenglühen'

Syn. *H. macrophylla* 'Alpenglow'. Bred by Brugger. From Tetnang, Germany, 1950

Obviously of great attraction for the garden, this cultivar is still offered for sale. It is a robust shrub with a rounded corymb, with individual florets nicely spaced to display the sepals in a not overcrowded flower head. The florets open wide but not flat. The sepals, generally four to a floret, are deltoid with a pointed tip. Their edges turn up, and they have a crease and sometimes also a green or whitish stripe down the centre. On maturity the colour of the stripe changes to a deeper shade of the general colour. The flowers remain a good red in soil of pH 6.5 for the whole of the season, before turning brown. The leaves are rugose, slightly leathery and wrinkled. The branch is almost plain, but where it is not, it colours to a dark stripe often extending, in autumn, beyond the distance between the nodes.

A similar cultivar, difficult to distinguish from *H. m.* 'Alpenglühen', is *H. m.* 'Deutschland' bred by Baardse in 1921, and which received an AM in 1927. The sepals of *H. m.* 'Alpenglühen' are slightly more lilacy in colour, the overall head shape is more rounded, and the sepals more tightly grouped, with more of an overlap at the base of the floret. The leaves of *H. m.* 'Deutschland' are a lighter green and glossy.

Flower
Head Shape: spherical
Head Size: medium to large
Sterile Flowers: cupped, overlapping
Sepal Number: 3–5, mainly 4
Sepal Immature: creamy or purply pink with red edges
Sepal Mature: rich red to rose
Fertile Flower Immature: cream
Fertile Flower Mature: white or blue
Peduncle: green with red speckles
Pedicel: pink/cream, red speckles
pH: 6.5

Leaf
Main Colour: mid-green
Edge Colour: sometimes slightly red
Texture: coarse, slightly rugose
Back of Leaf: paler than front
Veins: pale and recessed on front, prominent on back
Curvature: edges up
Branch: pale-green, fine-red speckles, long dark stripes in autumn
Petiole: green

Height: medium
Flowering Time: early to late

Above: *H. mac.* 'Alpengluhen', Windermere (pH 6.5)
Below: *H. mac.* 'Deutschland', Windermere (pH 6.5)

H. macrophylla 'Altona'

AM 1957. AGM 1992 (H3/4). Bred by H. Schadendorff, 1931

This quite common variety deserves to be more widely grown, if only for its chameleon qualities. Its immature flowers are cupped, formed by overlapping, serrated, undulating sepals. In maturity, some of the sepals become entire, in fact all the sepals in a whole flower head may do so, making identification somewhat precarious. Mature sepals often become wavy and develop a point. Some flowers change to a purplish plum colour while others change to a smoky blue, both tending to be lighter towards the centre of the floret. Autumn sees an even more startling change when most of the blooms change to a vibrant brick red. The shrub also produces, in autumn, some flower heads of an unusual dark bluey green where the sepals become twisted in relation to each other. It dries well in its autumn colours and is loved by flower arrangers. It propagates well from cuttings and is often used for pot work, where breeders manage to coax even more exotic colours. A single shrub grown as a specimen set in a lawn is a lovely sight. It grows well by the sea and tolerates full exposure to the sun. This variety should not be confused with *H. m.* 'Hamburg' whose flowers are more blue, and has fewer and larger flowers which often obscure the leaves. It does not colour as well in the autumn. Nor must it be confused with *H. m.* 'Europa', which has larger leaves and fewer flowers.

Flower

Head Shape: flattened globose
Head Size: medium
Sterile Flowers: variable, crowded
Sepal Number: 4–6
Sepal Immature: lilac, yellow/blue centre, blue eye
Sepal Mature: lilac/purple, blue centre
Sepal Autumnal: vibrant red or blue/green
Fertile Flower Immature: light blue/green
Fertile Flower Mature: blue
Peduncle: green, red dashes
Pedicel: cream/lilac, red dashes
pH: 6.5

Leaf

Main Colour: mid-green
Autumn Colour: tips darkening
Edge Colour: occasionally red brown
Texture: slightly rugose
Back of Leaf: lighter green
Veins: faint on front, mid-vein on back prominent
Curvature: edges up, tip down
Branch: pale green, red speckles
Petiole: green

Height: medium to large
Flowering Time: mid to late

H. mac. 'Altona', Windermere (pH 6.5)

H. macrophylla 'Amethyst'

Seedling of H. m. 'Europa'. Bred by M. Haworth-Booth, 1938

A delightful medium-sized and unusual mophead with single and double florets often on the same flower head. When immature, the flower head is very tight, opening to a delightful well-spaced-out corymb. Its colour varies from a pale lilac to shell pink with the edges of the sepals light pink, blending to deeper pink towards the centre of the floret. The double effect is created by a group of tiny sepals, of which the inner ones sometimes become twisted and deformed, making a whorl. This effect is not so apparent early in the season. The sepals are also serrated which gives the flower head even more added interest and attraction. The shrub flowers late in the season, and on the terminal buds only. The leaves are coarsely serrated and are retained until very late in the season. This plant is robust and deserves a position in the garden where the attractive flowers can be enjoyed at close quarters.

Flower

Head Shape: almost conical
Head Size: small
Sterile Flowers: single or whorls, serrated
Sepal Number: 4 or 8 when double
Sepal Immature: yellowy green
Sepal Mature: pale lilac or pale pink
Fertile Flower Immature: quite a deep blue
Fertile Flower Mature: deeper blue
Peduncle: green with dots and dashes
Pedicel: green
pH: 6.5

Leaf

Main Colour: mid- to light green
Autumn Colour: darker green
Edge Colour: as leaf
Texture: smooth, thin, slightly rugose
Back of Leaf: lighter green
Veins: central vein lighter green
Curvature: flat, edges up when immature
Branch: plain green
Petiole: plain green

Height: medium
Flowering Time: late

Above and below: *H. mac.* 'Amethyst', Logan Botanic Garden, Wigtownshire, Scotland

H. macrophylla 'Ami Pasquier'

AM 1953. AGM 1992 (H3/4). Seedling of *H. m.* 'Maréchal Foch'. Bred by E. Mouillère, 1930

This is a lovely, bright, vigorous mophead growing to about 120 cm (4 ft), and prefers semi-shade. It is easily confused with *H. m.* 'Westfalen', AGM 1992 (H3–4), which in many ways is remarkably similar. The flower head is small and reasonably crowded. It is composed of orbicular overlapping sepals which do not push against each other. This cultivar always seems to be in flower. The colour tends towards the red end of the spectrum but in acid soil of pH 6.5 can change to wine purple. It is a seedling of *H. m.* 'Maréchal Foch', so in very acid conditions it can also be blue (Haworth-Booth). Both varieties, in slightly alkaline soils, are a very bright red, with *H. m.* 'Ami Pasquier' being more crimson red and *H. m.* 'Westfalen' more vermilion red. The leaves are rounded and mid-green, but are rather small for the size of the bush.

According to the RHS Floral Committee B "When *H. m.* 'Ami Pasquier' and *H. m.* 'Westfalen' are grown together, with plenty of space between the plants, it is the habit which is important in distinguishing the two – *H. m.* 'Ami Pasquier' will become a vigorous plant to 120 cm (4 ft) across and high. On the other hand *H. m.* 'Westfalen' is a compact, slow-growing plant rarely exceeding 75 cm (2½ ft) tall which shows good autumn colour."

Flower

Head Shape: hemispherical
Head Size: small
Sterile Flowers: overlapping, flat
Sepal Number: 4–6
Sepal Immature: cream to lilac
Sepal Mature: pinky plum to purple
Fertile Flower Immature: pink
Fertile Flower Mature: blue
Peduncle: pink to green dashes
Pedicel: pink to blue
pH: 6.5

Leaf

Main Colour: mid-green
Edge Colour: occasionally red
Texture: fairly smooth
Back of Leaf: paler edge
Veins: front central prominent
Curvature: edges up
Branch: green, brown dashes
Petiole: pale green

Height: medium
Flowering Time: early to late

Above: *H. mac.* 'Ami Pasquier', Spinner's Garden, Lymington, Hants (pH 6.1)
Right: *H. mac.* 'Westfalen', Bank House, Borwick, Nr Carnforth, Lancs (pH 6.5)

H. macrophylla 'Ave Maria'

Bred by Brugger, 1951

Having been growing in Cumbria for over ten years this still maintains its compact form. A sturdy plant with a splendid covering of medium-sized mophead flowers so numerous that the leaves are scarcely seen. In an equally generous fashion, sterile florets are crowded on each flowerhead. Flowers open cream and turn to a pure white with a faint pink tinge developing as the season progresses. Fresh flowers continue to appear into September, giving an extended flowering season. Leaves show some red autumn tints.

As with most white hydrangeas, scorching from strong sunlight does occur and spoils the picture. However, given shelter from direct sun this shrub will provide around three months of garden decoration. Provided that the right location is found, this is one of the best summer to autumn shrubs for a small garden.

Flower

Head Shape: crowded mophead
Head Size: medium
Sterile Flowers: cupped, crowded
Sepal Number: 4–5, overlapped
Sepal Immature: cream
Sepal Mature: white
Sepal Autumnal: tinged pale pink
Fertile Flower Immature: cream
Fertile Flower Mature: cream
Peduncle: green, red dashes
Pedicel: cream/white
pH: 6.5

Leaf

Main Colour: mid-green
Autumn Colour: some red tints
Edge Colour: as leaf
Texture: matt
Back of Leaf: slightly lighter
Veins: light green
Curvature: edges up
Branch: green, many red marks
Petiole: short, pale green

Height: small
Flowering Time: early to mid-late

Above and below: *H. mac.* 'Ave Maria', Windermere (pH 6.5)

H. macrophylla 'Ayesha'

Syn. *H. m.* 'Silver Slipper'. AM 1974, AGM 1992 (H3/4).
Country of origin: Japan

This shrub has flowers so different from other cultivars of *H. macrophylla* that it is not readily recognized as belonging to the same species, but once seen it is never forgotten. It is an exceptionally free-flowering mophead. The large flattish flower head is composed of a very large number of tiny florets. Each sepal has raised edges, curving inwards, giving the overall appearance of flowers similar to lilac. The colour range is pale blue through white to pale pink, depending on the acidity of the soil. It has a reputation of being somewhat delicate but grows abundantly in Cornwall and the Lake District. This is one of the very few members of the genus which is scented, although not very strongly. It is ideal for conservatory work because of its possible delicacy, and because its scent is then contained. The leaves are mid-green, matt and smooth, with shallow serrations. Two similar cultivars called *H. m.* 'Terre de Feu' and *H. m.* 'Pink Lilac' have been noted in the Melbourne Botanic Gardens, Australia. These may be synonyms for the same cultivar. Also *H. m.* 'Scaring-Fielder Lilac' is found in England, which seems to be a larger version of this cultivar.

Flower

Head Shape: slightly convex
Head Size: medium
Sterile Flowers: tightly cupped, orbicular
Sepal Number: 4
Sepal Immature: cream
Sepal Mature: white, pink or pale blue
Fertile Flower Immature: creamy green
Fertile Flower Mature: blue or pink
Peduncle: green
Pedicel: cream
pH: 6.5

Leaf

Main Colour: mid-green
Autumn Colour: green until late December
Edge Colour: as leaf
Texture: matt, smooth
Back of Leaf: slightly lighter green
Veins: prominent on back
Curvature: flat
Branch: green with red dashes
Petiole: as branch

Height: large
Flowering Time: early to late

Above: *H. mac.* 'Ayesha', Mount Congreve, Kilmeaden, Co. Waterford, Ireland (pH 6.2 to pH 6.5)

Below: *H. mac.* 'Ayesha', Rosewarne, Cornwall

H. macrophylla 'Beauté Vendômoise'

French Cert of Merit 1909. Bred by E. Mouillère et Fils from
H. m. 'Mariesii Grandiflora' × *H. m.* 'Rosea'

One of the finest lacecaps, with individual florets being some of
the largest attained by any macrophylla. Haworth-Booth
described the bush as being of 'moderate growth', but his shrub
has grown over the years to 2.7 m (9 ft) in his own garden. The
size and generous spacing of the sepals make this shrub a most
distinctive and attractive lacecap. Like *H. m.* 'Mariesii', the ray
flowers often cover the fertile centre flowers and appear
through them, a fact which detracted, in its earlier days, from its
value as a pot plant. The large, wide, deltoid sepals do not
overlap and are white to palest blue in colour. The fertile
flowers are a deeper blue opening to mid-blue. The leaves are
smooth and lightish green, turning blotchy yellowy green before
turning brown. Although mid-season flowering, it is quite
decorative in November, provided it survives any early frosts.

'Brympton Mauve' was thought to be a similar but distinct
cultivar. After many years of observation, however, we believe
these two to be the same plant with different names.

Flower

Head Shape: shallow convex
Head Size: large
Sterile Flowers: large, flat, numerous
Sepal Number: mainly 4, occasionally 5
Sepal Immature: pale yellow
Sepal Mature: palest blue with deeper veining,
overall effect is white
Fertile Flower Immature: pink or lilac
Fertile Flower Mature: blue
Peduncle: green with dashes
Pedicel: lilac
pH: 6.5

Leaf

Main Colour: light green
Autumn Colour: blotchy, paler yellowy green
Edge Colour: as leaf
Texture: smooth
Back of Leaf: lighter
Veins: not conspicuous
Curvature: flat, tip down
Branch: green with slight brown dashes
Petiole: pale green

Height: large
Flowering Time: mid to late

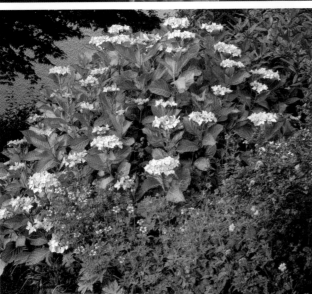

Above: *H. mac.* 'Beauté Vendômoise',
Windermere (pH 6.5)

Below: *H. mac.* 'Beauté Vendômoise' with
Photinia 'Red Robin' and geraniums (TN-C)
(pH 6.5)

H. macrophylla 'Bläuling'

Translation 'Blue Butterfly'. Bred at Wadensvil, 1984

One of the smallest of the 'Teller' series but also one of the most charming. Our plant is five years old and is only 60 cm (2 ft) high.

Flowering early in the hydrangea season the lacecap heads develop first one ring of florets, then another and later, the central fertile flowers can be almost hidden by even more sterile florets. Opening cream with a pale blue border, the blue of the florets intensifies until a beautiful contrast of deep blue and cream appears. Later, this becomes a more uniform colour. Fertile flowers are deep blue. On alkaline soil, the shrub is equally attractive with pale pink flowers.

Being both beautiful, sturdy and hardy this is an excellent shrub for a small garden. It would also make a suitable specimen for a container.

Flower
Head Shape: lacecap
Head Size: small
Sterile Flowers: numerous, two layers or more
Sepal Number: 3–5, usually 4
Sepal Immature: pale blue, cream centre
Sepal Mature: deeper blue, cream centre
Sepal Autumnal: mid blue, lilac streaks
Fertile Flower Immature: pale blue
Fertile Flower Mature: mid blue
Peduncle: green, red markings
Pedicel: blue
pH: 6.5

Leaf
Main Colour: light to mid-green
Autumn Colour: darker green
Edge Colour: fine red on maturity
Texture: thick, matt
Back of Leaf: lighter green
Veins: clearly defined
Curvature: edges up
Branch: thick, red marks on light green
Petiole: plain light green

Height: small
Flowering Time: early to mid

H. mac. 'Bläuling', Windermere (pH 6.5) (TN-C)

H. macrophylla 'Blaumeise'

Syn. 'Blue Sky' or 'Teller Blue'. Translation 'Blue Tit'. Raised in Wadensvil, 1979

A compact and sturdy, medium to large shrub bearing a generous covering of beautifully formed lacecap flowers. These have taken time, in our soil of pH 6.5, to settle to their final colour of deep royal blue. Some tints of pink and purple still show attractively beside the blue. New, fresh flowers adding highlights of cream and blue continue into September, while sepals on older flowers reverse to dusky pink. These sepals overlap each other so that the sterile florets form a characteristic square shape when pressed flat.

An exceptional plant which has stood the test of time and is spectacular on acid soil.

Above: *H. mac.* 'Blaumeise', Windermere (pH 6.5) (TN-C)
Below: *H. mac.* 'Blaumeise' with *H. mac.* 'Libelle',
Windermere (pH 6.5)

Flower

Head Shape: lacecap
Head Size: medium
Sterile Flowers: closely packed around the circumference of the head
Sepal Number: 4, occasionally 5, totally overlapped
Sepal Immature: pale blue, cream centre
Sepal Mature: deep royal blue
Sepal Autumnal: reversing to dusky pink
Fertile Flower Immature: cream
Fertile Flower Mature: mid blue
Peduncle: plain green
Pedicel: blue
pH: 6.5

Leaf

Main Colour: mid-green, broad, glossy
Autumn Colour: no change
Edge Colour: as leaf
Texture: thick
Back of Leaf: lighter green
Veins: central vein prominent
Curvature: edges slightly raised
Branch: thick, sturdy, few marks
Petiole: plain green

Height: medium to large
Flowering Time: mid to late

H. macrophylla 'Blue Wave'

Syn. *H. m.* 'Mariesii Perfecta'. AM 1965. FCC 1985. AGM 1992 (H3/4). Bred by V. Lemoine of Nancy, 1902. Seedling of *H. m.* 'Mariesii'

This shrub is widely grown, but a good clone is worth searching for. Many inferior lacecaps are so labelled, but the quality of the flower is poor. A good variety well grown in light shade is a glorious sight, coming into bloom in mid-August and still beautiful in late November, if not caught by an early frost. The plant is what everyone expects a lacecap to look like, being very regular in outline, some sepals having entire margins while others have slight serrations. Looking closely at a really good clone, the sepals, which can be either blue or pink, depending on the pH of the soil, deepen to a rich claret at the throat, and in maturity do not overlap. The bush can grow, over many years, by self-layering to an enormous size, but of course need not do so. The flowers bleach and the foliage scorches if grown in full sunlight. If picked at the right time, the flowers dry to a lovely silvery blue. The leaves are mid- to dark green, occasionally having red edges in maturity, and the branches have red speckles.

Flower

Head Shape: convex
Head Size: mid to large
Sterile Flowers: opening flat, facing outwards
Sepal Number: 4–5
Sepal Immature: cream
Sepal Mature: pale lilac/blue, darker centre
Sepal Autumnal: light silvery blue
Fertile Flower Immature: green to purple
Fertile Flower Mature: bright blue or lilac
Peduncle: pinky mauve
Pedicel: deep blue
pH: 6.5

Leaf

Main Colour: mid- to dark green
Edge Colour: red on mature growth
Texture: smooth, slightly glossy
Back of Leaf: smooth
Veins: prominent light veins on back
Curvature: edges up
Branch: green, red dots and dashes
Petiole: pale green, darker at nodes

Height: large
Flowering Time: late

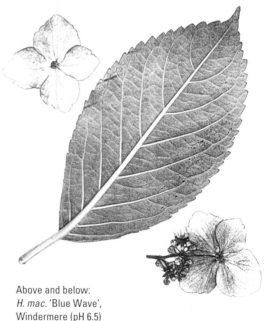

Above and below:
H. mac. 'Blue Wave',
Windermere (pH 6.5)

H. macrophylla 'Brunette'

Eye-catching because of its exceptionally dark flowers and leaves, this plant is known in France as *H. m.* 'Merveille Sanguine' or *H. m.* 'Folis purpurea'. The florets open cream with a purple edge and mature to a deep rich purple – the darkest hydrangea of any that we have seen. Sterile florets are pushed up tightly against each other and the sepals have a velvety texture. Bright blue fertile flowers appear both in the centre of each sterile floret and hidden beneath the florets. Foliage, as remarkable as the blooms, is coarse, rugose and a dark reddish-green. A sheltered place in the garden is needed for this lovely plant to give of its best. As it never grows large it would also be an excellent candidate for planting in a tub.

H. macrophylla 'Merveille'

Paris Medal 1937. Bred by H. Cayeux of Le Havre, 1927

This, a larger and strong-growing shrub, has many similarities of form but lacks the exciting colour of *H. m.* 'Brunette'. *H. m.* 'Merveille' has paler purple florets on acid soil and rosy-crimson ones on alkaline soil. Flowering lasts for an unusually long period. The leaves are lighter in colour but still coarse and rugose. Petioles and internodal distances are short.

Both these plants are subject to attack from capsid bugs, which can be controlled by the application of the appropriate chemical to the soil during winter.

Below: *H. mac.* 'Brunette', Windermere (pH 6.5)

Flower
Head Shape: flat, sepals bunched
Head Size: medium
Sterile Flowers: cupped, twisted
Sepal Number: 4–5
Sepal Immature: purple edge shading to cream with green centre
Sepal Mature: rich, deep velvety purple
Fertile Flower Immature: deep blue
Fertile Flower Mature: deep blue
Peduncle: green with dashes
Pedicel: deep purple
pH: 6.5

Leaf
Main Colour: very dark bronze
Autumn Colour: darker bronze
Edge Colour: darker bronze
Texture: deeply rugose
Back of Leaf: dark, muddy green
Veins: prominent on back
Curvature: edges up, concave
Branch: green, very mottled
Petiole: purple

Height: medium
Flowering Time: late

H. macrophylla 'Europa'

AGM 1992 (H3/4), Bred by H. Schadendorff, 1931

This shrub is very difficult to distinguish from *H. m.* 'Altona' and *H. m.* 'Hamburg', all three having been bred by the same breeder in the same year. *H. m.* 'Europa' has pink to lilac young flowers with cream centres. The young sepals are sometimes serrated, and are slightly marked with red spots or streaks which become more obvious with age. Because the flower heads and sepals are smaller and the leaves larger than those of *H. m.* 'Altona' and *H. m.* 'Hamburg', the impression is that the shrub has fewer flowers than the other two. These leaves of *H. m.* 'Europa' are also consistently the same shape. *H. m.* 'Hamburg' has deep-pink to dark-blue flower heads, sometimes both on the same bush at the same time. Flowering in mid- to late season, *H. m.* 'Hamburg' tolerates full sun or light shade. The autumnal colouring is very varied, even on one flower head, being brighter where the shrub is sheltered. The unusual blues and greens are interesting and loved by flower arrangers, especially when dried. The leaves vary in shape quite considerably, and are coarsely toothed. Neither of the above should be confused with *H. m.* 'Altona' (see p. 94) which has a more pointed leaf and does not turn so deep a blue on acid soils, but bright red in autumn. All are easily propagated from cuttings and dry well for winter decorations. Of these three, it is remarkable that *H. m.* 'Hamburg' has not received the AGM given to the other two in 1992.

Flower

Head Shape: hemispherical
Head Size: medium
Sterile Flowers: tightly packed, pushing up
Sepal Number: 4
Sepal Immature: yellow with pink edges
Sepal Mature: very deep pink
Sepal Autumnal: purply pink
Fertile Flower Immature: green to pale pink
Fertile Flower Mature: blue
Peduncle: green with red marks
Pedicel: pink or blue
pH: 6–6.5

Leaf

Main Colour: mid-green
Autumn Colour: brown
Edge Colour: turning brown
Texture: semi-matt
Back of Leaf: almost as front
Veins: recessed on front
Curvature: edges up
Branch: few long dashes
Petiole: red marks

Height: large
Flowering Time: mid to late

Above: *H. mac.* 'Europa', Royal Botanic Gardens, Kew, Wakehurst Place (pH 6.0 to 6.5)

Below: *H.mac.* 'Hamburg', Windermere (pH 6.5)

H. macrophylla 'Floralia'

There is a sense of gaiety and even coquettishness about this cultivar. The sepals are a distinctive boat shape, longer rather than wide. The acute tips tend to turn down and the edges up with a slight wave. They tend to twist on the floret and the florets push up against each other creating a rough outline. A gentler shape develops with maturity. The florets are shell pink with a white eye, with a hint of lilac in soil of pH 6.5. The leaves are mid-green with the edges turning red in old age. The serrations to the leaves are not very coarse. The branch has speckles and the petioles become tinged with brown later in the season.

Flower

Head Shape: convex
Head Size: large
Sterile Flowers: crowded
Sepal Number: 4 or 5
Sepal Immature: pale yellow-pink, boat-shaped
Sepal Mature: pink with red streak
Sepal Autumnal: pink
Fertile Flower Immature: cream
Fertile Flower Mature: blue
Peduncle: brown, many dashes on green
Pedicel: pink
pH: 6.5

Leaf

Main Colour: mid-green
Autumn Colour: turns brown early
Edge Colour: red with age
Texture: smooth
Back of Leaf: lighter green
Veins: obvious on reverse
Curvature: flat
Branch: speckled
Petiole: tinged brown when aged

Height: medium
Flowering Time: mid to late

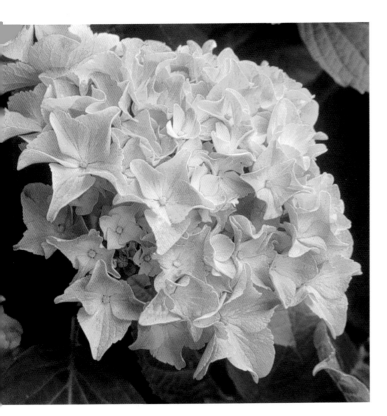

H. mac. 'Floralia', Windermere, pH 6.5

H. macrophylla 'Frillibet'

Bred by M. Haworth-Booth

A large mid-season shrub which is quite robust, flowering
profusely all season long with medium-sized heads on rather
inadequate stems. The flowers tend to droop but there is such
a profusion of them that they seem to form a continuous
curtain. A delicate-looking mophead, opening creamy yellow
and turning a delightful pale blue on acid soils. Unique
among mopheads, the sepals reverse in autumn as lacecaps
do. They also tend to a violet colour late in the season. The
highly serrated sepals give the almost spherical head a very
decorative effect, which is distinctive. The leaves are smooth
but not glossy. This variety is difficult to find, which is
regrettable as its numerous blooms make it an exceedingly
attractive plant. It is best grown in dappled shade.

Flower

Head Shape: hemispherical to spherical
Head Size: medium
Sterile Flowers: reverse in autumn
Sepal Number: 4, overlapped
Sepal Immature: pale blue, white centre
Sepal Mature: pale blue
Sepal Autumnal: pale blue/lilac
Fertile Flower Immature: pale yellow
Fertile Flower Mature: white
Peduncle: pale green, dark purple dash
Pedicel: white speckled purple
pH: 6.5

Leaf

Main Colour: mid-green
Edge Colour: as leaf
Texture: smooth, not glossy
Back of Leaf: lighter than front
Veins: recessed on front
Curvature: edges up
Branch: green, speckled
Petiole: plain green

Height: large
Flowering Time: early to late

H. mac. 'Frillibet', Windermere (pH 6.5)

H. m. 'Générale Vicomtesse de Vibraye'

AM 1947. AGM 1992 (H3/4). Bred by Mouillère, 1909, from *H. m.* 'Otaksa' × *H. m.* 'Rosea'

This is a very reliable, free-flowering mophead with pure, light-blue flowers on acid soil, readily pink in alkaline soil. It flowers on side shoots as well as on the terminal buds. The very tightly packed flower heads are composed of small overlapping sepals. Some manage to open flat, and some push against others and turn up, while in other cases the whole floret tilts. If the shrub is hard pruned, the flower heads can be large and, when heavy with rain, they tend to bend, sometimes to ground level. The shrub can layer itself, making huge bushes, smothering all weeds. It ages to a most unusual sea green or dusky lilac, and can be dried like this for flower arrangements, or sprayed for Christmas decorations. It is admirable by the sea and withstands full sun and exposure with equanimity. It makes an excellent pot plant and is used by nurseries for forcing. Several other varieties look similar to this shrub during part of their flowering cycle, notably *H. m.* 'Mme A. Riveraine' (with coloured nodes) and *H. m.* 'Blue Bonnet'. This is darker towards the centre of the floret and a slightly more lilac blue. In autumn *H. m.* 'Blue Bonnet' ages to shades of lime and purple.

1909 *Revue Horticole*, page 326, gives parentage as *H. m.* 'Rosea' × *H. m.* 'Souvenir de Claire'. Flowered for the first time in 1908, colour bright pink.

Flower

Head Shape: hemispherical/orbicular
Head Size: large
Sterile Flowers: overlapping, crowded
Sepal Number: 3 or 4
Sepal Immature: yellow to cream
Sepal Mature: pale blue, veins darker
Sepal Autumnal: sea green or lilac
Fertile Flower Immature: cream to pale blue
Fertile Flower Mature: pale blue
Peduncle: lilac with red dashes
Pedicel: pale blue
pH: 6.5

Leaf

Main Colour: pale green
Autumn Colour: dark mahogany eventually
Edge Colour: as leaf
Texture: matt
Back of Leaf: lighter than front
Veins: prominent on back
Curvature: flat, tip down
Branch: light green with dots and dashes
Petiole: plain green

Height: large
Flowering Time: early and continuous

Above left: *H. mac.* 'Générale Vicomtesse de Vibraye', Windermere (pH 6.5)
Above right: *H. mac.* 'Blue Bonnet', Tony Harrison, Southport
Below: *H. mac* 'Mme A. Riveraine', The Royal Horticultural Society's Garden, Wisley, where some alkaline pockets occur.

H. macrophylla 'Gentian Dome'

Syn. *H. m.* 'Enziandom'. Bred by Dr A. Steiniger of Vorst, 1940

On acid soil this shrub is an eyecatcher. It is a very bright, very deep, rich blue, (pink on alkaline soils). When immature the flowers have white centres, but as they mature, the colour changes to pure blue. With further ageing, a plum colour develops, caused by the sun. Shaded portions of the sepals remain bluey grey. The florets are cup-shaped when young but on maturity are almost flat, with some sepals twisting. Mid- to late season flowering, several good flowers can last into mid-October. It is excellent for cutting and dries well into its mature or autumnal plum colouring, sometimes both colours on the same head at the same time. This shrub is easy to propagate from cuttings or layerings, but surprisingly is only available from a very few nurseries. In maturity it can be confused with *H. m.* 'Hamburg' but the latter usually has other flower heads of a different colour, all of which are much larger. Other cultivars with which it may be confused are *H. m.* 'Mathilde Gutges', a smaller shrub, which changes colour more readily towards purple in autumn and carries its flowers well above the foliage, while *H. m.* 'Gentian Dome' is more recessive. *H. m.* 'Maréchal Foch' in peak maturity is very similar but flowers earlier and turns silvery grey from the tips of the sepals, with the blue intensifying towards the centre. It also has darker-blue fertile flowers, and requires shade as it bleaches in the sun. *H. m.* 'Maréchal Foch' is a very fine shrub when grown sympathetically.

Flower

Head Shape: hemispherical, crowded
Head Size: medium
Sterile Flowers: crowded, overlapping
Sepal Number: 3–5
Sepal Immature: cream centre, blue edge
Sepal Mature: bright, dark blue
Sepal Autumnal: blue to red purple
Fertile Flower Immature: cream/green
Fertile Flower Mature: light blue
Peduncle: green with red dashes
Pedicel: blue with red dashes
pH: 6.5

Leaf

Main Colour: mid- to dark green
Autumn Colour: dark red to copper
Edge Colour: dark red
Texture: coarse
Back of Leaf: light green
Veins: prominent on back
Curvature: edges up, tip straight
Branch: green with red speckles, black streaks later
Petiole: plain, light green

Height: small to medium
Flowering Time: mid to late

Above left: *H. mac.* 'Gentian Dome' In a pot of alkaline soil

Below left: *H. mac.* 'Gentian Dome', Windermere (pH 6.5)

Right: *H. mac.* 'Maréchal Foch', Fall City, Seattle, WA (pH 6.5) (TL-H)

H. macrophylla 'Grant's Choice'

Selected by James Grant of GrayswoodHill

This is a lovely, fresh and simple lacecap with a slightly unusual colour, being white with several sepals flushed with apple blossom-pink or lilac on an irregular flower head. The large sepals are mainly entire and wavy, but occasionally serrated ones are found on the same head. The sepals open wide, overlap each other and are sometimes tilted with an attractive twist. These surround a small fertile corymb which changes colour from mid-blue to pink, depending on the acidity of the soil. The leaves are large and rounded and with a distinct point and are coarsely serrated. They are a good, dark green and in one case were seen to turn copper very early; there is always a hint of copper either on their edges or on their tips. The mid-rib and veins of the leaves are a prominent cream and the petioles are very short.

Flower

Head Shape: slightly convex
Head Size: medium
Sterile Flowers: facing upwards, overlapping
Sepal Number: 4 and 5
Sepal Immature: cream
Sepal Mature: white, flushed pink/lilac
Fertile Flower Immature: green
Fertile Flower Mature: mid- to dark blue
Peduncle: many red dashes on green
Pedicel: white to lilac
pH: 6.5

Leaf

Main Colour: dark green
Autumn Colour: copper
Edge Colour: copper edge and tip
Texture: smooth, rugose
Back of Leaf: slightly lighter green
Veins: cream, prominent, unobtrusive on back
Curvature: flat
Branch: green with brown dots
Petiole: light green, short

Height: medium to large
Flowering Time: mid to late

Above: *H. mac.* 'Grant's Choice',
Windermere (pH 6.5) (TN-C)

Below: *H. mac.* 'Grant's Choice' with
H. mac. 'Pensée', *Rosa glauca* and *Photinia*
'Red Robin'

H. macrophylla 'Hanabi'

Translation 'Firework', named by T. Yamamoto. Introduced from Japan

Presented to us at Hampton Court Flower show in 1995, this plant has given us both pain and pleasure. Outdoors in Cumbria it survives but has not yet flowered. Kept in a conservatory it flowered well but became lax. A frost-free greenhouse would be ideal, or a warmer, sheltered garden site.

A large and vigorous plant, it makes a truly spectacular display. The inflorescence is lacecap in form but irregular in shape. The sterile florets are held on exceptionally long pedicels giving a lax appearance to the head. Each floret is formed from layer upon layer of white-tinged-pink elliptical sepals. The total flowerhead is large as are the erectly held leaves.

A truly beautiful plant to be treasured provided the right conditions can be maintained.

Flower

Head Shape: irregular, lax lacecap
Head Size: large
Sterile Flowers: eight-ten, large
Sepal Number: several layers, 4–5 per layer
Sepal Immature: cream
Sepal Mature: white tinged pink
Sepal Autumnal: white tinged pink
Fertile Flower Immature: green
Fertile Flower Mature: pale pink
Peduncle: green, red nodes
Pedicel: pink, up to 7 cm (3 in) long
pH: 6.5

Leaf

Main Colour: mid green
Autumn Colour: some red appears late in season
Edge Colour: as leaf
Texture: slight gloss
Back of Leaf: lighter green
Veins: well recessed
Curvature: almost flat
Branch: green, very few red marks
Petiole: long – 3 cm (1¼ in) or more

Height: medium–large
Flowering Time: mid to late

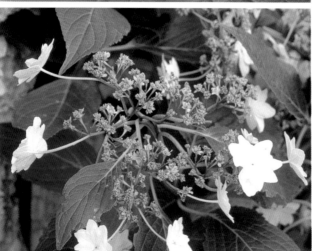

Above and below: *H. mac.* 'Hanabi', Windermere (pH 6.5)

H. macrophylla 'Harry's Red'

This is a lovely late-flowering mophead with compact stocky growth. The small but numerous flowers are composed of crowded, overlapping florets giving spherical heads. The sepals are slightly deltoid with entire edges and a centre crease. They overlap at the centre of the floret, where there is a white eye when immature. The florets open almost flat when mature and all open the same amount. Underneath there are, occasionally, blue fertile flowers. The sepals age to a deep cerise in soils of pH 6.5 and then turn brown. The leaves are mid-green in colour, turning darker green, then orange with red markings. The branches have very large blue/black stripes and the pedicels are purple and woody. This shrub remains more red than most macrophyllas in neutral and slightly acid soils and is of moderate size suitable for the smaller garden.

H. mac. 'Harry's Red', Windermere (pH 6.5)

Flower

Head Shape: spherical
Head Size: small
Sterile Flowers: crowded, cupped early, flat later
Sepal Number: 3–5
Sepal Immature: yellowy cream, pink edge
Sepal Mature: very deep rose madder
Fertile Flower Immature: creamy yellow
Fertile Flower Mature: deep blue
Peduncle: green with dashes
Pedicel: blue to purple and woody
pH: 6.5

Leaf

Main Colour: mid-green
Autumn Colour: darker green, turning orange with red marks
Edge Colour: as leaf turning red/brown
Texture: smooth
Back of Leaf: lighter green
Veins: unobtrusive
Curvature: flat
Branch: blue/black dashes on green
Petiole: pale green, short

Height: small
Flowering Time: mid to late

H. macrophylla 'Hörnli'

Bred by P. Meier, Wadenswil, Switzerland

This is a delightful small mophead with bright-red or pink sepals, which do not overlap. There are so many florets to the corymb, that the head becomes very crowded. Haworth-Booth refers to the shrub called *H. m.* 'Hornly' and dismisses it as 'a tiny dwarf, seldom flowers'. This has not been our finding. The shrub is recommended for the front of a bed, with its wealth of flowers in good years. It eventually reaches a height of 1 m (3 ft). The leaf edges turn up and both the edges and tips are red. It flowers late in the season. *H. m.* 'Tovelit' also found commercially as *H. m.* 'Tofelil' is very similar. Its tightly packed flower heads rot in excessive rain but if removed, they will be quickly replaced. A look at the leaf shape will remove all doubt as to the correct name as it is very distinctive, being narrow elliptic with a long acuminate tip.

Flower

Head Shape: convex, crowded
Head Size: small
Sterile Flowers: crowded, open flat
Sepal Number: 4
Sepal Immature: creamy white
Sepal Mature: red
Sepal Autumnal: purple
Fertile Flower Immature: almost green
Fertile Flower Mature: as sepal opening paler
Peduncle: plum with dashes
Pedicel: purple
pH: 6.5

Leaf

Main Colour: lightish green
Autumn Colour: brown blotches on edges
Edge Colour: red tinges
Texture: smooth, matt
Back of Leaf: lighter green
Veins: mid-rib prominent on back
Curvature: edges up, tip down
Branch: green with red dashes
Petiole: pale green

Height: small
Flowering Time: late

Above: *H. mac.* "Hörnlii', Windermere (pH 6.5)
Below left: *H. mac.* 'Tovelit', Windermere (pH 6.5)
Below Right: The same shrub ten years later

H. macrophylla 'Jogasaki'

Syn. 'Pink Firework'. Introduced from Japan

Similar in form to *H. macrophylla* 'Hanabi' but better suited to our climate.

The flowerhead, held well erect, is again somewhat irregular in outline, but quite compact. The sterile florets are formed of a double row of sepals and are held erect, around the perimeter of and often among the fertile flowers. On alkaline soil, the sterile florets are pale pink and the fertile flowers are deep crushed strawberry shade. On acid soil, the outer florets are a delightful lilac/blue, with deep blue fertile flowers. In each case, the combination is most attractive. Leaves are large and firmly held.

In Cumbria, our plant is now over 120 cm (4 ft) high and is flowering well in the garden. Unseasonal early or late frosts would probably set it back for a season, so a sheltered garden site would be wise once established. Maintaining the plant in a pot and taking it into a cold greenhouse for the winter would also be good practice until it grows to around 60 cm (2 ft) high. This attention in the early years is justified by the splendid display achieved.

Flower

Head Shape: irregular lacecap
Head Size: medium
Sterile Flowers: numerous, in and around head
Sepal Number: 10 or more
Sepal Immature: pink or lilac
Sepal Mature: pink or lilac/blue
Sepal Autumnal: pink or lilac/blue
Fertile Flower Immature: pink or lilac
Fertile Flower Mature: deep pink or deep purple/blue
Peduncle: brown, dark flecks
Pedicel: long, deep pink or lilac
pH: 6.5

Leaf

Main Colour: mid-green
Autumn Colour: going red
Edge Colour: red even when young
Texture: leathery
Back of Leaf: light green, sometimes suffused red
Veins: lighter green
Curvature: edges up, sometimes undulate
Branch: green, heavily flecked brown
Petiole: very short, light green

Height: medium
Flowering Time: late

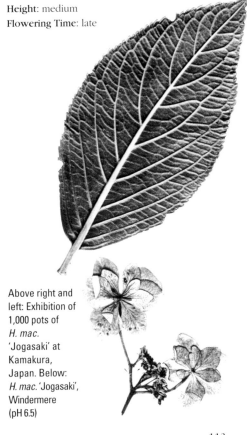

Above right and left: Exhibition of 1,000 pots of *H. mac.* 'Jogasaki' at Kamakura, Japan. Below: *H. mac.* 'Jogasaki', Windermere (pH 6.5)

H. macrophylla 'Joseph Banks'

Syn. *H. m.* 'Sir Joseph Banks'. Original Chinese clonal variety introduced in 1789

There is disagreement among botanists and Haworth-Booth as to the correct name for this shrub. Although the original plant from China was brought to Kew, there is no longer a plant of *H. m.* 'Joseph Banks' there. A dried specimen is in the Kew herbarium presented by Haworth-Booth in 1948. *The Plant Finder* gives *H. m.* 'Otaksa' as a synonym for *H. m.* 'Sir Joseph Banks', but the former is an ancient variety from Japan whereas *H. m.* 'Joseph Banks' came from China. The shrub thrives near the sea; and withstood undamaged the severe gales of 1987 in the Isle of Wight. It flowers on the terminal shoots only and if these are damaged by late frosts, the flower is lost for the whole season. The shrub is very vigorous, with strong stiff shoots. The flower head is hemispherical, large and tightly packed with small sepals of white, pale pink or very pale blue. The sepals are usually entire but sometimes slightly serrated and pointed. The leaves are large, smooth and glossy with acuminate tips.

H. m. 'Sea Foam' which Haworth-Booth considers to be a reversion of *H. m.* 'Joseph Banks', is a lovely very late-flowering white lacecap with a deep-blue fertile centre. The large, rather open shrub is sometimes reluctant to flower but manages to do so in September. The florets are composed of four or five white entire sepals which do not overlap and have a very light lilac or blue/lilac eye. The flower head is not regular in shape. The large elliptic leaves have long petioles, are mid-green and have a smooth texture. It is very useful as a late flowerer.

Flower

Head Shape: hemispherical
Head Size: large
Sterile Flowers: small, cupped,
Sepal Number: 4 or 5
Sepal Immature: green to deep cream
Sepal Mature: white or pale blue
Fertile Flower Immature: cream
Fertile Flower Mature: palest blue
Peduncle: green, brown spots
Pedicel: deep lilac pink
pH: 6.5

Leaf

Main Colour: mid-green
Autumn Colour: keeps leaves very late
Edge Colour: as leaf
Texture: smooth, glossy
Back of Leaf: lighter green
Veins: conspicuous on back
Curvature: flattish, edges up
Branch: green with red dashes
Petiole: light green

Height: large
Flowering Time: early to late

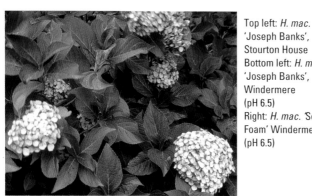

Top left: *H. mac.* 'Joseph Banks', Stourton House
Bottom left: *H. mac.* 'Joseph Banks', Windermere (pH 6.5)
Right: *H. mac.* 'Sea Foam' Windermere (pH 6.5)

H. macrophylla 'Lanarth White'

AM 1949. AGM 1992 (H4)

This shrub is sometimes simply referred to as 'Lanarth'. A really lovely lacecap with many sterile florets somewhat irregularly spaced around the corymb. The fertile flowers are green when immature opening to mid-blue or lilac. There are often blue or lilac fertile flowers in the centre of the florets. The sepals are purest white. It dries supremely well with the sepals turning cream, and towards the centre of the floret almost yellow. The really distinguishing feature of this cultivar is the absence of speckles on the branches, which are plain green. The leaves have extremely fine serrations and are paler and more yellow than most macrophyllas. The shrub flowers profusely in poor soil and prefers full exposure, so it is suitable for planting near the sea and is also convenient when a white hydrangea is wanted for a site with no shade.

Bartrum states that 'white lacecaps are common in Japan and resemble *H. m.* 'Lanarth'. If given a rich compost, they will produce large, irregularly shaped corymbs of entirely sterile flowers.' Haworth-Booth states that *H. m.* 'Lanarth' is of 'puzzling origin' which may be 'a hybrid of the subspecies *H. m. chinensis*'. Both agree that it was found at Lanarth, Cornwall.

Flower

Head Shape: flat
Head Size: small to medium
Sterile Flowers: irregularly placed round corymb
Sepal Number: 4–5, overlapping
Sepal Immature: green
Sepal Mature: pure white, touches of pink/purple in centre
Fertile Flower Immature: green
Fertile Flower Mature: blue or lilac
Peduncle: browny green
Pedicel: cream/palest blue
pH: 6.5

Leaf

Main Colour: greeny/yellow
Texture: glossy, rugose
Back of Leaf: a little lighter green
Veins: light green central vein
Curvature: flat, tip down
Branch: plain green
Petiole: light green

Height: medium
Flowering Time: early to late

Right and left: *H. mac.* 'Lanarth White', Windermere (pH 6.5)

H. macrophylla 'Leuchtfeuer'

Popular in Europe and the USA, this vigorous shrub is tight and compact. The medium-sized flower heads are held erect and are fairly tightly packed with florets. These are composed of red sepals in soil of pH 6.5, which age to a deeper lilac/red. The sepals overlap slightly; as they mature, they push up against each other, forcing themselves into cup shapes. Before fading, they change yet again and lie almost flat. The centre of each floret has a fertile flower, which is cream when immature, opening to a light blue. Because the corymb is not too overcrowded, the flower head is not affected by rain. The slightly glossy leaves are edged red/brown and are boat-shaped. This shrub should become more popular, being vigorous and flowering late into the autumn.

Flower
Head Shape: convex, full
Head Size: medium
Sterile Flowers: almost flat; cupped when mature; unaffected by rain
Sepal Number: mostly 4, a few 5
Sepal Immature: cream with red edge
Sepal Mature: red/deep purply pink
Sepal Autumnal: purple
Fertile Flower Immature: cream
Fertile Flower Mature: palest blue
Peduncle: green to brown, a few red marks
Pedicel: green to lilac
pH: 6.5

Leaf
Main Colour: light green
Edge Colour: red/brown
Texture: slightly glossy
Back of Leaf: little lighter than front
Veins: front recessed, back prominent
Curvature: edges up
Branch: mainly plain green, red at nodes
Petiole: pale green

Height: medium
Flowering Time: mid to late

Below: *H. mac.* 'Leuchtfeuer', Windermere (pH 6.5)

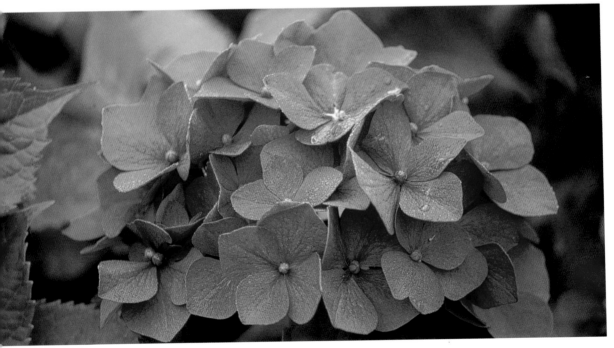

H. macrophylla 'Libelle'

Translation 'Dragon Fly'. Syn. Teller White, Snow. Raised
Wadensvil, 1964

A vigorous member of the Teller group. Large lacecap heads
are formed from attractively cupped white florets, jostling for
space – they appear among and around the fertile flowers
without obscuring them. The fertile flowers are cream,
opening deep blue and making a striking contrast to the pure
white of the sterile florets. Gradually the sepals flatten, some
red markings appear and in autumn they reverse to deep
pink. More fresh white blooms come late in the season to
continue the display.

This is a striking and beautiful plant, although its white
flowers do scorch in full sun, as do most white cultivars of *H.
macrophylla*. Some shade is therefore desirable. A high
canopy of deciduous trees would be ideal and the white
flowers would shine out boldly. In Cumbria the shrub has
taken time to flower but a background of rhododendrons
gives protection from north and east winds as well as some
shade. This has proved all that is necessary to give a good
display and we would not be without this excellent plant.

Flower

Head Shape: slightly domed lacecap
Head Size: medium–large
Sterile Flowers: cupped early, around and
through head
Sepal Number: 3, 4, 5
Sepal Immature: creamy white
Sepal Mature: white
Sepal Autumnal: white, red marks, pink reverse
Fertile Flower Immature: cream-pink-blue
Fertile Flower Mature: deep blue
Peduncle: green
Pedicel: cream, pale pink
pH: 6.5

Leaf

Main Colour: mid–light green
Autumn Colour: some red at tips
Edge Colour: as leaf
Texture: matt, rugose
Back of Leaf: lighter green
Veins: well recessed
Curvature: edges up
Branch: green, few red marks
Petiole: plain light green

Height: medium–large
Flowering Time: mid

Above: *H. mac.* 'Libelle', Windermere (pH 6.5) (TN-C)

Below: 'Teller' hydrangeas with 'Libelle'

H. macrophylla 'Lilacina'

AGM 2000 (H3/4). Bred by V. Lemoine, 1904

This is a large, strong-growing but compact bush. The ray flowers have boldly serrated sepals, one of which tends to be larger than the others on the same floret. When young, the flowers are dominated by the vigorous foliage, but when mature the shrub is a centre of attraction. The central flowers are mid-blue to lilacy pink. Obviously this variety readily changes colour depending on the pH of the soil. The ray flowers also change colour throughout the season, which is interesting if closely observed. Towards the centre and edges of each sepal, the colour is almost white, while the remaining parts are pale lilac when young. These turn, when older, to plum or deep lilac, often with a white streak and whitish edges, and reversing also to a deep plum. The pedicels are long, making the sepals stand well away from the fertile flowers. Mid- to late season flowering, the shrub flowers continuously for a very long time, and is not affected by rain. The flower heads dry beautifully in very many different colours and it is worth growing for this fact alone. The leaves are fairly slim for the *H. macrophylla* species, reminiscent of *H. serrata*, with occasional dark red edges turning reddish brown in the autumn. It is a chance-pollinated seedling of *H. m.* 'Mariesii' and is similar to many other varieties growing in Japan.

Flower

Head Shape: flat
Head Size: small
Sterile Flowers: rarely overlapping, sepal sizes mixed
Sepal Number: 3–5, mainly 4, one larger
Sepal Immature: lilac, white centre and/or edge
Sepal Mature: plum or deep lilac
Sepal Autumnal: reverses, grey to plum
Fertile Flower Immature: light blue or pink
Fertile Flower Mature: dark blue
Peduncle: green, small dashes
Pedicel: cream/purple and long
pH: 6.5

Leaf

Main Colour: mid-green
Autumn Colour: reddish brown
Edge Colour: dark red
Texture: slightly rugose
Back of Leaf: lighter green
Veins: central light green, prominent on back
Curvature: edges up
Branch: green, speckled dark red
Petiole: very short, slightly red

Height: large
Flowering Time: mid to late

H. mac. 'Lilacina', Windermere (pH 6.5)

H. macrophylla 'Madame Emile Mouillère'

Syn. *H. m.* 'Sedgewick's White'. AM 1910 and 1963. AGM 1992 (H3/4). Bred by E. Mouillère, 1909 from *H. m.* 'White Wave' × *H. m.* 'Rosea'

This shrub has stood the test of time, for it is one of the early cultivars and is still in production today. Its usefulness, both to gardeners and the nurserymen who grow for 'the pot trade', must be extremely good to have lasted so long. This lovely pure-white hortensia flowers in July/August and then successively until late in the season. Growing up to 180 cm (6 ft), it is very vigorous. Its large flower heads are composed of serrated or entire overlapping sepals in an overcrowded head. The florets, opening almost flat, push up against each other giving a frilly outline to the head shape. The flower heads when full of rain droop, like most mopheads, but perk up again on drying. The sepals turn blush pink or a lovely lime-green with age, and in these colours, especially the lime green, the flower heads can be dried. The flowers tend to turn brown if subjected to long drought or strong sunlight, so it prefers light shade, or a north wall, especially against a house. It is reliably identified by having unspotted stems and branches, and with red or blue eyes at the centre of the florets. It is easy to propagate and forces well. It is stocked by most nurseries.

H. m. 'Soeur Thérèse' is rather similar, but has a more lax open flower. The sepals are not so serrated when immature, nor are they as rounded. It is even whiter and does not have the red or blue central eye.

Flower

Head Shape: convex, crowded
Head Size: large
Sterile Flowers: crowded, overlapping
Sepal Number: 4 and 5
Sepal Immature: creamy green
Sepal Mature: clear white
Sepal Autumnal: bluish pink or lime green
Fertile Flower Immature: pale green
Fertile Flower Mature: red/blue (depends on pH)
Peduncle: green, white dashes on some
Pedicel: white/greeny white
pH: 6.5

Leaf

Main Colour: green
Edge Colour: pink
Texture: smooth, slightly glossy
Back of Leaf: paler green
Veins: prominent on back
Curvature: edges markedly up, tips down
Branch: plain green, purple nodes
Petiole: pale green

Height: large
Flowering Time: mid and successively

Above: *H. mac.* 'Mme Emile Mouillère', Tony Harrison, Southport
Right: *H. mac.* 'Soeur Thérèse', Mount Congreve, Kilmeaden, Co. Waterford, Ireland (pH 6.2 to 6.5)

H. macrophylla 'Mariesii'

AM 1938. FCC 1965. Introduced from Japan, 1879

A beautiful lacecap. It is a large strong upright shrub. This variety has more blooms than many others, flowering mid to late in the season and lasting well into November unless caught by early frost. The numerous sterile florets are white to palest lilac with blue fertile flowers. These occur haphazardly through the darker-blue central fertile corymb. The leaves taper and are unusually narrow, turning red from their tips in autumn. The significant feature of the leaves is the cupping of the edges, giving a spoon-shaped effect. The fact that it is much prized, confirms its garden-worthiness, although originally it was disliked by those who grew the shrub in pots and who thought that it had an untidy head. It is not very commonly found in nurseries. The seed from this variety gave rise to *H. m.* 'Lilacina', *H. m.* 'Blue Wave' and *H. m.* 'White Wave', all raised by Lemoine. *H. m.* 'White Wave' crossed with *H. m.* 'Rosea' produced *H. m.* 'Mme E. Mouillère'. Haworth-Booth thought that *H. m.* 'Tricolor' is a possible branch sport of this variety.

Flower

Head Shape: convex
Head Size: medium to large
Sterile Flowers: numerous, grow through fertile flowers also
Sepal Number: 4–5
Sepal Immature: cream to pale blue
Sepal Mature: white/palest blue
Fertile Flower Immature: green
Fertile Flower Mature: dark blue
Peduncle: green with dashes
Pedicel: lilac
pH: 6.5

Leaf

Main Colour: light green
Texture: smooth
Back of Leaf: light green
Veins: unobtrusive
Curvature: slow bend backwards
Branch: plain green
Petiole: plain green

Height: large
Flowering Time: mid to late

Above and below: *H. mac.* 'Mariesii', Windermere (pH 6.5)

H. macrophylla 'Mathilda Guges'

Bred by August Steiniger of Vorst, 1946

This delightful medium-sized shrub flowers in mid-season. It is better known in North America than France or Britain where it is only available from a few specialist nurseries. The flower heads are composed of small- to medium-sized florets on a compact head. The immature sepals are yellowy green with an almost entire purple edge, maturing to a mid-blue or rich violet/purple, with boldly serrated edge. These florets open nearly flat when mature becoming larger and pushing against each other later, giving a frilly appearance to the flower head. The leaves are elliptic with an acuminate tip. This is one of the best hortensias so it is surprising that it is not more widely available. As illustrated, this cultivar can change colour dramatically. The pink flower shown appeared in the first season after the shrub was planted in soil of pH 6.5. In subsequent years, the same shrub carried deep blue flowers.

Flower

Head Shape: hemispherical and crowded
Head Size: small to medium
Sterile Flowers: mature flat, but later cupped
Sepal Number: 4 or 5
Sepal Immature: yellow green, purple edge
Sepal Mature: blue
Sepal Autumnal: violet/purple
Fertile Flower Immature: blue/green
Fertile Flower Mature: blue
Peduncle: green with spots
Pedicel: green, red dashes
pH: 6.5

Leaf

Main Colour: mid-green
Autumn Colour: lighter green from tip
Edge Colour: slightly red
Texture: matt
Back of Leaf: lighter green
Veins: slightly darker than leaf
Curvature: edges up
Branch: green with dashes
Petiole: green

Height: medium
Flowering Time: mid to late

Above: *H. mac.* 'Mathilda Guges', Windermere (pH 6.5)
Below: *H. mac.* 'Mathilda Guges', Windermere, first year after planting (pH 6.5)

121

H. macrophylla 'Merritt's Supreme'

This compact semi-dwarf shrub can best be described as stocky with very thick branches. It has medium to large flower heads which are numerous and successional. The floret can be composed of up to six sepals. As the florets age, the sepals become quite large and serrated. They overlap to such an extent that it seems that each floret has become double. In soil of pH 6.5 the flower colour is lilac to purple with a crease down the centre of the sepal of a lighter tint of the flower colour. The centre of the floret is often cream. The leaves are slightly glossy. The branch has coloured nodes and the petioles are plain green. The shrub seems to be susceptible to attack by capsid bugs. This is another shrub thought highly of in the USA but not well known in Great Britain.

Flower

Head Shape: hemispherical
Head Size: medium
Sterile Flowers: cupped, creased, overlapped
Sepal Number: 4–6
Sepal Immature: purple with cream centre
Sepal Mature: purple with white centre
Sepal Autumnal: plum
Fertile Flower Immature: pale green
Fertile Flower Mature: dark blue
Peduncle: brown
Pedicel: blue
pH: 6.5

Leaf

Main Colour: mid-green
Edge Colour: as leaf or slightly lighter
Texture: smooth and glossy
Back of Leaf: paler green
Veins: recessed on face, prominent on reverse
Curvature: flat except when young
Branch: very thick, a few dark dots
Petiole: plain green, coloured nodes

Height: small
Flowering Time: early to late

H. mac. 'Merritt's Supreme', Windermere (pH 6.5)

H. macrophylla 'Mousseline'

Seedling of *H. m.* 'Rosea'. Bred by E. Lemoine, 1909

This is another shrub which should be more widely grown and is not readily available. The growth is tall and stout, branching out widely, flowering early and successively so prolonging the flowering season. It has above average resistance to frost. The flower head is large, pale, rose pink in alkaline soil, or pale light blue in acid. It is composed of many four-sepalled florets which eventually open flat. Some sepals collide against others and tip up, giving the head a frilly appearance, while the majority open fully flat and overlap adjacent florets like slates on a roof, giving a generally smooth outline. The flower heads tend to droop due to their size. In autumn the colour changes to a lovely blue/sea green, some becoming slightly blotched with vermilion. The nodes do not colour. The leaves are a little more yellowy than the average and tend to be blotchy.

Flower

Head Shape: convex, crowded
Head Size: large
Sterile Flowers: florets overlapping
Sepal Number: 4
Sepal Immature: cream
Sepal Mature: pale blue, not overlapping
Sepal Autumnal: blue/green
Fertile Flower Immature: pink
Fertile Flower Mature: lilac
Peduncle: plain, darkish green
Pedicel: pink
pH: 6.5

Leaf

Main Colour: yellowy green, blotched
Texture: smooth, thin, matt, velvety
Back of Leaf: light green
Veins: not prominent
Curvature: edges up, tip down
Branch: plain, light green
Petiole: plain, light green

Height: large
Flowering Time: early to late

Above: *H. mac.* 'Mousseline', Windermere (pH 6.5)
Below: *H. mac.* 'Mousseline', Windermere, recently moved (pH 6.5)

123

H. macrophylla 'Mousmée'

Cayeux, 1967

Similar in form to the 'Tellers' but from a French rather than a Swiss nursery. This is a large and vigorous plant although a little lax in growth. On soil of pH 6.5, the cupped sterile florets are a wonderful, eye-catching deep purple/pink with light centres. They attract attention additionally because they are borne on unusually long pedicels – often up to 5 cm (2 in). This means that the florets are held well away from and above the fertile flowers which form a deep royal blue centre to the large inflorescence. The colour combination is striking. Later the florets flatten, partially covering the fertile flowers and then reverse to show a pale lilac. A long season of colourful display.

Above and below: *H. mac. 'Mousmée'*, Windermere (pH 6.5) (TN-C)

Flower
Head Shape: irregular lacecap
Head Size: medium to large
Sterile Flowers: cupped early, in and around head
Sepal Number: 4–5, totally overlapped
Sepal Immature: rose, cream centre
Sepal Mature: purple/pink, cream centre
Sepal Autumnal: flat, reverses to pink
Fertile Flower Immature: pink/red
Fertile Flower Mature: deep royal blue
Peduncle: brown
Pedicel: long, red
pH: 6.5

Leaf
Main Colour: light green
Autumn Colour: darker
Edge Colour: as leaf
Texture: smooth
Back of Leaf: lighter green
Veins: more obvious on reverse
Curvature: edges up
Branch: green, speckled red
Petiole: plain green

Height: medium to large
Flowering Time: mid to late

H. macrophylla 'Möwe'

AGM 1992 (H3/4). Translation 'Seagull'. Bred Wadensvil, 1964

Work done by H. Bertrand and C. Lambert at INH, Angers, France has shown that *H. macrophylla* 'Geoffrey Chadbund' and *H. macrophylla* 'Möwe' are one and the same plant. They have the same morphological features, the same enzyomatic patterns and the same triploid chromosome number. The valid name is 'Möwe', being the earlier.

This has always been a good shrub – sturdy, vigorous, hardy and colourful. Early florets are cupped and appear around the perimeter of the head. Later, their totally overlapped sepals flatten and partially obscure the fertile flowers. Colours can be a dramatic red with pink fertile flowers on alkaline soil and purple with blue fertile flowers on acid soil. It is one of the last plants to fade in autumn in Cumbria, when the purple sepals reverse to deep lilac-pink.

Flower

Head Shape: flat lacecap
Head Size: medium
Sterile Flowers: 13 or more, in and around head
Sepal Number: 4–5
Sepal Immature: mauve with cream centre
Sepal Mature: purple/pink
Sepal Autumnal: deep purple/pink
Fertile Flower Immature: cream
Fertile Flower Mature: mid blue
Peduncle: red/brown
Pedicel: blue/lilac
pH: 6.5

Leaf

Main Colour: light green
Autumn Colour: brown at tips
Edge Colour: as leaf
Texture: rugose, slight gloss
Back of Leaf: lighter green
Veins: very obvious on back and front
Curvature: all edges up, tips flat
Branch: green, few red dashes
Petiole: purple from nodes

Height: medium
Flowering Time: mid to late

Above and below: *H. mac.* 'Möwe', Windermere (pH 6.5)

125

H. macrophylla 'Nigra'

FCC 1885. AGM 1992 (H3/4). Imported from China by Wilson as *H. m.* var. 'Mandshurica'

A good late season mophead with pink, mauve or blue flowers. Each flower head is small. Early in the season the florets are tightly packed and forced one against the other. As the season progresses, the pedicels lengthen and the flower head develops a loose, shaggy appearance. The sepals are entire and do not overlap. The whole head has a speckled look because the immature and mature florets are distributed throughout the same corymb at the same time. The immature sepals are cream maturing to a lovely pinky lilac with a darker centre, but the colour is dependent on the pH of the soil. The colour of the sepals is pale blue with a lilac centre in soil of pH 5.5. The deep red pedicels are eye-catching and help identification. The leaves are a lightish green, turning bronze from the tip in autumn. The branches are black or dark purple, and it is this which makes its identification certain.

Flower
Head Shape: convex
Head Size: small
Sterile Flowers: very crowded, forced up; lax later
Sepal Number: 4 or 5, not overlapping
Sepal Immature: cream
Sepal Mature: pink/lilac or blue
Sepal Autumnal: pale blue to pinky lilac at centre
Fertile Flower Immature: yellow
Fertile Flower Mature: cream
Peduncle: black
Pedicel: deep red
pH: 6.5

Leaf
Main Colour: light green
Autumn Colour: turning bronze from tip
Texture: fairly smooth
Back of Leaf: lighter green
Veins: not prominent
Curvature: flat, some edges up, tips down
Branch: red turning black (characteristic)
Petiole: deep bronzy red on underside

Height: medium
Flowering Time: late

Above: *H. mac.* 'Nigra', Windermere (pH 6.5), early flower
Right: *H. mac.* 'Nigra', Windermere (pH 6.5) (TN-C)

H. macrophylla 'Oregon Pride'

Raised by Oregon Hydrangea Company, USA

Originally bred for the pot plant trade in the USA, this has become a popular garden plant there. It is a medium-sized shrub with noticeably upright growth. The rounded mopheads are packed with sepals which turn and twist to find space. Opening with cream centres, they develop to a deep purple with a vivid blue fertile flower in the centre of each floret. Fresh heads with cream centres to the sterile florets continue to appear among the established purple blooms, making a splendid display. The strong, erect glossy stems are a most striking feature of the plant as they are dark red, almost black and quite conspicuous. This shrub has been seen growing in the new Hydrangea Walk in the Sir Harold Hillier Gardens and Arboretum near Romsey in Hampshire, England, where it was thriving. It is a plant which we should like to get into the trade in the UK.

Flower

Head Shape: well domed mophead
Head Size: medium
Sterile Flowers: crowded, often twisted
Sepal Number: 4, 5, overlapped
Sepal Immature: deep pink, cream centre
Sepal Mature: deep pink going mauve
Sepal Autumnal: dusky mauve
Fertile Flower Immature: blue
Fertile Flower Mature: deep blue
Peduncle: deep red
Pedicel: red
pH: 6.5

Leaf

Main Colour: mid-green, going darker
Autumn Colour: brown tips
Edge Colour: red later
Texture: rugose, slight gloss
Back of Leaf: light green
Veins: well recessed on front
Curvature: edges up, flattening later
Branch: red-brown/black-conspicuous
Petiole: green edged red, short

Height: medium
Flowering Time: mid to late

H. mac. 'Oregon Pride', Windermere (pH 6.5])

H. mac. 'Oregon Pride', Windermere (pH 6.5) four years later

H. macrophylla 'Parsival'

AM 1922. AGM 1992 (H3/4). Bred by J. Wintergalen of Munster, 1922

The shrub is of small to medium height with quite a large spread. It is a very distinctive and continuous-flowering plant, from early June to October, holding up some of its heads well. The facility to change colour is very pronounced. The small flower heads are often seen divided into two different colours. This occurs even on fifty-year-old shrubs. The colours are in the red/lilac to purple range at pH 6.5, but the colour changes to a deep blue on very acid soil. Most florets open flat with an open fertile flower of light blue in the centre. The sepals overlap and are both entire and serrated when young, becoming more serrated as they age. The overlapping of the sepals and the florets gives the whole head a smooth appearance, although the serrated edges to the sepals are very evident. The distance between the nodes is small and the branches are thick. It is easy to dry for winter decoration retaining its colour well.

Flower

Head Shape: hemispherical
Head Size: small
Sterile Flowers: cupped, flat when mature with big overlap
Sepal Number: 4 and 5
Sepal Immature: yellow green/lilac, or red pointed, some serrated, white radiating lines and white eye
Sepal Mature: red/lilac, serrated and entire
Sepal Autumnal: retaining colour late
Fertile Flower Immature: pinky cream
Fertile Flower Mature: light blue
Peduncle: pink/purple with red dashes
Pedicel: pink/purple, red dashes
pH: 6.5

Leaf

Main Colour: mid- to dark green
Texture: smooth
Back of Leaf: lighter than front
Veins: recessed on front, light green and conspicuous on back
Curvature: tip bending backwards
Branch: many small red dashes on green
Petiole: light green

Height: small to medium
Flowering Time: early and continuous

Above and below: *H. mac.* 'Parsival', Windermere (pH 6.5)

H. macrophylla 'Pfau'

Translation 'Peacock'. Bred Wadensvil, 1983

A small but sturdy shrub, this is one of the National Collection's most striking plants. The inflorescence is a beautifully formed lacecap with sterile florets distributed around the circumference. On the slightly acid soil their colour is the most intense purple/blue. Their form too is eye-catching, as the edges of each sepal are raised along a line from tip to base, producing a boat shape. Add to this a slight twist, and every floret becomes uniquely attractive. The fertile flowers complete the picture, changing from pale to deep blue as the season progresses. In autumn the sterile florets reverse to show dusky pink backs. At this point, they droop slightly on their long pedicels, as if their job of attracting insects was over. The leaves are almost covered by the mass of blooms.

Above : *H. mac.* 'Pfau',
Below: *H. mac.* 'Pfau', Windermere (pH 6.5) (TN-C)

Flower

Head Shape: lacecap
Head Size: small-medium
Sterile Flowers: 12–15, raised above centre
Sepal Number: 4, 5 total or partial overlap
Sepal Immature: lilac, light centre
Sepal Mature: intense purple/blue
Sepal Autumnal: reversing to pink
Fertile Flower Immature: pale blue
Fertile Flower Mature: vivid blue, going cream
Peduncle: mauve
Pedicel: blue
pH: 6.5

Leaf

Main Colour: mid-green
Autumn Colour: red at tips
Edge Colour: red
Texture: rugose, slight gloss
Back of Leaf: lighter green
Veins: conspicuous both back and front
Curvature: edges slightly up, tips down
Branch: green, red dashes
Petiole: plain green

Height: medium
Flowering Time: mid

H. macrophylla 'Pia'

This is one of the smallest varieties in the species and is useful on rockeries and also for containers, growing up to 30 cm (12 in) high. The florets are crowded when young but open almost flat later. They are composed of three or four serrated sepals which hardly overlap and are pink to pale red when mature. They have red lines radiating from the centre and have quite a point when immature, losing this when older. They do, however, twist and curl in a most becoming way. The leaf colour is mid-green which develops red/brown marks in the autumn. The shrub, though, needs to be carefully watched as it may revert to a rather taller ordinary plant. Any stems which tend to do this should be cut out at the base.

Flower
Head Shape: immature conical and tight, more open when mature
Head Size: small
Sterile Flowers: cupped crowded, overlapping
Sepal Number: 3 or 4
Sepal Immature: white with red edges
Sepal Mature: red radiating lines
Fertile Flower Immature: cream
Fertile Flower Mature: pinky brown
Peduncle: pink
Pedicel: cream
pH: 7.0

Leaf
Main Colour: mid-green
Autumn Colour: red to brown
Edge Colour: red on some leaves
Texture: slightly rugose
Back of Leaf: lighter green
Veins: not prominent
Curvature: edges up, tips down
Branch: green with tiny dots
Petiole: plain, light green

Height: dwarf
Flowering Time: mid to late

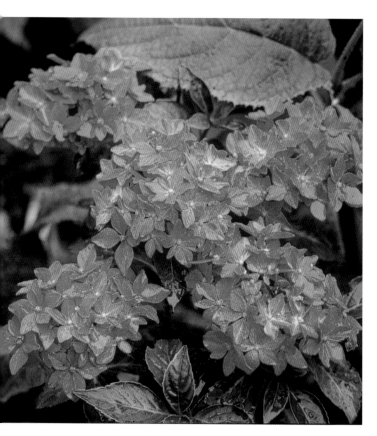

H. mac. 'Pia', Windermere [pH 6.5]

H. macrophylla 'Quadricolor'

A delightful medium-sized shrub. The flower head has lilac, fertile flowers in the centre of the corymb, while surrounding and through these are pale pink to white sterile florets. These have four or five well-separated sepals on long, lilac pedicels. The shrub is also prized by flower arrangers as the variegated leaves have four colours, hence the name. These are light and dark green and creamy white with thin patches of brightest yellow in varying amounts on the edges of most leaves. In garden centres it is frequently misnamed 'Tricolor' but the yellow splashes on the leaf edges are a sure means of identifying *H. m.* 'Quadricolor'. These are absent from *H. m.* 'Tricolor'. The latter has been given an FCC in 1882 and an AGM in 1992 (H3-4) but the authors find that this cultivar reverts whereas *H. m.* 'Quadricolor' has not been known to do so. Young cuttings are quite difficult to strike and slugs and snails are immediately attracted to them. The shrub prefers shelter from frost and searing cold winds, but soon regenerates. *H. m.* 'Maculata' is another variegated cultivar, not to be confused with *H. m.* 'Immaculata' (which is a white mophead, and does not have variegated leaves). The majority of leaves on *H. m.* 'Maculata' are variegated, and an occasional branch bears speckled leaves. The variegation, when it appears, comprises white and two shades of green, with the white showing mainly on the edge of the leaf. It is a vigorous but rather shy flowering lacecap. This is considered, by Haworth-Booth, to be a sport of *H. m.* 'Sea Foam'.

Flower

Head Shape: variable, amorphous
Head Size: medium
Sterile Flowers: invade central corymb
Sepal Number: 4 or 5, widely spaced
Sepal Immature: creamy yellow
Sepal Mature: pale pink to white
Fertile Flower Immature: greeny lilac
Fertile Flower Mature: lilac
Peduncle: green with small dashes
Pedicel: lilac
pH: 6.5

Leaf

Main Colour: mid-green, light green, white
Edge Colour: as leaf and occasionally yellow (characteristic)
Texture: smooth, dull
Back of Leaf: almost same as the front
Veins: inconspicuous
Curvature: flat
Branch: green, few brown specks
Petiole: pale green

Height: medium
Flowering Time: mid to late

Above: *H. mac.* 'Tricolor', Windermere (pH 6.2)
Below left: *H. mac.* 'Quadricolor', Windermere (pH 6.5)
Below right: *H. mac.* 'Maculata', John F. Kennedy Arboretum, Co. Wexford, Ireland (pH 6.2)

H. macrophylla 'Rotschwanz'

Translation 'Redstart'. Wadensvil, 1987

A small member of the Teller series, this shrub is hardy
and sturdy given the conditions it needs. Like many
H. macrophylla cultivars it prefers some shelter, such as that of
large deciduous trees or planting at the edge of woodland.
Then it responds with startling brilliance. The numerous sterile
florets are a vivid red on alkaline soil, but a deep crimson on
acid soil. They are positioned mainly around the circumference
of the head, with a few appearing in the centre. Rather like
H. macrophylla 'Pfau' the sepals are grooved and twisted
which adds greatly to the attraction. Fertile flowers are pink on
alkaline soil and blue on acid soil. Suitable for a small garden,
this is one of our most popular plants.

Flower

Head Shape: lacecap
Head Size: small-medium
Sterile Flowers: up to 20, well above fertile
flowers
Sepal Number: 4, 5
Sepal Immature: red, cream centre
Sepal Mature: deep crimson red
Sepal Autumnal: darker purple/crimson
Fertile Flower Immature: pink-lilac
Fertile Flower Mature: blue
Peduncle: purple
Pedicel: purple
pH: 6.5

Leaf

Main Colour: mid-green
Autumn Colour: red edge
Edge Colour: red on mature leaves only
Texture: rugose, glossy
Back of Leaf: lighter green
Veins: recessed on front, prominent on back
Curvature: edges up
Branch: green, many long red dashes
Petiole: short, green

Height: small, medium
Flowering Time: mid to late

Above: *H. mac.* 'Rotschwanz',
Windermere (pH 6.5)
Below: *H. mac.* 'Rotschwanz',Windermere (pH 6.5)
six years later (TN-C)

H. macrophylla 'Seascape'

This plant came to us from Rosewarne, Cornwall, England where a collection had been made around 1960. We have been unable to trace its provenance but we include it because of its merits. The growth is open to lax, but vigorous, resulting in a shrub (after twelve years) that is twice as wide as it is high. Mophead inflorescences are very large and the lower ones tend to bend to the ground. Sepals are cream, suffused with lilac as they mature and there is a turquoise blue fertile flower in the centre of each floret. The head is full but not crowded. Fresh white blooms continue well into September. Other than flopping somewhat due to size, heads withstand exposure without scorching, which is unusual for such delicate colouring.

A truly beautiful plant for those who have the space. We hope to get this shrub into commercial production.

Flower

Head Shape: slightly irregular mophead
Head Size: medium-large
Sterile Flowers: full head, mixed sizes together
Sepal Number: 3, mostly 4
Sepal Immature: cream
Sepal Mature: white to palest pink
Sepal Autumnal: white, lilac streaks
Fertile Flower Immature: cream
Fertile Flower Mature: blue
Peduncle: green, big red dashes
Pedicel: pale green
pH: 6.5

Leaf

Main Colour: mid-green
Autumn Colour: darker green
Edge Colour: red in autumn
Texture: smooth
Back of Leaf: lighter green
Veins: unobtrusive
Curvature: flat
Branch: plain green
Petiole: light green

Height: medium (but twice as wide)
Flowering Time: mid to late

Above and below: *H. mac.* 'Seascape', Windermere (pH 6.5)

133

H. macrophylla 'Tokyo Delight'

AGM 2000 (H3/4)

The name 'Delight' exactly evokes the character of this shrub. It is colourful, attractive, strong, vigorous, large, yet with a lovely light character. The very many smallish lacecap flower heads rise tier upon tier, composed of soft-pink central corymbs of fertile flowers which are raised above the encircling white sepals, which face outwards. These sterile florets start their flowering cycle pure white with a red eye; the sepals, like *H. s.* 'Grayswood' turn pink with red blotches. Eventually the whole head turns bright crimson. The effect is quite enchanting in its earlier stages of development and looks like apple blossom. These leaves are set off by mid- to dark green leaves often with red tips and cream central veins. The leaves then turn russet and eventually purple in the autumn. This shrub should be sought, and would be beautiful in most garden situations.

Flower

Head Shape: convex
Head Size: small
Sterile Flowers: overlapping, facing outwards
Sepal Number: 4, a few 5
Sepal Immature: white
Sepal Mature: white, blush pink, red spots
Sepal Autumnal: bright crimson
Fertile Flower Immature: pink
Fertile Flower Mature: blue/lilac
Peduncle: palest green, purple dashes
Pedicel: palest green
pH: 6.4

Leaf

Main Colour: mid- to dark green
Autumn Colour: turning purple/russet
Edge Colour: red
Texture: matt, slightly rugose
Back of Leaf: pale green
Veins: white on upper surface
Curvature: flat occasional edges up
Branch: green with red dashes
Petiole: light green

Height: large
Flowering Time: early to late

Above: *H. mac.* 'Tokyo Delight', Windermere (pH 6.5) (TN-C)

Below: *H. mac.* 'Tokyo Delight', Mount Congreve, Kilmeaden, Co.Waterford, Ireland [pH 6.2 to 6.5]

H. macrophylla 'Veitchii'

AGM 1992 (H3/4). Imported from Japan by Maries about 1861. Exhibited by Veitch at The Temple Show, 1903

This is a mid-season-flowering lacecap with large flattish flower heads. The bush tends to be straggly. The mainly three, but occasionally four, sepals are remarkably large and white and have a lilac tint. Sometimes, when grown in sunlight, one ray flower can be partly shaded by another, causing part of the sepal to be white, and part pinkish. The sepals age to a striking lime-green colour in autumn and reverse when the fertile flowers have been fertilized. The reverse turns a lovely pale lilac, then red/brown. The fertile flowers are pink in bud but open, surprisingly, to a mid-blue on acid soils. It dries well in its white colouring or its attractive lime-green and lilac autumn colouring, for winter decoration. This variety is easy to propagate. Although not mentioned by Mallet, the French have used it as a progenitor for other varieties, according to Haworth-Booth. Bartrum also stated that 'along with . . . 'rosea' [sic] and 'Otaksa' . . . were mostly used by European nurseries in the breeding of many of our lovely Hortensias.' As it was not mentioned by Möhring it seems unlikely to have been used much for pot work.

Flower

Head Shape: convex, irregular
Head Size: large
Sterile Flowers: very large, overlapping
Sepal Number: 3, occasionally 4
Sepal Immature: cream
Sepal Mature: white to palest lilac
Sepal Autumnal: lime green, lilac on back, turning red/brown
Fertile Flower Immature: green then pink
Fertile Flower Mature: blue
Peduncle: greeny brown
Pedicel: very pale lilac
pH: 6.5

Leaf

Main Colour: light green to darker green
Texture: rugose
Back of Leaf: very slightly lighter
Veins: deeply recessed
Curvature: some flat, mostly tips down
Branch: light green speckled
Petiole: light green

Height: large
Flowering Time: mid to late

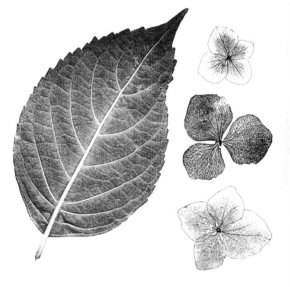

Above: *H. mac.* 'Veitchii', Windermere (pH 6.5)
Below: *H. mac.* 'Veitchii' in autumn after the sepals have reversed

H. macrophylla 'White Wave'

AM 1948. AGM 1992 (H3/4). Bred by V. Lemoine of Nancy, 1902

Originally named *H. m.* 'Mariesii Grandiflora' but altered to 'White Wave' by Haworth-Booth as the name was invalid. The original name does indicate that this cultivar was bred from *H. m.* 'Mariesii'. The growth is sturdy, growing to a mid- to large shrub. The flower head is similar to 'Mariesii' too, with pearly white entire, but later serrated, sepals occasionally invading the central mass of fertile flowers. (Although this fact is not mentioned by other authorities, it is to be expected, knowing the parentage.) These fertile flowers are pale pink when immature, opening to pink or pale-blue on maturity. The size of the fully open florets and the size of the sepals is larger than average. The shrub flowers on the majority of the side shoots as well as on the main stem. In shade it is less free-flowering and is of more compact habit. In late September, the sepals reverse and change from shell pink on the face to creamy green on the reverse, now uppermost. The leaves are mid-green in colour and have coarse serrated edges. These turn in autumn to red/brown from the tips. A really lovely lacecap.

H. mac. 'White Wave', Windermere (pH 6.5)

Flower

Head Shape: flat, amorphous
Head Size: large
Sterile Flowers: occasionally invading central corymb
Sepal Number: 3 to 5, usually 4
Sepal Immature: greeny yellow
Sepal Mature: white, slightly pink tinge
Sepal Autumnal: creamy-green, edges serrated
Fertile Flower Immature: pink
Fertile Flower Mature: pink, opens blue
Peduncle: green with minute dashes
Pedicel: pinky white with dashes
pH: 6.5

Leaf

Main Colour: mid-green
Autumn Colour: turns red/brown on tips
Texture: smooth, becomes coarse as it ages
Back of Leaf: almost the same as the front
Veins: not obtrusive
Curvature: edges up
Branch: green with brown dashes
Petiole: pale green

Height: mid to large
Flowering Time: mid to late

H. serrata 'Blue Bird'

AM 1960. AGM 1992 (H4). Old Japanese cultivar

A very interesting and highly decorative shrub growing to about 1.5 m (5 ft), and as much across, flowering continuously from early June to early October. The sepals are entire and, depending on the acidity of the soil, may be blue or pink. The central corymb of fertile flowers also changes colour according to the soil acidity. When the central corymb has been fertilized, the sepals turn over and the reverse turns bright pink, irrespective of the pH of the soil. Fresh flowers with deep-blue central corymbs appear among those with pink reversed florets. The leaves are green to start with but change from the tips to a lovely red brown and, together with the changing flowers, a multitude of colour continues well into the autumn. It is easy to propagate. The leaves outlined with hoar frost are also a lovely sight.

Flower

Head Shape: concave
Head Size: medium
Sterile Flowers: no overlap, facing upwards and outwards
Sepal Number: 4–6
Sepal Immature: pink
Sepal Mature: white, pale blue
Sepal Autumnal: reverses to pink
Fertile Flower Immature: pink
Fertile Flower Mature: blue
Peduncle: reddy brown
Pedicel: white/cream
pH: 6.5

Leaf

Main Colour: mid-green to reddish brown
Autumn Colour: dark red/brown
Edge Colour: touched with dark red
Texture: matt, deeply quilted
Back of Leaf: light green, even when front is red
Veins: not conspicuous
Curvature: bending backwards, edges up
Branch: green to red brown
Petiole: dark green

Height: medium to large
Flowering Time: early and continuous

Above left: *H. serrata* 'Blue Bird' in a garden setting (TN-C)
Above right: Autumn leaves
Below: Flower head of *H. s.* 'Blue Bird', Windermere (pH 6.5)

H. serrata 'Blue Deckle'

Bred by M. Haworth-Booth

This delightful lacecap was developed 'with the aim of producing a dwarf rival to *H. m.* 'Générale Vicomtesse de Vibraye' (Haworth-Booth). The shrub is certainly beautiful, but the colour much lighter than 'Vibraye'. The flowers are composed of numerous sepals, most of which are serrated, although some entire ones can be found. These surround the fertile central flowers which are the same colour or a slightly deeper blue than the sepals. It flowers prolifically starting in July and still produces blooms in September. The flower head turns slate green, with the sepals reversing and the underside, now sometimes uppermost, turning lilac purple, giving a remarkable iridescent effect: quite gorgeous. The leaves are ovate, light green turning red in the autumn, with the edges turning purple. It is also superb in its strong uniform pink colouring.

Flower

Head Shape: hemispherical
Head Size: small
Sterile Flowers: overlapping, invading central corymb
Sepal Number: 4 and 5
Sepal Immature: pale blue, or pink, cream centre
Sepal Mature: pale blue, serrated edges
Sepal Autumnal: sea green, reverse lilac purple
Fertile Flower Immature: green/very pale blue
Fertile Flower Mature: deeper blue than sepals
Peduncle: green, many dark red dashes
Pedicel: pale blue
pH: 6.1

Leaf

Main Colour: light green
Autumn Colour: red
Edge Colour: as leaf, purple in autumn
Texture: smooth, matt
Back of Leaf: lighter than front, smooth
Veins: not prominent
Curvature: edges up
Branch: green, many red dashes
Petiole: short and red

Height: small
Flowering Time: early and continuous

Above: *H. serrata* 'Blue Deckle', Windermere (pH 6.1)
Below: *H. serrata* 'Blue Deckle', Windermere, recently moved (pH 6.5)

H. serrata 'Diadem'

PC 1962. AM 1963. AGM 2000 (H3/4)

This shrub is a very early flowering lacecap which is ideal for small gardens or pot work, flowering from June to August and having occasional further flowers later in the season. Smothering all weeds, it is wider than it is high, but remains very compact. The flowers are composed of a beautiful pale to mid-blue ring of sterile florets surrounding the central, fertile, light-blue flowers. Both are pink on alkaline soils, where it is just as pretty. The sepals reverse after the flowers have been fertilized and eventually turn a very deep purple lilac. The leaves are at first a yellowy green but soon have brown tips. Most then turn a lovely deep plum which sets off the delightful flowers. This shrub is hardy and is ideal for the front of borders where it is always the centre of attraction.

Flower

Head Shape: convex
Head Size: small
Sterile Flowers: opening flat, starlike
Sepal Number: mainly 4, some 5
Sepal Immature: cream
Sepal Mature: light blue
Sepal Autumnal: reverses to purple lilac
Fertile Flower Immature: purple
Fertile Flower Mature: pale blue
Peduncle: purple
Pedicel: pale blue
pH: 6.1

Leaf

Main Colour: yellow green, brown tips
Autumn Colour: bright red to dark purple
Edge Colour: some bronze
Texture: matt, smooth, slightly quilted
Back of Leaf: lighter green
Veins: prominent mid-rib on reverse
Curvature: edges up, tips slightly down
Branch: green, pink at nodes
Petiole: as leaf but very short

Height: small to medium
Flowering Time: very early and continuous

Above and below: *H. serrata* 'Diadem', Windermere (pH 6.5)

H. serrata 'Grayswood'

AM 1948. AGM 1922 (H4). Introduced by Mr Chambers of Grayswood Hill, 1888

A tall, rather sparse shrub in its earlier years, it eventually bushes out. Growing to a height of about 2 m (6 ft) the shrub is very showy throughout its quite long flowering season. It starts flowering about the beginning of August and its autumnal colours are bright well into October. The lacecap flower head has a centre of pink or blue fertile flowers surrounded by about nine sterile ray florets opening white, but due to the action of sunlight, soon turning brilliant red from the tips. The florets are composed of mainly three, occasionally four, sepals, one of which is distinctly larger than the others. The sepals do not overlap. When aged, the sepals reverse and turn a very rich deep crimson and the flower head dries well at this stage. The leaves are acuminate and are yellowish-green when young, turning dark green later with reddish brown edges. In autumn, they develop reddish patches. *H. s.* 'Intermedia' is a similar but more spindly shrub that has a concave, smaller flower head. The sepals, which are highly serrated, face upwards and turn from white through pink to red, very quickly reversing to a duller red, paler towards the centre. The flower head has a square or triangular look, depending on the number of sepals in the floret. These surround a mid-blue to lilac fertile centre. The leaves are rugose and dark green, turning to a rich red/brown with the backs remaining green and the central vein remaining red. The petiole is a mahogany colour.

Flower
Head Shape: convex
Head Size: small
Sterile Flowers: facing outwards, not upwards, one sepal larger
Sepal Number: 3 or 4
Sepal Immature: white
Sepal Mature: pink with red blotches
Sepal Autumnal: reverses crimson
Fertile Flower Immature: green
Fertile Flower Mature: pale pink or blue
Peduncle: purplish red
Pedicel: pink/lilac
pH: 6.4

Leaf
Main Colour: pale green to dark green
Autumn Colour: red tints to dull bronze
Edge Colour: reddish brown
Texture: smooth
Back of Leaf: slightly lighter green
Veins: central raised on back
Curvature: flat
Branch: a few red dots
Petiole: short, reddish at nodes

Height: large
Flowering Time: mid to late

Above: *H. serrata* 'Grayswood", Windermere (6.5 pH) (TN-C)
Below left: *H serrata*, 'Grayswood', Windermere (pH 6.5) in autumn colour
Below right: *H. serrata* 'Intermedia', Windermere (pH 6.5)

H. serrata 'Kiyosumi'

Syn. 'Kiyosumisawa'. Bred by Y. Hayashi, 1950

A charming and easily recognized plant; it is from Mt. Kiyosumi in Japan. The shrub is lax in growth but the numerous small blooms are held firmly on the slim, woody stems. Vigour has increased considerably as the shrub has grown, and we anticipate that its move to a slightly sunnier area will be beneficial – dappled shade would be its natural environment in Japan, but with more warmth there than in Cumbria, England.

The sterile florets are carried on long pedicels. At first they are held in a vertical plane but they flatten later in the season. The sepals are most attractive, with white/cream centres surrounded by a narrow frame of strong pink/red. This deep colour tends to percolate some way towards the centre of the floret with time. In the autumn, florets reverse to display a deep pink colour on the backs of the sepals. Fertile flowers, pink at first, quickly open and dry to brown. The leaves are also striking, being green when young but quickly suffusing to dark red with light green veins.

The interesting colour combinations of both flower and leaf make this a most attractive plant. It benefits from close inspection so is especially suitable for a small garden.

Flower

Head Shape: lacecap
Head Size: small
Sterile Flowers: up to 12, around circumference
Sepal Number: 4 and 5
Sepal Immature: white/cream, pink border
Sepal Mature: white, broader pink/red border
Sepal Autumnal: reverse to deep pink
Fertile Flower Immature: pink
Fertile Flower Mature: brown
Peduncle: pink base, cream tip
Pedicel: long, cream
pH: 6.5

Leaf

Main Colour: light yellowy green
Autumn Colour: dark red suffusing from edge
Edge Colour: dark red, few green in shade
Texture: matt
Back of Leaf: grey green
Veins: light green, conspicuous against red
Curvature: flat
Branch: light green flecked red
Petiole: dark red

Height: medium
Flowering Time: mid

Above and below: *H. serrata* 'Kiyosumi', Windermere (pH 6.5)

H. serrata 'Kurohime'

Translation 'Black Princess'. Distributed by T. Yamamoto

A small shrub of somewhat lax growth, carrying large numbers of small lacecap flowerheads. The very pointed sepals give the florets a star-like quality. On soil of pH 6.5, floret colour has changed slowly from pale pink to deep purple pink. More purple/deep blue blooms are gradually appearing. On more acid soils the florets can be a strong purple. There is a constant succession of new flowerheads, giving a very long season. The fertile flowers are purple and retain this colour until autumn. Leaves are a light green early with some red colour developing. The stems (presumably giving the name to the plant) are darkest purple, almost black. This is a colourful, hardy and most attractive plant.

Flower

Head Shape: lacecap, domed centre
Head Size: small
Sterile Flowers: small, held away from centre
Sepal Number: 4–5
Sepal Immature: pink
Sepal Mature: deep purple pink
Sepal Autumnal: fading
Fertile Flower Immature: pink
Fertile Flower Mature: purple
Peduncle: green, red marks
Pedicel: lilac pink
pH: 6.5

Leaf

Main Colour: light green
Autumn Colour: many turning red
Edge Colour: red
Texture: matt
Back of Leaf: lighter green
Veins: lighter green than leaf
Curvature: flat
Branch: green, dense red marking
Petiole: dark red

Height: small, wider than tall
Flowering Time: early, mid and late

Above: *H. serrata* 'Kurohime', Windermere (pH 6.5), young plant
Below: *H. serrata* 'Kurohime', Japan, acid soil (T. Yamamoto)

H. serrata 'Miranda'

AGM 2000 (H3/4). Selected seedling, Haworth-Booth

This is a lovely, delicate, small- to medium-sized lacecap with a ring of sterile florets surrounding a centre composed of clusters of fertile flowers, which are very distinct from each other. The sterile florets have four or five overlapping sepals, their colour varying from pale blue through white to pale pink, depending on the pH of the soil. Sometimes blue and pink appear on the same bush at the same time. When mature they become the same colour throughout the shrub. Fertile central flowers are pinky lilac when unopened, but open to a light blue. The leaves are yellowy green with red edges and eventually turn blotchy red all over. The central vein is much lighter when immature but, characteristically, all the veins change to red when the leaves are older. Ideal for containers, this shrub will enhance patios.

Flower

Head Shape: flat or convex
Head Size: small
Sterile Flowers: facing upwards, overlapping
Sepal Number: 4–5
Sepal Immature: mauve with white centre
Sepal Mature: deeper mauve, pink or blue with occasionally red dots
Sepal Autumnal: reverses, same colour on back
Fertile Flower Immature: lilac
Fertile Flower Mature: light blue
Peduncle: light brown
Pedicel: cream/mauve
pH: 6.5

Leaf

Main Colour: light yellowy green
Autumn Colour: mottled yellow, red veins
Edge Colour: fine red margin
Texture: matt, rugose with age
Back of Leaf: lighter greeny yellow
Veins: central vein light green, all veins turn red on ageing
Curvature: edges up, tip down
Branch: green with fine red speckles
Petiole: short, green, slight red tint

Height: small to medium
Flowering Time: early and continuous

Above and below: *H. serrata* 'Miranda', Windermere (pH 6.5) (TN-C above)

H. serrata 'Preziosa'

PC 1961. AM 1963. FCC 1964. AGM 1992 (H4). Bred by G. Ahrends, 1961

A very showy and sought after shrub as it is usually reliably red, even on acid soils. It forms a compact and rounded bush. Although a *serrata*, this shrub has a head like a small mophead. It forms an erect bush flowering in mid-season with a hemispherical small head. Its immature sepals are cream with pale pink edges maturing to a bright red. This colour is variable, even on the same plant, from pink through pinky red to lilac and even violet, especially when late in the season. The leaves are light green but darkening towards the edges, with red veins, petioles and branches. These features are instantly recognizable and characteristic. If frosted early, the leaves turn a brilliant red and remain so for the rest of the season, when they will turn bronze. This shrub is ideal for growing near the house or against a wall and is also suitable for containers.

Although most authorities classify this shrub under *H. serrata*, others give it a varietal name of its own. C. Mallet states that it is a hybrid between *H. serrata* and *H. macrophylla*. The authors have plants on which some flower heads revert to a lacecap form in late summer. The sterile flowers fall away from the centre revealing fertile flowers in the centre of the flower head.

Flower

Head Shape: hemispherical
Head Size: small
Sepal Number: usually 4
Sepal Immature: cream with pale pink edges
Sepal Mature: red, pink or lilac, never blue
Sepal Autumnal: bright red
Fertile Flower Immature: greeny brown
Fertile Flower Mature: blue
Peduncle: dark red
Pedicel: pink, sometimes lilac
pH: 6.5

Leaf

Main Colour: light green, darker centre
Autumn Colour: red, later bronze
Edge Colour: red
Texture: rugose, dull, matt
Back of Leaf: lighter green
Veins: red
Curvature: edges slightly up
Branch: red
Petiole: pink

Height: small to medium
Flowering Time: mid to late

Above and below: *H. serrata* 'Preziosa', Windermere (pH 6.5)
Right: *H. serrata* 'Preziosa', Windermere (pH 6.5) showing tendency to lacecap form

H. serrata 'Rosalba'

AM 1939. AGM 1992 (H4)

This is a useful front-of-border plant, being vigorous and decorative. It tolerates light shade and flowers throughout the season. The pink, immature flowers in the centre of the corymb mature to pink or lilac and are encircled with a few sterile florets. These appear haphazardly around the edge of the corymb. Opening almost white at the start of the season, they soon start turning pink from the tips of the sepals. Increasingly with age, red dots appear on these. This is a salient feature of the variety. The sepals eventually turn deep pink. The serrated-edged leaves are bright mid-green, developing red/brown tips with age.

H. s. 'Beni Gaku' was given as a synonym of *H. s.* 'Rosalba' by Ohwi 1965 and Makino 1989. Both these Japanese authorities describe a plant of medium stature with white sterile florets. These change colour gradually, from the outer edge of the sepal towards the centre, until the whole floret is vivid red. The fertile flowers are white. While this is a plant with clear identity and striking appearance, it does not match with our understanding of *H. s.* 'Rosalba'.

Flower

Head Shape: flattish, slightly irregular
Head Size: small
Sterile Flowers: irregularly spaced
Sepal Number: 3 or 4
Sepal Immature: yellowy cream
Sepal Mature: whitish, blush pink, red dots
Sepal Autumnal: deep pink, red dots
Fertile Flower Immature: pink
Fertile Flower Mature: pink or lilac
Peduncle: lilac
Pedicel: white or pale pink
pH: 6.2–6.5

Leaf

Main Colour: bright green
Autumn Colour: turning brown from tips
Texture: matt
Back of Leaf: slightly lighter green
Veins: light on front
Curvature: mainly flat
Branch: current season's growth: green
Petiole: green

Height: medium
Flowering Time: early to late

Above: *H. serrata* 'Rosalba', Mount Congreve, Kilmeaden, Co. Waterford, Ireland (pH 6.2 to 6.5)
Below left: *H. s.* 'Rosalba', Ivy Hatch, Ightham, Kent (pH 6.0)
Below right: *H. s.* 'Beni Gaku', Windermere (pH 6.5)

H. serrata 'Schichidanka'

From T. Yamamoto, Japan

This small plant from the wooded mountains of Japan has been known since the sixteenth century. It disappeared and was then rediscovered after World War II in Mount Rokko, Kobe, Japan.

It is delicate in every detail but nevertheless quite hardy. The inflorescence displays the daintiest of all hydrangea flowers. Comprised of many tiny sterile florets on long pedicels, each floret has concentric layers of narrow, pointed sepals. Massed on the head, in either the pink or pale blue version, the effect is star-like and eye-catching. By late summer, the florets reverse to show a red or mauve colour. Turning the floret by hand, one finds the original top surface has become bright green. The green leaves quickly suffuse to dark red.

This shrub is small and its flowers are quite different from other hydrangeas. It should be sited in the garden where it can be easily seen and its merits appreciated. It would be suitable for planting in a container.

Flower
Head Shape: slightly domed lacecap
Head Size: small
Sterile Flowers: numerous, up to 10
Sepal Number: 9–10 in double layer, inner rows smaller
Sepal Immature: cream
Sepal Mature: pale blue
Sepal Autumnal: reverse to lilac
Fertile Flower Immature: lilac
Fertile Flower Mature: dry up or wither
Peduncle: grey green
Pedicel: as flower
pH: 6.5

Leaf
Main Colour: mid-green suffusing red
Autumn Colour: dull dark red
Edge Colour: red tips
Texture: matt
Back of Leaf: rugose
Veins: raised on back
Curvature: edges up on young, tips down on old
Branch: woody, green
Petiole: very short, brown

Height: small
Flowering Time: early

Above left: *H. serrata* 'Schichidanka', Knightshayes, Devon, England
Below left: *H. serrata* 'Schichidanka', Windermere (pH 6.5)

H. serrata 'Shishiva'

From Japan via USA

This rather lax plant grew with great vigour but was slow to flower. Once flowering began, it was prolific. There were masses of small lacecap heads composed of pale pink florets and, surprisingly, vivid red fertile flower buds. Even more surprising, the fertile flowers open blue. At this stage the colour-contrasts throughout the shrub are bright, perhaps even harsh. As the pink colour of the florets deepens with age and the blue of the fertile flowers fade, the whole becomes a harmonious and spectacular display. Leaves contribute to the show, as some become totally red and all have bright red veins. Unusually too the leaves are held in threes on the stem. Altogether a hardy and colourful plant with characteristics making it easy to recognise.

Flower
Head Shape: domed lacecap
Head Size: small
Sterile Flowers: numerous around the circumference
Sepal Number: 4–6, mostly 5
Sepal Immature: cream, pink edge
Sepal Mature: pink, white centre
Sepal Autumnal: deep red
Fertile Flower Immature: green
Fertile Flower Mature: red, opening to show blue filament
Peduncle: green
Pedicel: cream
pH: 6.5

Leaf
Main Colour: bright green, held in threes
Autumn Colour: many bright red
Edge Colour: red tips
Texture: rugose
Back of Leaf: light green
Veins: centre one bright red, back and front
Curvature: tips arched back
Branch: red
Petiole: short, red

Height: small-medium
Flowering Time: mid

Above and below: *H. serrata* 'Shishiva', Windermere (pH 6.5)

147

H. serrata f. thunbergii

Given to us by T. Yamamoto, as *H. thunbergii*

This is certainly one of the hydrangeas from which Japanese make tea and which are all known as 'amacha'. Our plant may be 'koamacha' or small tea hydrangea, which was described by Siebold in *Flora Japonica* and is sometimes grown for domestic tea in Japan. Other 'amacha' are now grown commercially for tea crops.

The shrub growing in Cumbria is hardy in an edge of woodland setting. Charming small lacecap blooms are held upright on the slim, woody stems. Opening in July, the sterile florets are pink with white centres. The colour gradually deepens but the white centres remain until later when the florets reverse to show dusky pink backs. Sepals are rounded and they overlap entirely. The fertile flowers, of which there are fewer than in many lacecaps, are deep pink opening to blue. Leaves are small, narrow and tapered like the species *H. serrata*. They change from green to dark red and are carried on very short red petioles. They have a sweet taste. An unusual plant: dainty, colourful and a good talking point!

Flower
Head Shape: very flat lacecap
Head Size: small
Sterile Flowers: held around circumference
Sepal Number: 3, 4
Sepal Immature: pink, white centre
Sepal Mature: deeper pink, white centre
Sepal Autumnal: reverse to dusky pink
Fertile Flower Immature: deep pink
Fertile Flower Mature: blue
Peduncle: red
Pedicel: pink
pH: 6.5

Leaf
Main Colour: light green
Autumn Colour: dark red
Edge Colour: as leaf
Texture: matt
Back of Leaf: lighter green
Veins: red on backs
Curvature: flat
Branch: red
Petiole: very short, red

Height: small
Flowering Time: early to mid

Above and below: *H. serrata* f. *thunbergii*, Windermere (pH 6.5)

H. serrata 'Tiara'

M. Foster 1990. AGM 2000

This is a welcome addition to the small group of cultivars of *H. serrata*, which flower pink on alkaline soil and blue on acid soil. It is similar to *H. serrata* 'Diadem' but makes a more vigorous statement. The many flowerheads are held well above the foliage and are eye-catching in the garden. The sterile florets, beautifully formed, are so plentiful that they sometimes obscure the fertile flowers in the centre of the head. Colour is particularly exciting. On slightly acid soil, sterile florets open pale pink and change gradually to a clear deep pink with some red markings. The buds of the fertile flowers are coral pink opening to display purple filaments. On more acid soil, pale blue florets surround pale blue fertile flowers. Either combination is equally charming, and is accompanied by bright green narrow tapered leaves which turn dark red and finally vivid red in autumn. Flowering continues well into September in Cumbria, which is unusual for a *serrata*. This plant well deserves its AGM and is a must for hydrangea lovers.

Flower
Head Shape: slightly domed lacecap
Head Size: small
Sterile Flowers: numerous, some in centre of head
Sepal Number: mostly 4, some 5
Sepal Immature: pale pink
Sepal Mature: deep pink
Sepal Autumnal: deep pink, red marks
Fertile Flower Immature: coral red
Fertile Flower Mature: pink or purple filaments
Peduncle: green/red
Pedicel: red
pH: 6.5

Leaf
Main Colour: bright red
Autumn Colour: dark red, some vivid red
Edge Colour: as leaf
Texture: matt
Back of Leaf: green, even when red on front
Veins: light green on red leaf
Curvature: edges up, tips down
Branch: light green, red marks
Petiole: very short

Height: small-medium
Flowering Time: early, mid and late

Below: *H. s.* 'Tiara', Windermere (pH 6.5), young plant (TN-C)

Above and below: *H. s.* 'Tiara', Knightshayes, Devon (GL-H)

H. serrata ssp. yezoensis

Syn. *serrata megacarpa* (Ohwi)

Found in the most northerly Japanese island of Hokkaido (early named Ezo) and in the northern parts of Honshu, this plant thrives on severely cold winters. Its taxonomy is uncertain but it has come to our collection in Cumbria from two different sources – by seed gathered on an expedition to Seibu, Japan, and from a cutting given by T. Yamamoto. I include it because it thrives in cool areas, does not like a lot of sun, is hardy and decorative.

After ten years' growth, the shrub is of medium height but considerably more in width. The small lacecap blooms are numerous and well supported on the slim stems. Sepals can be pink or blue, with entire or serrated borders. The fertile flowers, again either pink or blue, attract masses of bees. Leaves are a yellowish green with sharply denticulate borders and are broader than most *H. serrata* cultivars. The flowering season is earlier than other hydrangeas and in Cumbria is over by August. This is an interesting plant, useful for its resistance to cold and an attractive addition to the early summer garden.

Flower

Head Shape: lacecap
Head Size: small
Sterile Flowers: 6–12 around circumference
Sepal Number: 4, 5
Sepal Immature: pale blue
Sepal Mature: pale blue
Sepal Autumnal: reverse to creamy white
Fertile Flower Immature: pale blue
Fertile Flower Mature: pale blue
Peduncle: light green, red marks
Pedicel: cream or pale blue
pH: 6.5

Leaf

Main Colour: light green
Autumn Colour: red colour on some
Edge Colour: as leaf, sharply denticulate
Texture: matt
Back of Leaf: lighter green
Veins: light on front
Curvature: flat
Branch: light green, red spots
Petiole: red from node

Height: small-medium
Flowering Time: early

Above and below: *H. serrata* ssp. *yezoensis*, Windermere (pH 6.5)

H. paniculata 'Floribunda'

AM 1953. AGM 1992 (H4). Introduced from Japan, 1868

This is a very striking plant. Left unpruned, it can form a shrub or, more accurately, a small tree several metres high and wide, but its size can of course by controlled by spring pruning. Starting to open in late July, the flowers continue well into the autumn.

The elegant panicles are slender and pointed, and above average height. Those on the top of the bush are held erect, while peripheral stems bow down under the weight of flowers. Sterile and fertile flowers occupy roughly equal amounts of space in each panicle, and are evenly distributed, giving a balanced, open effect. The mature colouring is a mixture of cream and pink, the pink colouring coming mainly from the back of the sepals as they fade. A pruned version will display the same attractive panicles, however, and will be an asset in a smaller garden.

A similar cultivar is *H. paniculata* 'Tardiva', introduced by Haworth-Booth from Chenault's nursery, and given an AM in 1966. This is at its flowering peak in mid-September, and continues well into October. Colouring is white, lightly tinged with pink/cream as the season progresses. The panicles are shorter than those of *H. p.* 'Floribunda' and the sterile florets are fewer and concentrated more towards the base of the panicle. Another excellent plant, and advantageous because of its very late flowering.

Flower

Head Shape: tall slim panicle
Head Size: up to 36 cm (14 in) high, up to 20 cm (8 in) diameter base
Sterile Flowers: evenly dispersed
Sepal Number: 4, often 5
Sepal Immature: cream
Sepal Mature: cream, touch of pink
Sepal Autumnal: creamy-green, reverse pink
Fertile Flower Immature: cream
Fertile Flower Mature: open cream, closed green
Peduncle: brown, light green tip
Pedicel: cream/green
pH: 5.5–6.0

Leaf

Main Colour: dark green
Autumn Colour: as leaf
Texture: matt, slightly hairy
Back of Leaf: lighter colour, hairy
Veins: slightly recessed
Curvature: mainly flat
Branch: old: rough; new: mid-brown, lighter streaks
Petiole: light green, short

Height: large
Flowering Time: mid to late

Left: *H. p.* 'Floribunda', Hemelrijk, Belgium (pH 6.5)
Right: *H. p.* 'Tardiva', Windermere (pH 6.5)

H. paniculata 'Grandiflora'

FCC 1869. AGM 1992 (H4). Country of origin: Japan

Grown first in Japanese gardens and introduced to the West by Siebold, this is the most popular of the paniculatas. In the USA, where it is known as the 'pee-gee' hydrangea, it is so widely grown that it has escaped from cultivation and become naturalized in the wild. It can grow unpruned as a large and vigorous shrub, smothered in bloom; it can be pruned to produce fewer and larger flowers on a smaller bush; or it can be trained as a single-stemmed standard.

The panicles appear to be composed entirely of massed sterile florets. The fact that many bees visit the plant, however, indicates the error of this assumption, and closer examination will reveal the partly hidden fertile flowers. The bees forage these for nectar, using the sterile florets as landing platforms. The sepals, evenly elliptic with little overlap, open creamy white. They develop a pale-pink tinge around their margins as they mature, and this colour gradually suffuses the whole floret. A deep pink 'eye' adds a decorative finish. The flowering season lasts from July to September, in Britain.

Gales are the chief hazard. On a hard-pruned shrub, the heavy heads get buffeted by wind and stems can snap, while heavy rain can turn the mature flowers an ugly brown colour. These slight drawbacks are easily outweighed by the many advantages of this splendid plant.

Flower

Head Shape: broad panicle
Head Size: up to 25 cm (10 in) high, up to 20 cm (8 in) diameter base
Sterile Flowers: densely packed
Sepal Number: 4, on cupped floret
Sepal Immature: white, slightly capped
Sepal Mature: cream, pink edge
Sepal Autumnal: deep cream/pink
Fertile Flower Immature: pink
Fertile Flower Mature: cream
Peduncle: cream/red
Pedicel: cream/red
pH: 6.5

Leaf

Main Colour: light green
Autumn Colour: slightly lighter
Texture: matt, slightly hairy
Back of Leaf: lighter green
Veins: central vein red on back and all veins prominent
Curvature: edges up
Branch: brown, raised pale markings
Petiole: green, short

Height: large
Flowering Time: mid to late

Right and left: *H. p.* 'Grandiflora', Windermere (pH 6.5)

H. paniculata 'Kyushu'

AGM 1992 (H4)

A cultivar which is reminiscent of the species, this mid-season variety is in full flower by the end of July, a time when there can be a shortage of colour in the garden. The growth is erect and the panicle compact, pointed and broad at the base. The green tint, apparent early in the season, is superseded by creamy white colouring as the fertile flowers open. The white sterile florets are distributed sparingly, mainly at the panicle base. The leaves are dark and, unusually for an *H. paniculata*, glossy. The colour scheme throughout the season is entirely white and green, and the effect is light, open and elegant.

Another cultivar displaying green and white, is *H. paniculata* 'Green Spire', selected by J. and R. de Belder. This is capable of becoming a very large shrub – 2 m (7 ft) high and 4 m (14 ft) wide has been seen. Growth is rather lax, with the majority of branches and panicles on a mature bush growing nearer to the horizontal than the vertical. One might expect, from the name, to find all green flowers, but it is the massed, unopened, fertile flowers which impart the green coloration, especially at the tip where they remain closed throughout the season. Towards the base of the panicle, fertile flowers open to give a froth of creamy white. Many white sterile florets are dispersed around the lower part of the panicle, and a few scattered towards the tip. These tend to light green as the season progresses, adding to the generally verdant appearance. The leaves are dark, slim and, once again, glossy.

Flower

Head Shape: slim open panicles
Head Size: 20 cm (8 in) tall × 15 cm (6 in) diameter base
Sterile Flowers: sparse, more at base
Sepal Number: 4
Sepal Immature: deep cream
Sepal Mature: creamy white, fine grey lines
Sepal Autumnal: cream
Fertile Flower Immature: creamy green
Fertile Flower Mature: creamy white
Peduncle: cream/pale green
Pedicel: cream
pH: 6.5

Leaf

Main Colour: dark green
Edge Colour: as leaf
Texture: smooth, glossy
Back of Leaf: lighter, glossy
Veins: raised on back
Curvature: flat, wavy edge
Branch: green, white marks
Petiole: red

Height: large
Flowering Time: early to mid

Left: *H. p.* 'Kyushu', Windermere (pH 6.5)
Right: *H. p.* 'Green Spire', Hemelrijk, Belgium (pH 5.5 to 6.0)

H. paniculata 'Pink Diamond'

Selected by J. and R. de Belder, Kalmthout, Belgium

Grown unpruned, this cultivar forms an enormous bush while, like other paniculatas, huge heads can be produced on a smaller plant by pruning. On the 'natural' shrub, tall panicles of interspersed fertile and sterile cream flowers open in late summer. The panicles are well shaped with slightly rounded tips and are carried in profusion. The upper ones are held erect, the peripheral ones bend their stems to the horizontal. At this stage, there is no evidence of the plant living up to its name! However, starting from the panicle base, the florets gradually develop a pink coloration which advances towards the tip, deepening as it progresses until the whole is a deep shade of rose. The backs of the sterile flowers can become a strong red, and the whole metamorphosis is quite dramatic. The colouring shows up to advantage with a background of dark or grey foliage, and against a clear sky the panicles are especially beautiful.

Growing without any difficulties, this is a plant to be prized.

Flower

Head Shape: tall open panicle
Head Size: up to 30 cm (12 in) high, up to 20 cm (8 in) base diameter
Sterile Flowers: evenly distributed
Sepal Number: 4, slight overlap
Sepal Immature: cream
Sepal Mature: rose pink
Sepal Autumnal: deep pink, red on back
Fertile Flower Immature: cream
Fertile Flower Mature: red
Peduncle: light green/pale pink
Pedicel: cream going pink
pH: 5.5–6.0

Leaf

Main Colour: mid- to dark green
Edge Colour: as leaf
Texture: matt
Back of Leaf: lighter green
Veins: front recessed, back raised
Curvature: flat
Branch: woody, white marks
Petiole: brown/red

Height: large
Flowering Time: mid to late

Above: *H. p.* 'Pink Diamond', Hemelrijk, Belgium (pH 5.5 to 6.0)
Below: *H. p.* 'Pink Diamond', Windermere (pH 6.5)

H. paniculata 'Praecox'

AM 1956. FCC 1973. AGM 1992 (H4). Introduced by C.S. Sargent from Japan, 1893

This well-established cultivar differs from others in many respects, most obviously in its flowering time which, beginning in June, is usually over by the end of July. However, it has an extra bonus. In April, well before the flowers open, the leaves begin unfolding to a lovely golden yellow. This is surprisingly eye-catching and attractive in a garden which is somewhat bare at this time. The plant develops slowly to a tree-like shrub. The 'panicles' are short and broad, resembling a rather domed lacecap. Fertile flowers are in the majority, especially in the centre of the bloom, where they open to form a creamy mound. Sterile florets are scattered around the periphery and towards the base of the panicle. They stand out with distinction, as their sepals are separate and pure white. These are elongated, and careful inspection will often show that one sepal is longer than others of the same floret.

The leaves are long and narrow, with raised, undulate edges and, by the time the flowers appear, the leaves are a glossy mid-green.

Any necessary pruning should be done after the flowers fade, as earlier pruning would remove the current season's blooms.

For all its short flowering period, this is a shrub well worth including in any but the smallest gardens.

Right: *H. p.* 'Praecox', Windermere (pH 6.5)
Left: Early leaves of *H. p.* 'Praecox', Windermere (pH 6.5)

Flower

Head Shape: flattened panicle
Head Size: up to 20 cm (8 in)
Sterile Flowers: widely spaced
Sepal Number: 4–5, one often larger
Sepal Immature: white
Sepal Mature: white, fine grey lines
Fertile Flower Immature: green/white
Fertile Flower Mature: matt/cream
Peduncle: cream/green
Pedicel: cream
pH: 6.5

Leaf

Main Colour: yellow, goes mid-green
Autumn Colour: yellow
Edge Colour: slightly lighter
Texture: smooth, glossy
Back of Leaf: lighter green
Veins: inconspicuous
Curvature: all edges up
Branch: light green, light marks
Petiole: red

Height: large
Flowering Time: early

H. paniculata 'Unique'

AM 1990. AGM 1992 (H4). Selected by J. and R. de Belder, 1968, Kalmthout, Belgium

Capable of growing to over 3 m (10 ft) high, with both upright and arching branches, this can also be pruned to produce a striking feature plant in a small garden. True to its name, it can be easily recognized: although it is a seedling of *H. p.* 'Floribunda', it bears some resemblance in form to *H. p.* 'Grandiflora' and in colour to *H. p.* 'Pink Diamond'. It is the shape of the panicle which identifies *H. p.* 'Unique'. This can be large on a mature shrub, quite broad at the base and markedly blunt or rounded at the tip. Although the numerous fertile flowers can be seen through gaps in the coverage of sterile florets, no fertile flowers appear at the tip where, on many other *paniculata* cultivars, they form a sharp point. The sterile florets are large with rounded overlapping sepals. They jostle for space on the panicle surface. Opening white in mid-July, the flowers gradually develop a pink tinge, intensifying as the season progresses. The red 'eye' of *H. paniculata* 'Grandiflora', however, is absent.

The shrub is vigorous, trouble-free and highly recommended.

Flower

Head Shape: broad panicle, rounded tip
Head Size: up to 30 cm (12 in) high, up to 20 cm (8 in) base diameter
Sterile Flowers: large: cover complete head
Sepal Number: 4–5, occasionally 6
Sepal Immature: white
Sepal Mature: creamy white
Sepal Autumnal: cream/pink
Fertile Flower Immature: palest green
Fertile Flower Mature: green/cream
Peduncle: pale green/red
Pedicel: pale green/cream
pH: 6.5

Leaf

Main Colour: mid-green
Edge Colour: as leaf
Texture: matt, slightly hairy
Back of Leaf: similar colour to front
Veins: raised on back
Curvature: edges often raised
Branch: red
Petiole: dark red

Height: large
Flowering Time: mid to late

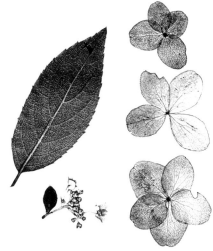

H. p. 'Unique', Windermere (pH 6.5)

H. paniculata 'White Moth'

Selected by J. and R. de Belder, Kalmthout, Belgium

A vigorous and prolific plant. One mature example was seen in Savill Gardens, Windsor and another in Belgium. The shrub at Windsor was pruned annually to two buds of the previous year's growth. The result was an erect bush bearing huge blooms of broad, clearly defined panicles. The Belgian plant, older and unpruned, was a large, lax and spreading bush. Its panicles were irregularly shaped, with the fertile flowers clearly visible through a light covering of sterile florets. Both were beautiful, and it was interesting to see the contrast created by pruning. Flowering starts in July and continues well into the autumn, the flowers maintaining their creamy white colour throughout. However treated, this is a striking and excellent shrub.

Another *H. paniculata* cultivar which is atypical in appearance is *H. p.* 'Brussels Lace', selected by J. and R. de Belder. Seen growing freely to maturity in Belgium, the effect was of massed cream flowers, so closely packed on a huge bush that foliage was partly obscured. The shape of the panicle is not obvious from a distance but, seen close up, is short and irregular, with a high proportion of tightly grouped fertile flowers. It is these which give the bush its predominant colour, from deep cream to lighter cream as they open. Cream sterile florets are sparsely scattered, mainly at the panicle base.

Flower

Head Shape: short, irregular panicle
Head Size: (unpruned) up to 30 cm (12 in) overall diameter,
(pruned) c. 40 cm (16 in) high, 25 cm (10 in) base diameter
Sterile Flowers: large, cupped, evenly throughout panicle
Sepal Number: 4–5
Sepal Immature: white
Sepal Mature: cream
Sepal Autumnal: greenish cream
Fertile Flower Immature: green
Fertile Flower Mature: cream
Peduncle: cream
Pedicel: cream
pH: 5.5–6.0

Leaf

Main Colour: mid-green
Edge Colour: as leaf
Texture: matt, slightly hairy
Back of Leaf: lighter colour, rough
Veins: prominent on back
Curvature: flat or bending back
Branch: brown, white marks
Petiole: pink/green

Height: large
Flowering Time: mid to late

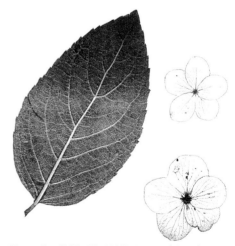

Above: *H. p.* 'White Moth', Windermere (pH 6.5)

Below: *H. p.* 'Brussels Lace', Hemelrijk, Belgium (pH 5.5 to 6.0)

H. quercifolia 'Harmony'

Found in Attalla, Alabama, USA at Harmony Baptist Church Cemetery, by J.C. McDaniel

This is a shrub with a difference. The broad, rounded bush is instantly recognized, because of the striking, white conical flowers. These are like none other, especially in texture. Broad-based and round-tipped, the panicle is composed of densely packed sterile florets. These are so close that there is absolutely no space between them, giving the flower head an air of solidity. Emerging pale green, the florets mature to dazzling white, then mellow to cream before the sepal edges turn pink. The pink and cream autumn shades gradually deepen and finally fade to brown, the plant having already given two months of colour and change. Heads gathered in the autumn will dry well.

The mid-green, coarsely rugose-lobed leaves last late into the autumn before developing rust and purple shades, which again serve to prolong the season.

Although the results in Great Britain will probably be less dramatic than in the USA, the plant will benefit from a sheltered spot, will provide eye-catching interest in late summer and autumn, and make a fine conversation piece.

Flower

Head Shape: broad, blunt panicle
Head Size: up to 21 × 16 cm (8$^1/_2$ × 6 in)
Sterile Flowers: cupped, densely crowded
Sepal Number: 4
Sepal Immature: pale green
Sepal Mature: white
Sepal Autumnal: cream/pink/brown
Fertile Flower Immature: none found
Fertile Flower Mature: none found
Peduncle: pale green
Pedicel: pale green
pH: 7.0

Leaf

Main Colour: mid-green
Autumn Colour: rusty-red/burgundy
Edge Colour: as leaf
Texture: matt, rugose
Back of Leaf: greyish green, hairy
Veins: recessed front, raised back
Curvature: edges slightly raised
Branch: old: peeling; young; red
Petiole: hairy, light brown

Height: medium, large in warm areas
Flowering Time: late in GB, early in USA

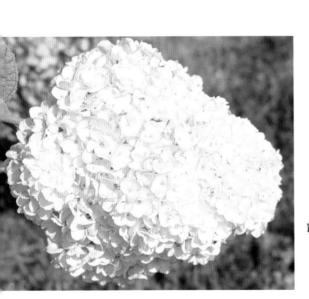

H. quercifolia 'Harmony', Snowflake Nurseries, Alabama, USA (pH 7.0)

H. quercifolia 'Snowflake'

Protected by Plant Breeders Rights in USA and France.
Raised in Alabama, USA by C. Aldridge, 1960s

A spectacular and successful plant. Raised in the area which is native to *H. quercifolia*, it grows to perfection in the warm climate of south-eastern USA. It can, however, do well in Great Britain, given good drainage, and a sheltered position in full sun. Flower heads may not be as large or as numerous, but the shrub is irresistibly attractive and well worth growing.

The long, slim panicles are laden with multiple florets, some carrying a whorl of as many as forty-five sepals. Each sepal goes through a series of colour changes as it matures, from pale green, through white, to pale pink, deeper pink and finally brown. As the outer sepals of each floret mature before the inner ones, there is a constant blend and succession of colour contrasts. These shades can be captured by drying the flower heads for striking indoor decoration.

The bright-green young leaves darken gradually, then begin to develop deep red tints. As young leaves are often found alongside mature ones, the foliage alone provides an eye-catching spectacle. Even the bark has interest, being cinnamon coloured on young stems, while older wood has darker bark which peels off in strips during the winter.

Flower

Head Shape: long, slim panicle
Head Size: up to 30 × 10 cm (12 × 4 in)
Sterile Flowers: double, cover whole head, do not obscure fertile fl.
Sepal Number: up to 45
Sepal Immature: cream
Sepal Mature: cream
Sepal Autumnal: pink, brown
Fertile Flower Immature: none found
Fertile Flower Mature: none found
Peduncle: pale green
Pedicel: pale green
pH: 6.5

Leaf

Main Colour: dark green
Autumn Colour: scarlet, purple
Edge Colour: as leaf
Texture: matt, rugose
Back of Leaf: hairy, green
Veins: light, recessed on front, raised on back
Curvature: flat, some tips back
Branch: brown bark, peels in winter
Petiole: hairy, light brown

Height: medium, large in warm areas
Flowering Time: late in GB, early in USA

Above: *H. q.* 'Snowflake' in Aldridge Garden, Hoover, Alabama, USA (E. Aldrige)
Right: Flower head of *H. q.* 'Snowflake', Windermere (pH 6.5)

159

H. quercifolia 'Snow Queen'

Styer Award of Garden Merit 1989. Plant Patent No. 4458.
Found on Princeton Nurseries, New Jersey

This is an elegant plant, less flamboyant than *H. quercifolia* 'Snowflake', but beautiful in its own right. The flower, a gently tapered panicle, is a refined version of the species bloom, and is held erect on stiff stems. The many sterile florets, pure white maturing through cream to pink, lie flat. The smooth outline thus formed, has occasional gaps, through which the cream fertile flowers can be seen. The attractive leaves turn from dark green to shades of red-purple in autumn, and remain late on the plant. In winter, peeling bark and orange buds prolong the season of interest.

Although it will grow in shade and in full sun, *H. q.* 'Snow Queen' will flower better with more warmth than is usually found in northern Britain. However, it is hardy and undemanding, and well worth trying in any sunny, sheltered site.

Flower

Head Shape: slim, smooth panicle
Head Size: 21 cm (8 in) tall × 12 cm (5 in) diameter base (approx)
Sterile Flowers: many, flat, overlapping
Sepal Number: 3–5, mostly 4
Sepal Immature: greeny cream
Sepal Mature: white
Sepal Autumnal: pink
Fertile Flower Immature: green
Fertile Flower Mature: cream
Peduncle: pale green
Pedicel: white
pH: 7.0

Leaf

Main Colour: dark green
Autumn Colour: purple/red
Edge Colour: sometimes brown
Texture: coarsely rugose
Back of Leaf: hairy, green
Veins: white, recessed on front
Curvature: edges up
Branch: young green, old brown peeling
Petiole: slightly hairy, pink/red

Height: medium, large in warm areas
Flowering Time: late in GB, early in USA

Above: *H. q.* 'Snow Queen', Princeton Nurseries
Below: *H. q.* 'Snow Queen', The Sir Harold Hillier
Garden and Arboretum , Romsey, England

Flower Head Types of Subspecies and Cultivars

1. Globose

Rounded head; many sterile florets, fertile flowers usually present

H. arborescens	'Annabelle'		'Heinrich Seidel'
	'Grandiflora'		'Hörnli'
H. macrophylla	'All Summer Beauty'		'Joseph Banks'
	'Alpenglühen'		'Leuchtfeuer'
	'Altona'		'Madame A Riveraine
	'Amethyst'		
			'Madame E Mouillère
	'Ami Pasquier'		
			'Maréchal Foch'
	'Ave Maria'		'Mathilda Gutges'
	'Ayesha'		'Merveille'
	'Blue Bonnet'		'Mousseline'
	'Brunette'		'Nigra'
	'Deutschland'		'Oregon Pride'
	'Europa'		'Parsival'
	'Fisher's SilverBlue'		'Pia'
	'Floralia'		'Rosea'
	'Frillibet'		'Seascape'
	'Générale Vicomtesse		'Soeur Thérèse'
	de Vibraye'		'Tovelit'
	'Gentian Dome'		'Westfalen'
	'Hamburg'	*H. serrata*	'Preziosa'
	'Harry's Red'		

2. Composite
Shallower head; sterile florets usually encircling central corymb of fertile flowers.

H. anomala	ssp. anomala		'Maculata'
H. aspera	'Kawakami'		'Mariesii'
	'Macrophylla'		'Mousmée'
	'Mauvette'		'Möwe'
	'Peter Chappell'		'Pfau'
	ssp. sargentiana		'Quadricolor'
	'Villosa'		'Rotschwanz'
H. heteromalla	'Bretschneideri'		'Sea Foam'
	'Jermyn's Lace'		'Tokyo Delight'
	'Snowcap'		'Tricolor'
	'Wilsonii'		'Veitchii'
	'Xanthoneura'	*H. serrata*	'Beni Gaku'
	'Yalung Ridge'		'Blue Bird'
H. involucrata	'Hortensis'		'Blue Deckle'
H. macrophylla	'Beauté Vendômoise'		'Diadem'
	'Blauling'		'Grayswood'
	'Blaumeise'		'Intermedia'
	'Blue Wave'		'Kiyosumi'
	'Geoffrey Chadbund'		'Kurohime'
	see 'Möwe'		'Miranda'
	'Grant's Choice'		'Rosalba'
	'Hanabi'		'Schichidanka'
	'Jogasaki'		'Shishiva'
	'Lanarth White'		f.thunbergii
	'Libelle'		ssp. yezoensis
	'Lilacina'		

3. Panicle

Cone-shaped head; sterile florets always apparent, fertile flowers usually present.

H. paniculata	'Brussels Lace'		'Tardiva'
	'Floribunda'		'Unique'
	'Grandiflora'		'White Moth'
	'Green Spire'	*H. quercifolia*	'Harmony'
	'Kyushu'		'Snowflake'
	'Pink Diamond'		'Snow Queen'
	'Praecox'		

Flowering Times

Flowering times of species and cultivars may vary with climate, season and planting position.
E = early; M = mid; L = late

	E	M	L
H. anomala	*		
ssp. petiolaris	*		
H. arborescens	*	*	*
'Annabelle'	*	*	*
'Grandiflora'	*	*	*
H. aspera		*	*
'Kawakami'			*
'Macrophylla'		*	*
'Mauvette'	*	*	
'Peter Chappell'		*	*
ssp. sargentiana	*	*	
'Villosa'		*	*
H. heteromalla	*		
'Bretschneideri'	*		
'Jermyn's Lace'	*		
'Snowcap'	*		
'Wilsonii'	*		
xanthonura	*	*	
'Yalung Ridge'	*		
H. hirta	*		
H.integrifola	*	*	
H. involucrata		*	*
'Hortensis'		*	*
H. macrophylla		*	
'All Summer Beauty'	*	*	*
'Alpenglühen'	*	*	*
'Altona'		*	*
'Amethyst'			*
'Ami Pasquier'	*	*	*
'Ave Maria'	*	*	*
'Ayesha'	*	*	*
'Beauté Vendômoise'		*	*
'Blauling'	*	*	
'Blaumeise'		*	*
'Blue Bonnet'	*	*	

	E	M	L
'Blue Wave'			*
'Brunette'			*
'Europa'		*	*
'Floralia'		*	*
'Frillibet'	*	*	*
'Généralé Vicomtesse de Vibraye'	*	*	*
'Gentian Dome'		*	*
'Grant's Choice'		*	*
'Hamburg'		*	*
'Hanabi'		*	*
'Harry's Red'		*	*
'Hörnli'			*
'Jogasaki'			*
'Joseph Banks'	*	*	*
'Lanarth White'		*	*
'Leuchtfeuer'		*	*
'Libelle'		*	
'Lilacina'		*	*
'Madame E. Mouillère'	*	*	*
'Maréchal Foch'		*	*
'Mariesii'		*	*
'Mathilda Gutges'		*	*
'Merritt's Supreme'	*	*	*
'Merveille'	*	*	*
'Mousseline'	*	*	*
'Mousmée'		*	*
'Möwe'		*	*
'Nigra'			*
'Oregon Pride'		*	*
'Parsival'	*	*	*
'Pfau'		*	
'Pia'		*	*
'Quadricolor'		*	*
'Rotschwanz'		*	*
'Sea Foam'		*	*
'Seascape'		*	*
'Tokyo Delight'	*	*	*
'Tovelit'			*
'Tricolor'			*
'Veitchii'		*	*

'Westfalen'	*	*	
'White Wave'		*	*
H. serrata			
'Beni Gaku'	*	*	*
'Blue Bird'	*	*	*
'Blue Deckle'	*	*	*
'Diadem'	*	*	*
'Grayswood'		*	*
'Intermedia'	*	*	*
'Kiyosumi'		*	
'Kurohime'	*	*	*
'Miranda'	*	*	*
'Preziosa'	*	*	*
'Rosalba'	*	*	*
'Schichidanka'	*		
'Shishiva'		*	
f. thunbergii	*	*	
'Tiara'	*	*	*
ssp. yezoensis	*		

H. paniculata			*
'Brussels Lace'	*	*	
'Floribunda'			*
'Grandiflora'		*	*
'Green Spire'		*	*
'Kyushu	*	*	
'Pink Diamond'		*	*
'Praecox'	*	*	
'Tardiva'			*
'Unique'		*	*
'White Moth'	*	*	*
H. quercifolia			*
(all early in USA)			
'Harmony'			*
'Snowflake'			*
'Snow Queen'			*
H. scandens	*		
H. seemanii		*	*
H. serratofolia	*		
H. sikokiana	*	*	

Glossary of Terms

ACUMINATE   tapering to a long pointed tip

ACUTE   coming to a short, sharp point

ADVENTITIOUS   growing from an atypical position, e.g. roots arising from the stem, as in ivy

AGM   award of garden merit, given by the RHS to a plant of outstanding excellence for the garden. Reinstituted in 1992, and subject to periodic review. Reviewed 2003

AM   award of merit, given by the RHS to 'a plant of great merit for exhibition'. Instituted in 1888

APPRESSED   of hairs, pressed close to the surface

ATTENUATE   of convex sides, narrowing concavely to the base

AXIL   angle between leaf and stem, or between mid-rib and vein in a leaf

BRACT   modified leaf at the base of a flower stalk, giving the new growth protection

BRANCH   lateral stem, arising from main stem or trunk

CALYX   collective term for all the sepals of a flower

CAPSULE   dry fruit, containing seeds

CILIATE   fringed with hairs

CLONE   new plant, formed by vegetative reproduction from a parent plant, to which it is genetically identical

CONCAVE   lower in the centre

CONVEX   raised in the centre

CORDATE   of the base of a leaf, having two equally rounded lobes, forming a heart shape

CORYMB   flat-topped or domed cluster of flowers, the stalks of which arise one above the other, from a vertical stem. The lower pedicels are longer than the upper

CULTIVAR   a plant arising or maintained in cultivation, which, while not meriting botanical recognition, is clearly distinguishable. Its distinct characteristics are retained in reproduction

CUNEATE   with straight sides converging at the base

CYME   inflorescence in which each main stem ends in a flower

DELTOID   triangular, approximately equilateral

DENTICULATE   with a fine, tooth-shaped edge, projections straight out

ELLIPTIC   widest at the centre, and narrowing equally at both ends

ENTIRE   of leaf, sepal, petal – the edge or margin is free from teeth or divisions

EYE   in a flower, the centre part, especially when of a different or contrasting colour

FCC   first class certificate, given by the RHS to a plant of outstanding excellence for exhibition. Instituted in 1859

FERTILE   of a flower – having reproductive parts

FLORET   individual small 'flower' of an inflorescence

FLOWER   that structure of the plant concerned with sexual reproduction

GENUS   botanical category denoting a group of allied species

HORTENSIA (1)   the name commonly used in continental Europe for all hydrangeas.

HORTENSIA (2)   used by M. Haworth-Booth, and now accepted in English-speaking countries to mean the globose-headed cultivar of *H. macrophylla*, composed mainly of sterile florets. English common name: 'mophead'.

INFLORESCENCE   the part of the plant bearing flowers

INTERNODE   that part of the stem between two nodes

LACECAP   form of *H. macrophylla*, having a composite corymb with central, fertile flowers and marginal sterile 'ray flowers'

LANCEOLATE   long and slim in shape, widest at the base, and tapering gradually to a point

LAYER   new plant formed, when the stem of the parent plant bends to touch the ground and roots there

LOBE   area (of a leaf) which is partly divided, but still united to the main surface

MOPHEAD   common name, used mainly in Britain, for the globose-headed cultivar of *Hydrangea macrophylla*

NODE   slightly enlarged part of a stem or joint, from which other shoots, leaves or buds arise

OBOVATE   shaped as an inverted egg, wider above the centre

OBTUSE   blunt, rounded

OPPOSITE   of leaves, when they arise in pairs from the node

ORBICULAR   rounded

OVATE   egg-shaped, broader towards the base

PANICLE   branched inflorescence, made up of several racemes, commonly pyramidal

PARASITE   plant which derives its nourishment from another, live host plant. The parasite cannot exist independently

PC   Certificate of Preliminary Commendation, awarded by the Royal Horticultural Society

PEDICELS   the stalk of one flower in an inflorescence

PETAL   one of the inner floral leaves of a flower, usually modified and coloured. In a hydrangea, the petals are very small

PETIOLE   stem joining leaf to branch

pH   a logarithmic scale measuring acidity/alkalinity of soil, calculated on an aqueous solution; pH 7 is neutral. A higher pH number is alkaline; a lower pH number is acid

PINNATELY LOBED   of a leaf, when divided into several lobes, but not totally separated (e.g. oak leaf)

PUBESCENT   covered with soft downy hair

RACEME   inflorescence with individual flowers on stalks from a tall, central axis

RAY FLOWER   common name for the sterile florets which appear, usually round the margin, of a composite corymb

RHIZOMORPH   root-like strands associated with some fungi

RUGOSE   wrinkled, quilted, with many ridges

SAPROPHYTE   plant which gains its nourishment from dead and decaying organic matter

SCANDENT   climbing, twining

SEPAL   outer part of a flower – in hydrangeas, often enlarged and coloured

SERRATE   of indentations along a margin, sharp, saw-like and pointing forward

SERRULATE   as serrate, only finer

SPECIES   plants within a genus, which have similar, distinctive characteristics

SPORT   variant from the type

STERILE   unable to reproduce – does not set seed (some hydrangea flowers do have sexual parts, but do not set seed)

SUCKER   underground shoot, which appears above ground as a new plant

TERMINAL   topmost, of shoots and flowers

TERNATE   of leaves, when three arise from the same node

UMBEL   inflorescence in which all pedicels arise from the tip of the main axis

UNDULATE   wavy in outline

VEGETATIVE PROPAGATION   asexual plant reproduction, achieving offspring which are copies of the parent plant

WHORL   arrangement of organs from a common axis, at the same level, and encircling the axis

Illustrations of some terms used in the text

Shapes of leaves and sepals

1. Ovate   2. Obovate   3. Orbicular   4. Elliptic   5. Lanceolate   6. Deltoid

Tips

1. Acute   2. Acuminate   3. Obtuse   4. Retuse

Bases

1. Cuneate   2. Attenuate   3. Obtuse   4. Cordate

Margins

1. Entire   2. Serrate   3. Serrulate   4. Double serrate   5. Denticulate   6. Ciliate   7. Undulate

Arrangements of flowers and leaves

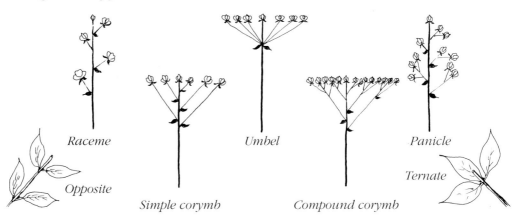

Raceme   Umbel   Panicle

Opposite   Ternate

Simple corymb   Compound corymb

List of Gardens

Gardens open to the public, and with a good display of hydrangeas. These gardens have been visited by, or are known to, the authors who apologize to any other garden owners who would like to have been included. The authors would be delighted to hear from these enthusiasts. National Trust properties are marked 'NT'.

England

Coleton Fishacre, Kingswear, Dartmouth, Devon, TQ6 0EQ
Tel. 01803 752466 (NT)

Dunham Massey, Altrincham, Cheshire, WA14 4SJ
Tel. 0161 941 1025 (NT)

Darley Abbey Park, Derby, DE22 1DS (National Collection of Viburnum and Hydrangea)
Tel. 01332 255828

Furzey Gardens, Minstead, nr Lyndhurst, Hampshire, SO43 7GL
Tel. 01703 812464

Hidcote Manor Garden, Hidcote Bartrim, Chipping Campden, Gloucestershire, GL55 6LR
Tel. 01386 438333 (NT) *Please avoid* popular opening times

The Sir Harold Hillier Garden and Arboretum, Jermyns Lane, Ampfield, nr Romsey, Hampshire SO51 0QA
Tel. 01794 368787
www.hilliergardens.org.uk

Royal Botanic Gardens, Kew, Richmond, Surrey, TW9 3AB
Tel. 020 8940 1171
www.rbgkew.org.uk

Kiftsgate Court, Chipping Campden, Gloucestershire, GL55 6LW
Tel. 01386 438777
www.kiftsgate.co.uk

Knightshayes Court, Bolham, Tiverton, Devon EX16 7RQ
Tel. 01884 257381 (NT)

Lakeland Horticultural Society Garden, Holehird, Patterdale Road, Windermere, Cumbria, LA23 1NP (National Collection of Hydrangea)
Tel. 01539 446008
www.cragview.demon.co.uk

Lanhydrock, Bodmin, Cornwall, PL30 5AD
Tel. 01208 73320 (NT)

Marwood Hill, Barnstaple, North Devon, EX31 4EB
Tel. 01271 42528

Montacute House, Montacute, Yeovil, Somerset, TA15 6XP
Tel. 01935 823289 (NT)

Nymans Garden, Handcross, nr Haywards Heath, West Sussex, RH17 6EB
Tel. 01444 400321 (NT)

Overbecks Museum and Garden, Sharpitor, Salcombe, Devon, TQ8 8LW
Tel. 01548 842893 (NT)

Savill and Valley Gardens, The Great Park, Windsor, Berkshire, SL4 2HT
Tel. 01753 860222
www.crownestate.co.uk/estates/windsor/gardens.shtml

Sheffield Park, Uckfield, East Sussex, TN22 3QX
Tel. 01825 790655 (NT)

Spinner's Garden, School Lane, Boldre, Lymington, Hampshire, SO41 5QE
Tel. 01590 673347

Stourton House Flower Garden, Stourton, Warminster, Wiltshire, BA12 6QF
Tel. 01747 840417

Trebah Garden, Mawnan Smith, nr Falmouth, Cornwall, TR11 5JZ
Tel. 01326 250448
www.trebahgarden.co.uk

Trelissick, Feock, nr Truro, Cornwall, TR3 6QL
Tel. 01872 862090 (NT)

Trengwainton, nr Penzance, Cornwall, TR20 8RZ
Tel. 01736 362297 (NT)

Royal Botanic Gardens Kew, Wakehurst Place, Ardingly, Haywards Heath, West Sussex, RH17 6TN
Tel. 01444 892701
www.rbgkew.org.uk

Royal Horticultural Society's Garden, Wisley, Woking, Surrey, GU23 6QB
Tel. 01483 224234
www.rhs.org.uk/gardens/wisley

Wales

Bodnant Garden, Taly-y-Cafn, Colwyn Bay, Clywd, LL28 5RE
Tel. 01492 650460 (NT)

Plas Newydd, Llanfairpwll, Anglesey, Gwynedd, LL61 6DQ
Tel. 01248 714795 (NT)

S. Wingett, The Garden House, Erbistock, Wrexham, LL13 0DL (National Collection of Hydrangea)
Tel. 01978 780958
www.borderlands.co.uk/garden-house/

Scotland

Mrs. A. Greenall, Lagg House, Dunure, Ayrshire, KA7 4LE (National Collection of Hydrangaceae, view by appointment)
Tel. 01292 500286

Royal Botanic Garden, Inverleith Row, Edinburgh, EH3 5LR
Tel. 0131 552 7171
www.rbge.org.uk

Logan Botanic Garden, Port Logan, Stranraer, Wigtownshire, DG9 9ND
Tel. 01776 860231

Younger Botanic Garden, Benmore, by Dunoon, Argyll, PA23 8QU
Tel. 01369 6261

Ireland

John F. Kennedy Arboretum, New Ross, Co. Wexford, Republic of Ireland
Tel. 00 353 51 88171

Mount Usher, Ashford, Co. Wicklow, Republic of Ireland
Tel. 00 353 404 40116/40205
www.mount-usher-gardens.com

Rowallane, Saintfield, Ballynahinch, Co. Down, Northern Ireland, BT24 7LH
Tel. 00 353 28 9751 0131 (NT)

Belgium

Arboretum Kalmthout, B-2180 Kalmthout, Belgium
Tel. 00 32 3 666 67 41
www.arboretumkalmthout.be

France

11, résidence du Cardonnay, 76150 St Jean du Cardonnay
Tel. 00 33 35 33 83 57 By appointment only; Wednesdays, May–September only

Le Jardin Botanique de Cournouaille, Comrit, 29120 Pont-L'Abbé
Tel. 00 33 98 87 34 56 or 0033 98 56 44 93

Le Vasterival, 76119 Ste-Marguerite-sur-Mer (nr Dieppe)
Tel. 00 33 35 85 12 05 Visit by prior appointment only

Parc de Pignerolles, District de l'Agglomeration Angevine, St Barthélemy d'Anjou, Angers
Tel. 00 33 41 86 52 21 (La Direction du Service des Espaces Verts d'Angers)

Parc des Moutiers, 76119 Varengèville-sur-Mer (nr Dieppe)
Tel. 00 33 35 85 10 02

Parc du Domaine de Beaurepaire, 50690 Martinvast (nr Cherbourg)
Tel. 00 33 33 52 02 23

Shamrock Hydrangea collection, route de l'Eglise, 76119 Varengèville-sur-Mer. By appointment only
Tel. 00 33 35 85 14 64

USA

Aldridge Gardens, Hoover, Alabama 35236
Tel. 001 205 682 8019
www.aldridgegardens.com

The Arnold Arboretum of Harvard University, 125 Arborway, Jamaica Plain, Massachusetts 02130-3519
Tel. 001 617 524 1718
www.arboretum.harvard.edu

Atlanta Botanical Garden, Piedmont Park at the Prado, Atlanta, Georgia 30605
Tel. 001 404 876 5859
www.atlantabotanicalgarden.org

Brooklyn Botanic Garden, 1000 Washington Avenue, Brooklyn, New York 11225–1099
Tel. 001 718 622 4433
www.bbg.org

The Morton Arboretum, Route 53, Lisle, Illinois 60532–1293
Tel. 001 708 968 0074
www.mortonarb.org

The Scott Arboretum of Swarthmore College, 500 College Avenue, Swarthmore, Pennsylvania 19081 1397
Tel. 001 215 328 8025
www.scottarboretum.org

The University of Georgia Botanical Garden
2450 South Milledge Avenue, Athens, Georgia 30605
www.uga.edu/~botgarden.home2.html

US National Arboretum, 3501 New York Avenue NE, Washington, DC 20002
Tel. 001 202 245 4523
www.usna.usda.gov

Washington Park Arboretum, University of Washington, XD-10 Seattle, Washington 98195
Tel. 001 206 543 8800
www.depts.washington.edu/wpa

Canada

The University of British Columbia Botanical Garden, 6804 S.W. Marine Drive, Vancouver, BC
Tel. 001 604 822 3928
www.ubc.botanicalgarden.org

VanDusen Botanical Garden, 5251 Oak Street, Vancouver, BC V6M 4H1
Tel. 001 604 266 7194

Australia

Royal Botanic Gardens and National Herbarium, Birdwood Avenue, South Yarra, Victoria 3141
Tel. 00 61 3 6552300

Busker's End, St Clair Street, Bowral, NSW 2576
Tel. 00 61 48 612942

New Zealand

Auckland Regional Botanic Gardens, 102 Hill Road, Manurewa, Auckland
Tel. 00 64 09 267 1457

Christchurch Botanic Gardens, 7 Rolleston Avenue, Christchurch 1
Tel. 00 64 366 1701

Sources and Further Reading

Allaby, M. (ed.) *Concise Oxford Dictionary of Botany*, OUP, 1992

Anderson Horticultural Library, *List of Plants and Seeds*, Minnesota Arboretum, 3675 Arboretum Drive, Box 39, MN 55317

Asen, S., Stuart, N.W., Siegelman, H.W. 'Effect of concentration of Nitrogen, Phosphorus and Potassium on *Hydrangea macrophylla*'. *Proc. Amer. Soc. Hort. Sciences*, 73, (1959) 495–501

Asen, S., Stuart, N.W., Specht, A.W. 'Colour of *Hydrangea macrophylla* sepals'. *Proc. Amer. Soc. Hort. Sciences*, 76 (1960), 631–6

Bailey, D.A. *Hydrangea Production*, Timber Press, 1989

Bartrum, D. *Hydrangeas and Viburnums*, John Gifford, 1958

Bean, W.J. *Trees and Shrubs, Hardy in the British Isles*, 8th edn, M. Bean and J. Murray, 1970

Beckett, K.A. 'Selfclinging Evergreen Climbers', *Journal of the RHS*, May 1975

Bertrand, H. 'Une Collection d'Hydrangea macrophylla Ser.' *PHM. Revue Horticole*. 316 (April 1991), 22–5

Bertrand, H. '*Hydrangea* – nom de cultivar, nom de marque, synonym, que choisir?' *PHM. Revue Horticole* 333 (Dec. 1992), 36–7

Brickell, C.D. 'Notes from Wisley', *Journal of the RHS, Aug. 1964*

Brickell, C.D. *'Botany or gardening?'* The Garden, Nov. 1970

Buswell, G. 'For peat's sake', *The Lakeland Gardener*, Vol. IX No. VIII, 1992

Chenery, E.M. 'The Problem of the blue Hydrangea', *Journal of the RHS* (July 1937), 304–20

Christian, R. *Well dressing in Derbyshire*, Derbyshire Countryside Ltd, 1987

Church, G. *Hydrangeas*, Cassell 1999

Cooper, M. and Johnson, A. *Poisonous Plants and Fungi*, HM Stationery Office for MAAF, 1988

Cordier, F. et J.P. *20,000 Plantes – Ou[2] et Comment les Acheter?*, Société Nationale d'Horticulture de France, La Maison Rustique, 1992

Dixon's *World of Photography – How to photograph nature*, Eaglemoss, 1984–5

Ebel, M. *Hydrangea et Hortensia*, Librairie J.B. Baillière et Fils, 2nd edn, 1948

Fisher, J. *The Origins of Garden Plants*, Constable, 1982

Gibbons, B. 'Photographing flowers and plants', *The Garden*, May 1983

Gill, W. 'High-Tech Greenfingers', *The Lakeland Gardener*, Vol. IX, No. 1, 19–21

Gregory, Dr S.C. 'Honey Fungus in gardens', *The Garden*, Nov. 1987

Halevy, A.H. and Arena, J.M. *Human poisoning from Nature and Cultivated Plants*, Duke Univ. Press, 1969

Haworth-Booth, M. 'My new shrub garden', *Journal of RHS*, Nov. 1949

The Hydrangeas, The Garden Book Club, 1st edn, 1955

The Hydrangeas, Constable, 5th edn, 1984

Effective Flowering Shrubs, Collins, new revised edn, 1962

H. macrophylla 'White Wave', *The Garden*, July 1971

'Natural Regeneration', *The Garden*, June 1972

Hay, R. and Synge, P. *Dictionary of Garden Plants in Colour*, RHS and Ebury Press, 1969

Henry Doubleday Research Association, *Alternatives to Peat*, 1990

Hillier, H.G. *Colour Dictionary of Trees and Shrubs*, David and Charles, 1981

Manual of Trees and Shrubs, David and Charles, 1991

'Late flowering trees and shrubs', *Journal of the RHS*, March 1961

Hughes, S. *Washi – The World of Japanese Paper*, Kodansha Int. 1978, 2nd printing 1982

Japanese National Tourist Organization, *The New Official Guide*, 1975

Jiaxi, W. and Yue, M. *China's Rare Flowers*, Morning Glory Press, Beijing 1988

Knight, F.P. 'Summer and Autumn Flowering Shrubs', *Journal of the RHS*, Jan. 1950

Krussman, G. *A Manual of Cultivated Broad Leaved Trees and Shrubs*, B.T. Batsford Ltd/Timber Press, 1984

Lémoine, V. *Catalogues*, 1870–1914

Lloyd, C. *Foliage Plants*, Collins, 1975

The Adventurous Gardener, Penguin, reprint 1987

'Long-lived Hydrangeas', *Country Life* (April 1958), 126–7

Lovell, C.R. *Plants and the Skin*, Blackwell (1993), 138

Lowe, J. *Into Japan*, J. Murray, 1985

MAAF *Commercial Production of Pot Plants*, HMSO (1969), 50–3

McClintock, D. 'The common ground of wild and cultivated plants', *The Garden*, Aug. 1972

McClintock, E., 'The cultivated hydrangeas' *Baileya*, 4 (1956), 165–75

'A monograph of the genus *Hydrangea*', *Proc. Californian Academy Sciences*, 29 (Nov. 1957), 147–256

'Climbing Hydrangeas', *Californian Horticultural Journal*, 34 (1973), 141–5

Makino, T. *Flora of Japan*, 1949

Mallet, C. *Hydrangeas – Species and Cultivars*, Centre d'Art Floral, 1992/Vol. 2 1994

Mansfield, T.C. *Shrubs in Colour and Cultivation*, Collins, 1946

Meier, F. *Tellerhortensien-Zuchtungen*, Flugschrift, 120, Juni 1990. Eidgenossische Forschungsanstalt fur Obst, Wein und Gartenbau, CH 8820 Wadenswil

Nevling, L.I., jnr. 'Climbing hydrangeas and their relatives', *Bulletin of the Arnold Arboretum*, 24 (June 1964), 17–39

Ohwi, J. *Flora of Japan*, Smithsonian Institute, Washington DC, 1965

Palmer, The Hon. L. 'A cold chalk garden throughout the year', *Journal of the RHS*, Jan 1967

Philip, C. and Lord T. *The Plant Finder*, Headmain Ltd, 1993

Phillips, R. and Rix, M. *Shrubs*, Pan Books Ltd, 1989

Pilatowski, R.E. 'A taxonomic study of the *Hydrangea arborescens* complex', Paper 6582, *Journal Series of the N. Carolina Agricultural Research Service*, Raleigh, 1982

Puttock, A.G. *The Hydrangea*, W.G. Foyle, Ltd, 1958

Ramsbottom, J. *Mushrooms and Toadstools*, Collins New Naturalist Series, 7th imp., 1977

Reader's Digest *Encyclopedia of Garden Plants*, 2nd edn, 1973

Rehder, A. *Hydrangea in Plantae Wilsonianae*, Vol. I (1913), 25–41, C.S. Sargent

Rehder, A. *Manual of Trees and Shrubs Hardy in N. America*, 2nd edn, 1956

Richards, B. and Kaneko, A. *Japanese Plants*, Shufonotomo Co. Ltd, Tokyo, 1989

RHS *The New Dictionary of Gardening*, Macmillan, 1992

Gardeners' Encyclopaedia of Plants and Flowers, C. Brickell (ed.), Dorling Kindersley, 1989

Russell, Sir E.J. *The World of the Soil*, Collins New Naturalist Series, 3rd imp., 1969

Sandwell, I. 'Finding a substitute for peat', *The Lakeland Gardener* Vol. IX, No. VIII, 1992

Sargent, C.S. *Forest Flora of Japan*, Haughton Mifflin and Co., 1894

Satake, Y., Hiroshi Hara, Shunji Watari and Tado Tominari *Wild Flowers of Japan – Woody Plants*, 1989

Shaw, J. *The Natural Photographers*, American Photographic Publications, 1984

Siebold and Zuccarini *Flora Japonica*, Vol. I, re-print 1935

Sjogren, E. *Acores Flores*, Madeira Regional Tourist Dept, 1982

Slinger, L.S. 'Gardens at Rowallane', *Journal of the RHS*, Nov. 1956

Spoerke, D.E. and Smolinske, S.C. *The Toxicity of House Plants*, CRC Press (1990), 156–7

Stearn, W.T. *Botanical Latin*, David and Charles, 1989

Tinker, Dr M.A. 'The Influence of soil factors in the growth of plants', *Journal of the RHS*, May 1936

Treseder, N.G. 'A new climbing hydrangea', *Journal of the Cornwall Garden Society*, 32 (March 1989), 117

Turner, A. 'Propagation of Hardwood Cuttings', *The Garden*, Sept. 1973

Turner, N.J. and Szezawinski, A.F. *Common Poisonous Plants and Mushrooms of N. America*, Timber Press, 1991

Walker, E.H. *Flora of Okinawa and S. Ryukyu Islands*, Smithsonian Institute, 1976

Wallace, A. and Wieland, P.A.T. 'Mineral nutrition associated with flower colour in hydrangea', Journal of Plant Nutrition 2 (1980), 217–20

Weiler, T.C. 'Hydrangea' *Introduction to Floriculture*, Larson, R.A. (ed.), Academic Press Inc., 1980

Wilson, E.H. 'The Hortensias', *Journal of the Arnold Arboretum* IV (1923), 233–46

Yamamoto, T. 'Hydrangeas and Japanese Iris', *Chabana Series* 4, Sekai Bunkasha, 1985

Useful Addresses

The Royal Horticultural Society (RHS)
80 Vincent Square, London SW1P 2PE
Tel: 020 7834 4333
www.rhs.org.uk

The National Council for the Conservation
of Plants and Gardens (NCCPG)
The Stable Courtyard, Wisley Garden,
Woking, Surrey GU23 6QB
Tel: 01483 211465
www.nccpg.com

The National Trust
36 Queen Anne's Gate,
London SW1H 9AS
Tel: 020 7222 5097
www.nationaltrust.org.uk

American Horticultural Society
7931 East Boulevard Drive
Alexandria, VA 22308, USA
Tel: 001 703 768 8700
www.ahs.org

The American Hydrangea Society
PO Box 11645, Atlanta, GA 30355–1645,
USA
www.americanhydrangeasociety.org

Société Nationale d'Horticulture de France
(SNHF)
84 rue de Grenelle, 75007 Paris
Tel: 00 33 1 44 39 78 78
www.snhf.asso.fr

Association des Amis de la Collection
d'Hydrangea 'Shamrock'
(Shamrock Association)
route de l'eglise, 76119 Varengeville-sur-
Mer, France
Tel: 0033 2 35 85 14 64

Ornamental Plant Conservation Association
of Australia, Inc. (OPCAA)
Royal Botanic Gardens, Melbourne,
Birdwood Avenue, South Yarra, Victoria
3141, Australia
Tel.: 00 61 3 650 5639
www.opcaa.rbg.vic.gov.au

Index

Bold numbers indicate a main entry.

allergy **78**
aluminium 51, **52**
aluminium sulphate **52**
ammonium sulphate 50, 55, 56
aphids 61
Armillaria mellea (honey fungus) **62–63**
autumn colour, flower 54, 94, 107, 108,
    123, 134, 135, 137, 138, 139, 140,
    143, 152, 154, 156
autumn colour, leaf 32, 81, 111, 137, 138,
    139, 143, 144, 147, 148, 149, 158,
    159, 160

bark 50, 56
Bertrand, Hélène **53**
boot-lace fungus (honey fungus) **62–3**
botrytis 61

capsid bug 61
climbers 22, 27, 33, 34–35, 43, 81
coir 50
Comber, H. F. 34
composite flower (lacecaps) **162**
Cornidia 12, 33–34
cuttings
    bud 71
    compost for 64
    feeding 68
    growing-on 69
    hairy-leaved hydrangeas 65
    hardwood **69–70**
    potting-on 68
    softwood **64–69**
    taking 64

dead-heading 57
diseases **60–61**
division of shrubs 74
drying hydrangea flowers **75–76**

evergreen hydrangeas 27, 33, 34, 40, 43
evergreen shrubs 42, 47
exposure to elements 94, 114, 115

feature plants 42, 43
fertilizers 52, **56**
flowers
    colour change 37, **51–54**
    cut fresh 75
description, general 12–14
    fertile **13**
    sterile **13**
frost
    damage **48, 56, 60**
    pockets 44, 49
    resistance 48

garden compost 50, 56
genus, structure of **12**
globose flowers (mopheads) **161**
grass cuttings 56
ground cover 45

Hani Matsuri (tea ceremony) **79**
hardiness **38–39**
hardiness zones 48, **22–23** (maps)
Haworth-Booth, M. **6**, 8, 11, 36
honey fungus, see *Armillaria mellea*
hortensia 36
humidity 49
hydrangea
    distribution, natural 10–11
    fossils 10
    name derivation 10
    tea 79
hydrangea
    acuminata 36
    amacha 79, **148**
    anomala 11, 16, **22–23**, 43
        ssp. *petiolaris* 23, 43, 45, **81**

arborescens 11, 13, 16, **23–25**, 45, **59,** 72, 79
  ssp. *arborescens* 24
  ssp. *discolor* 24
  ssp. *radiata* 24
  'Annabelle' 42, **82**
  'Grandiflora' 44, **83**
aspera 11, 12, 16, **25–26**, 43, 44, 45, 65, 76
  'Kawakami' 43, **84**
  'Macrophylla' **85**
  'Mauvette' **85**
  'Peter Chappell' 43, **86**
  ssp. sargentiana 43, 72, **87**
  'Villosa' 43, **88**
'Azisai' 36
heteromalla 11, 17, **26**, 43, 45
  'Bretschneideri' **89**
  'Jermyn's Lace' **90**
  'Snowcap' **89**
  'Wilsonii' **89**
  xanthoneura **90**
  'Yalung Ridge' **90**
hirta 17, **26–27**, 45
hortensia 36
hortensis 11, 36
  'Otaksa' 36, 37
integerrima 35
integrifolia 17, **27**, 43, 40
involucrata 11, 17, **27–28**, 45, 65
  'Hortensis' 41, 46, 72, **91**
japonica 36
macrophylla 10, 11, 12, 13, 14, 18, **28–30**, **35–39**, **41**, **42**, **43**, 45, 46, 47, 51, 57
  f. *normalis* 29
  ssp. *macrophylla* **29**
  ssp. *serrata* **29–30**, **42**
  'All Summer Beauty' 42, **92**
  'Alpenglühen' (Alpenglow') 41, 54, **93**
  'Altona' 42, 54, 76, **94**
  'Amethyst' 41, **95**
  'Ami Pasquier' **96**
  'Ave Maria' 41, **97**
  'Ayesha' ('Silver Slipper') 41, **98**
  'Beauté Vendômoise' 43, **99**

'Blauling' ('Blue Butterfly') **100**
'Blaumeise' ('Blue Tit') 41, 44, **101**
'Blue Bonnet' **107**
'Blue Sky', see 'Blaumeise'
'Blue Wave' 42, **102**
'Brunette' 41, **103**
'Brympton Mauve' 99
'Deutschland' 54, **93**
'Dragon Fly' ('Libelle') **117**
'Enziandom' ('Gentian Dome') 41, 47, 54, **108**
'Europa' **104**
'Floralia' **105**
'Folis Purpurea', see 'Brunette'
'Frillibet' 43, **106**
'Générale Vicomtesse de Vibraye' 42, 54, 72, 76, **107**
'Gentian Dome' see 'Enziandom'
'Grant's Choice' **109**
'Hamburg' 43, 94, **104** 108
'Hanabi' ('Firework') **110**
'Harry's Red' 54, **111**
'Hörnlii' 38, 41, **112**
'Jogasaki' **113**
'Joseph Banks' ('Sir Joseph Banks') 43, 47, **114**
'Lanarth White' 47, **115**
'Leuchtfeuer' **116**
'Libelle' ('Dragon Fly') 43, **117**
'Lilacina' 42, 76, **118**
'Mme A. Riveraine' **107**
'Mme E. Mouillère' 41, 47, **119**
'Mandshurica', see 'Nigra'
'Maréchal Foch' 47, 54, 76, **108**
'Mariesii' 37, 42, **120**
'Mariesii Perfecta', see 'Blue Wave'
'Mathilda Gutges' **102**, 108
'Merritt's Supreme' 43, **122**
'Merveille' **103**
'Merveille Sanguine', see 'Brunette'
'Mouillère', see 'Mme E. Mouillère'
'Mousseline' 43, **123**
'Möwe' ('Sea Gull') 44, **125**
'Nigra' 41, **126**
'Oregon Pride' **127**
'Parsival' **128**

'Pfau' (Peacock) 41, **129**
'Pia' 41, **130**
'Quadricolor' 41, **131**
'Red Start' see 'Rotschwanz'
'Riveraine', see 'Mme A. Riveraine'
'Rosea' 37
'Rotschwanz' ('Red Start') 41, **132**
'Sea Foam' 42, 47, **114**
'Seascape' **133**
'Sedgewick's White', see 'Mme E.
    Mouillère'
'Silver Slipper', see 'Ayesha'
'Sir Joseph Banks' ('Joseph Banks')
    114
'Snow' ('Libelle') **117**
'Soeur Thérèse' 41, **119**
'Teller Blue', see 'Blaumeise'
'Teller White', see 'Libelle'
'Tokyo Delight' 43, **134**
'Tovelit' 41, **112**
'Tricolor' **131**
'Veitchii' 42, 76, **135**
'Westfalen' 41, **96**
'White Wave' **136**
maritima 29, 36
opuloides 36
    'Otaksa' 34
paniculata 11, 19, **30–31**, 40, 42, 44, 45,
    60, 73, 77
    'Brussels Lace' **157**
    'Floribunda' **151**
    'Grandiflora' 42, **152**
    'Green Spire' **153**
    'Kyushu' **153**
    'Pink Diamond' **154**
    'Praecox' **155**
    'Tardiva' 42, **151**
    'Unique' 42, **156**
    'White Moth' **157**
petiolaris, see *anomala* ssp. *petiolaris*
quercifolia 11, 14, 19, **31–32**, 43, 45
    'Harmony' 43, **158**
    'Snowflake' 43, **159**
    'Snow Queen' 43, **160**
radiata see *arborescens ssp. radiata*
scandens 20. **32**, 45

seemanii 20, **33–34**, 43
serrata 18, **29–30**
    'Beni Gaku' 54, **145**
    'Blue Bird' 41, 44, **137**
    'Blue Deckle' 42, 54, **138**
    'Diadem' 41, 44, 54, **139**
    'Grayswood' 43, 54, 76, **140**
    'Intermedia' **140**
    'Kiyosumi' **141**
    'Kurohime' **142**
    'Miranda' **143**
    'Preziosa' 41, 54, **144**
    'Rosalba' 37, 43, **145**
    'Schichidanka' **146**
    'Shishiva' **147**
    f. *thunbergii* **148**
    'Tiara' 42, **149**
    ssp. *yezoensis* **150**
    seemannii 20, **33–34**, 40, 43
serratifolia 20, **34–35**, 40, 43
sikokiana 21, **35**, 45, 65

Japanese plants 38
Joseph Banks 11

lacecap **13**
lacecaps (composite flowers) **162**
layering **72**, 88
leaf mould 50, 55, 56
leaves, general **16–21**
    drooping 49

McClintock, Elizabeth 6
Mallett, Corrine 6
manure 50, 56
mildew, powdery 61
moisture **49**
mophead 13
mopheads (globose flowers) **161**
moving hydrangeas **45**, 51
mould, see botrytis
mulching **55–57**
mycoplasma 62

name confirmation 7, 53
national collections 7, 39